Cricket

FOR

DUMMIES

A Wiley Brand

2ND EDITION

Cricket

FOR

DUMMIES

A Wiley Brand

2ND EDITION

by Julian Knight

FOR

DUMMIES

A Wiley Brand

Cricket For Dummies®, 2nd Edition

Published by: **John Wiley & Sons, Ltd.,** The Atrium, Southern Gate, Chichester, www.wiley.com

This edition first published 2013

© 2013 John Wiley & Sons, Ltd, Chichester, West Sussex.

Registered office

John Wiley & Sons Ltd, The Atrium, Southern Gate, Chichester, West Sussex, PO19 8SQ, United Kingdom

For details of our global editorial offices, for customer services and for information about how to apply for permission to reuse the copyright material in this book please see our website at www.wiley.com.

Wiley publishes in a variety of print and electronic formats and by print-on-demand. Some material included with standard print versions of this book may not be included in e-books or in print-on-demand. If this book refers to media such as a CD or DVD that is not included in the version you purchased, you may download this material at http://booksupport.wiley.com. For more information about Wiley products, visit www.wiley.com.

Designations used by companies to distinguish their products are often claimed as trademarks. All brand names and product names used in this book are trade names, service marks, trademarks or registered trademarks of their respective owners. The publisher is not associated with any product or vendor mentioned in this book.

For general information on our other products and services, please contact our Customer Care Department within the U.S. at 877-762-2974, outside the U.S. at (001) 317-572-3993, or fax 317-572-4002.

For technical support, please visit www.wiley.com/techsupport.   796.358

A catalogue record for this book is available from the British Library.

ISBN 978-1-118-48032-8 (paperback); ISBN 978-1-118-48035-9 (ebk);

ISBN 978-1-118-48036-6 (ebk); ISBN 978-1-118-48034-2 (ebk)

Printed in Great Britain by TJ International, Padstow.

10 9 8 7 6 5 4 3 2 1

MIX
Paper from
responsible sources
FSC   FSC® C013056
www.fsc.org

Contents at a Glance

Table of Contents

Introduction

Welcome to the fascinating world of cricket, a sport loved around the globe by millions of die-hard fans.

To the casual observer cricket can appear complex and at times, well, just plain bizarre. What other sport is there which involves people dressing all in white and then throwing themselves around a muddy, grassy field? But those in the know treasure the game as simply the supreme test of brains and brawn.

I've written this book so that newcomers to cricket can get to know the game quickly, without feeling overwhelmed or intimidated. I also explain the history of the game and show you how to get out there and play . In double quick time you'll be appreciating fully the great game of cricket, whether as a player or a spectator.

About This book

This book provides you with everything you need to know about the sport of cricket. All the information you need to get started as a player or become an A1 fan is here between the pages of this book. But the good news is that you don't have to read this book from cover to cover. You can easily just dip into those chapters that catch your interest. Perhaps you'll be watching a game of cricket on television or listening to radio coverage and you'd like to know more about a particular aspect of the game and its history then just turn to the chapter which does the job.

If you're keen to get playing cricket there is lots in this book for you. section dedicated to developing batting, bowling and fielding techniques as well as explaining the tactical nuances of cricket captaincy. In addition, there is a chapter on training which is essential reading for anyone looking to develop their playing technique and all round physical conditioning.

If playing the game isn't for you, – and you'd rather be a fan,this book has an enormous amount to offer. The domestic and international cricket scene is laid out in full for you and there is a whole chapter dedicated to showing you how to get to watch big match cricket.

Whatever draws you to the sport, *Cricket For Dummies* will have something for you.

How to Use This book

Don't be restricted by the order in which the contents of this book appear. Flip through it, maybe starting with Chapter 1 where we explain the basics of the game. The book contains diagrams, drawings and tables to make it easy for you to immediately understand the most important aspects of the game.

You may find that in a discussion of a particular aspect of cricket in one chapter, we refer to another aspect of the game. Whenever this happens we tell you which chapter to turn to for more information about that other aspect. For example, when we talk about fielding positions we will tell you which chapter to turn to for more detailed information on positions.

Conventions Used in This Book

To help you navigate this book, I use the following conventions:

- *Italic* text is used for emphasis and to highlight new words and terms that we define in the text.
- **Bold** text is used to indicate key words and phrases in bulleted lists or the action parts of numbered steps.
- Sidebars are shaded grey boxes containing text that's interesting to know but not necessarily critical to your understanding of the chapter or topic.

Foolish Assumptions

While writing this book, I've made some assumptions about you. First of all, I've assumed you're human. Cricket is played by both men and women, though the men's game grabs the lion's share of the headlines. Throughout this book, for convenience, I have used terms such as 'batsman' and 'fieldsman', and the associated pronoun 'he', even though I know it won't cover everyone who reads this book.

Don't feel intimidated if you know nothing about cricket. This book will bring you up to speed, fast. Cricket can be a complex game and even some cricketers have difficulty grasping some aspects. But before long – after reading this book – you're going to be transformed into a cricket expert.

✔ Why are some cricket matches done with in a single day, while others last five whole days?

✔ How does spin bowling work?

✔ What does all the jargon mean? What on earth is *bowling a maiden over*, a *new cherry* and a *silly mid-off*?

✔ Why are Australia so good at cricket?

This book answers these questions, and many, many more. Our assumption is that you know nothing and we take it from there.

How This Book Is Organised

To make things easier for you, this book is divided into four parts. Each part focuses on an important aspect of the game of cricket.

Part 1: Getting Started with Cricket

This part arms you with the basics. The basic rules are explained, as are the pitch, and the roles of individual players. Also I examine the different formats of the game from five-day test matches to quick-fire Twenty20 cricket. I also explain how you can get in on the action and start playing the game. This part ends with handy hints on what you need to kit yourself out with to play cricket.

Part 11: Playing the Game

If you want to take up the game, this part is full of must-know tips and explanataions. But even if you just want to appreciate the skills of professional players, then this part is a real eye-opener. The first chapter explores batting, from starting out through to how to play aggressive and defensive shots. Bowling is the subject of the next chapter. Read this chapter and you could soon become a batsman's worst nightmare. The art of fielding the ball – catching the ball or stopping the batsmen from scoring runs through athletic stops and accurate throws – used to be overlooked by many cricketers, even some professionals. But nowadays fielding is seen as a key skill and in this part there is a whole chapter dedicated to showing you how to be a top class fielder. Next, captaining a cricket team and the tactical side of the sport are explored. This really is a must-read for would-be players and fans alike. The part ends with a chapter on how to train properly for cricket.

Part III: Welcome to Planet Cricket

This part tells you about all the competitions and tournaments played around the globe. In particular, what makes Test cricket so special – where the best players from around the world square off against each other – is honed in on. Cricket's greatest contest – The Ashes – is also looked at in depth as are some of the past and present heroes of the game. A light is also shined on other great global rivalries – such as between Pakistan and India. If that wasn't enough, this part also talks about the cricket scene in the UK, we look at the county championship and one day competitions. This part ends with an indispensable guide to be a cricket fan – where you can see top class cricket in the UK and abroad.

Part IV: The Part of Tens

The part without which no For Dummies book would be complete. This part is packed full of fascinating bits of information that you can store away and draw on whenever you feel like impressing everyone you know at the cricket club. It contains our unique take on the great cricketers and matches which have illuminated the history of cricket.

Icons Used in This Book

To help your navigation through this book keep an eye out for the icons, the little pictures that sit in the margin. They guide you to particular types of information. This list tells you what the icons in this book mean.

This Icon highlights tips and snippets of advice that can help you, whether you aim to become a better player or a better spectator.

Paragraphs with this icon attached contain information that is especially useful to remember.

You won't see this icon very often, but, when you do take heed, because it indicates areas which may cause concern.

This icon indicates a technical discussion is under way. You can skip this stuff if you want, because it isn't necessary for an understanding of the basics. If you read it, though, your cricket know-how will be boosted.

 This icon highlights the laws of the game, the sort of lingo you'll hear other players, umpires and commentators using, and those intricate little facts that all sports fans love to know about their game.

 Every so often I look in-depth at a great player from today or the past or just a quirky cricketing character; the idea is to give you an idea of the big names in the sport.

Where to Go from Here

What direction you take depends on your needs. Take a look at the table of contents because it's very detailed and gives you an excellent overview of the book and the way in which it's structured.

For the beginner, the best place to start is the beginning! But if you want to familiarise yourself with the basics of the game, go to Part I. If you're an aspiring player, Part II is the place for you, while if you want to know more about Test cricket – the ultimate contest in the sport – then go seek out Part III. In short, it's up to you, go enjoy the greatest sport of all!

Part I
Getting Started with Cricket

Go to www.dummies.com/extras/cricket for online bonus content.

In this part . . .

- ✔ Getting to know the rules and regulations.

- ✔ Finding your way round the field of play.

- ✔ Understanding the different formats of the game.

- ✔ Kitting yourself out with the right gear.

- ✔ Go to `www.dummies.com/extras/cricket` for online bonus content, including an extra Part of Tens chapter: 'Ten Great Cricket Controversies'.

Chapter 1

Taking In the Joy of Cricket

. . . .

In This Chapter

▶ Assessing the gulf between pros and amateurs

▶ Looking at the battle between bowler and batsman

▶ Exploring the strange, strange world of cricket speak

▶ Discovering what you need to be a cricket fan

▶ Understanding the role of the umpires

. . . .

*M*illions of people around the globe follow cricket. For many, cricket is the number one sport, offering a unique blend of physical strength, lightning reflexes, huge skill and tactics galore. In fact, there is a strong case for the game which, first spread by the British empire in the eighteenth and nineteenth century is the world's second most popular sport behind football.

When the best cricketers in the world do battle you won't see anything like it for nail-biting tension and excitement.

Glancing at Cricket's Global Appeal

Cricket has spread around the globe on the back of the British Empire.

Despite the best efforts of cricket's global administrators – the International Cricket Council (ICC) – cricket has never managed the trick of breaking out of this traditional heartland. For example, no Chinese cricket team exists and even the USA team actually consists mostly of expatriate West Indians living in Florida.

But the British Empire – which at its height covered a third of a globe – isn't a bad heartland for a sport. India, Pakistan, Australia, New Zealand, South Africa, West Indies, Zimbabwe and Bangladesh all play test cricket (the top echelon of the game: See Chapter 3 for more on test cricket).

Doing a quick bit of maths, that covers about 1.5 billion people – around a fifth of the world's population. Although not as big as football, this coverage dwarfs some other world sports such as rugby, hockey and international tiddlywinks! And cricket isn't a minority sport in the countries that play it: Far from it.

In India, Pakistan, Sri Lanka and Bangladesh, cricket is the number one sport; and in Britain cricket is still one of the major national sports, along with football and rugby.

Buoyed by a recent Ashes triumph, cricket is going through a renaissance in England. Unlike premiership football, cricket has no seven-figure annual salaries or swearing at the officials. And a good thing too, some would say. Hey, being a cricketer or a cricket fan may even be considered hip! One indication of English cricket's 'new golden age' is the news from the English and Welsh Cricket Board (ECB) that big match ticket sales are at an all time high.

National teams compete against each other in both test and one-day international matches. Tests involve each side having two innings and can last up to five days. One-day internationals, as the name suggests, are completed in a single day. Each side gets just one innings which is limited to a set number of overs, say 50 of 20. See Chapter 3 for more on the differences between test and one-day international matches.

Gauging the Difference: Amateur and Professional Cricket

Cricket, like most major sports, is divided between the amateur and the professional game. The amateurs play for fun, the professionals play for pay.

The key differences between amateur and professional cricketers fall into four main areas:

- **Fitness standards:** Professional cricketers are fitter than amateurs. They are put on special diets and fitness regimes and have an army of coaches to tell them what to do to get the most from their bodies. Even the most committed amateur is unlikely to be able to approach the sheer athleticism of a professional player.

- **Skill levels:** Professional cricketers are way ahead when it comes to their skill levels. They get to practise most days and dedicate themselves to honing their talents.

- ✔ **Commitment:** Amateurs have jobs and can, usually, only play at weekends. They may only get to train once a week during the cricket season, and perhaps not at all in the winter. For professionals, on the other hand, cricket is what they do for a living. They play matches on most days during the summer and may even travel abroad to play during the winter months.

- ✔ **Match length:** Because the skill levels of professionals are so high, completing some games of cricket in a day can be difficult. Therefore, longer formats of the game have been devised; some games taking anything up to five days to finish. See Chapter 3 for more on match formats. Amateurs only play one-day games, or very occasionally two-day games across weekends.

An estimated 300–400 professional cricketers earn their livings playing in Britain, whereas tens of thousands of amateur players play for fun each weekend during the summer months. Even more play the occasional game of cricket – perhaps they have their cricket bat and clothing stuffed under the stairs, getting everything out when asked to take part in a friendly match at work or the local village cricket club.

The cricket season runs from April to September in Britain. But because cricket is a global sport and other parts of the world have their summers at different times of the year, even when no cricket is being played in Britain – because the weather's cold and wet – cricket is being played somewhere else in the world. For example, in Australia the cricket season runs from late October through to March.

Understanding the great divide: Amateurs and professionals

Over time, the skill and fitness standards of professional cricketers have raced away from those of amateurs.

A long time ago, when test match cricket had just started to be played, many top players were amateurs. Often they were members of the upper classes who didn't have to work and had enough spare time on their hands to play cricket. However, back then a lot of sham amateurism went on with top players claiming to be amateur but receiving great big 'expenses' payments. See Chapter 17 for more on the sham amateur controversy.

Even in the relatively recent past seeing a few beer bellies among professionals wasn't unusual – going back to the 1980s, former England captains Mike Gatting and Ian Botham both carried a bit of extra padding around their midriffs! Even the Australians had their fair share of rotund cricketers such as Tasmanian David Boon and mustache wearing Fast bowler Merv Hughes. Nowadays, though, beer bellies are as rare as hen's teeth among professionals: They are athletes. As a result, performance levels in the professional ranks have raced away even farther from amateurs, especially when it comes to fielding. Go to watch any club cricket match and you can bet that before long you'll see a fielder misfield the ball or miss it altogether. Such moments of enjoyable farce are few and far between in the professional ranks.

But not only physical fitness and playing standards mark the growing gulf between professional and amateur. Some of the rules now differ between top-notch-professional and amateur matches.

In part the difference in rules is down to the inevitable march of new technology. In professional cricket matches, broadcast on television, the umpires can call on the help of video replay technology. They do this by requesting that a third umpire, sat on the sidelines, review the video evidence in order to give a decision – usually on whether a batsman has been caught, run-out or stumped. See Chapter 2 for more on the third umpire and modes of dismissal. The third umpire then radios his decision back to the two umpires on the pitch and the decision is given. Under the decision review system (DRS), see chapter two for more on this, a batsman who has been dismissed caught or leg before wicket can call for the third umpire to look again at the video footage and technology such as hawkeye and hotspot to check that the on-field umpire's decision was correct. Of course in amateur games – where rustling up a cricket ball and two sets of stumps can sometimes be hard enough – you won't find video replays or extra umpires.

Some experts suggest that by adopting such new technology the professional game is in danger of pulling away from the roots of the game. Ultimately, some argue, this could undermine the popularity of the professional game because amateur cricketers – who make up a sizeable proportion of fans at matches – may become unable to relate to the game as played by the professionals. In short, alienation could prove a big turn off.

Other people see no harm in the introduction of new technology as long as it helps the umpires make the right call.

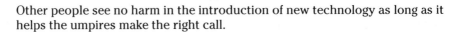

A cricket match involves two teams of 11 players and two on-pitch umpires.

An innings is completed when ten of a team's 11 batsmen have been dismissed by the fielding side. Once the batting team's innings is complete the fielding team takes their turn to bat. Therefore, the fielding team becomes the batting side and the batting side becomes the fielding team. Confused? Well check out Chapter 2 for the full low-down on an innings in cricket.

The umpire's job is to interpret and apply the laws of the game to the match situation. Among other things, this means that the umpires get to decide whether a batsman is out and whether a bowler has broken the game's laws. See Chapter 2 for more on the role of the umpire and the calls he has to make in a match situation.

Getting involved in the amateur game

Cricket can be played anywhere. All you need is a few willing bodies, a bat, a ball, something to act as stumps (an upturned box will do) and a bit of open space and, Bob's your uncle, you're away.

Many people's first encounter with cricket is through an informal game in a garden, a park, or even in the street. This can be tons of fun, but sooner or later, if the cricket bug bites, you'll want to take things a touch more seriously.

This is when cricket clubs – pardon the pun – come into play!

Joining is easy – not like some golf clubs. Just contact someone who is involved with the club, go along to a practice session, or a match, and see if you like what you see. Are they a friendly bunch, and is the standard right for you?

Clubs are mostly for amateurs but like professional teams they love to orga- nise themselves into leagues and play in cup competitions. Some competi- tions in which club sides compete have been going for donkey's years. Local newspapers usually report on club matches. Club sides play at weekends. Depending on how many players a club can rustle up, it may field several dif- ferent sides catering to a range of player abilities, from the very good player to the pure enthusiast who may not be blessed with oodles of talent.

The best players in the club (or the captain's mates) play for the first eleven. The next group play in the second eleven and so on downwards. One club I was a member of boasted six teams of eleven playing in different competi- tions. Leagues tend to be organised so that players of similar abilities square off against each other, so the second eleven at one club play other second eleven teams from the local area.

In short, club cricket is amateur and supposed to be fun, but at the same time a competitive streak runs through its heart. Trophies are at stake!

If you want to find out more about your local cricket club, you'll probably find that in this Internet savvy age it has a Web site. You can also find out information such as ground location and who the players are by checking out local newspapers. If you want a definitive list of all the clubs in a particular area, log onto the Web site of the club cricket conference at `www.club-cricket.com`.

Club cricket can be a breeding ground for the professional game. County sides scout club teams to check out any promising youngsters making their way in the game. If they like what they see they may invite the youngster to join them for practice or even offer them a contract to turn professional.

Joining a club isn't that expensive. Expect to play between £80 and £150 in annual subscription fees as well as a small fee for each match played. The fees are charged so that the club can hire pitches, when needed, and arrange for rather delicious cricket teas to be laid on for the players. Yum!

Exploring the Strange World of Cricket Speak

Eavesdropping on a couple of cricketers or cricket fans having a natter can be a surreal experience. They can seem to use their very own unique language more akin to Esperanto than English.

Some of the characteristics of cricket speak are:

- **Arcane words:** Cricket has been around for centuries and words that have fallen out of everyday usage long ago still have a foothold in cricket speak. For example, sometimes you hear the phrase *bowling a maiden over*; this may sound like something from a romantic novel but in fact refers to the bowler delivering an over without the batsman scoring a run.

- **Slang:** Perhaps no other sport is as wedded to the use of slang as cricket. Over time cricketers have developed their own words to describe on field actions and phenomena. Some of this slang has been adopted around the globe, and some is so bizarre that it stays put in its own country of origin. Most of the slang is fairly logical when you think of it. For example, a brand new cricket ball is referred to as a *cherry* because the ball is at its most red in colour when new and before the covering lacquer has worn away.

- **Multiple usages:** Nothing confuses non-cricket followers more than the habit among players and fans of using the same word to describe very different things. For example, the word *wicket* is often used to describe the following: The strip of turf between the two sets of stumps, the stumps themselves, and the act of dismissing the batsman. Have a look at this passage:

The bowler delivered the ball which bounced off the wicket. The batsman missed the ball which struck the wicket. The batsman had lost his wicket.

The good news is that in this book I avoid multiple usages of words like the plague.

Looking at Batsman Against Bowler

Watch a cricket match for any length of time and you soon understand that the main on-field contest is between the batsman and the bowler. This is because:

- ✔ The bowler's job is to get the batsman out – or *dismiss* him. The bowler can do this in a number of ways, for example by bowling balls that hit the stumps or by tempting the batsman into hitting the ball into the air to a fielder who then takes a catch.

- ✔ The batsman's job is to prevent the bowler from dismissing him and to score runs off the bowler's deliveries to add to the team's total.

The eyes of everyone – the batsman, bowler, fielders, umpires and spectators – are glued on the small cricket ball as it travels towards the batsman.

Understanding That Cricket is a Dangerous Game

Cricket can be dangerous. A cricket ball is 5½ ounces of cork wrapped in leather, and believe me, if you get hit by one you certainly know about it. In fact, each year lots of people around the globe are seriously injured, or in some rare cases killed, by cricket balls.

A player is most at risk of being hit when he is batting or fielding close to where the batsman plays his shots. Why batsmen are at risk is fairly obvious. The bowler is trying to hit the stumps and the batsman stands in the way trying to hit the ball to stop that from happening. Sometimes, though, the batsman's torso, head, hands or legs are inevitably struck by the ball.

Close fielders – including the wicket-keeper – are at risk of injury because they don't have long to react to the ball if the batsman hits it towards them. If the batsman hits the ball hard, it can travel at great speed and cause nasty injury to hands, body and even – gulp! – the face.

However, don't get the impression that cricket is like a heavyweight boxing bout with the players finishing the match all bloodied and bruised. Injuries, fortunately, are relatively rare. This is thanks, in no small part, to the amount of padding worn by batsmen (in particular) and close fielders. The ins and outs of cricket equipment, what you need, how much it costs and where to find it, is covered extensively in Chapter 4.

Taking in the Dark Side: Cricket Frustrations

Even the most ardent of fans accept that cricket is a sport not suited to everyone. Some people – around 280 million Americans for a start – just can't get their head around the game.

The people who aren't fans think that the idea of grown men putting on white clothing, hitting a ball around the place, chasing it for up to five days, and at the end of it all maybe still settling for a draw is, put simply, a bit daft.

Here are some things that drive cricket's detractors up the wall:

- Players leave the field if it starts to rain and even if the light is bad.
- Matches can last for days and still end in a draw.
- Cricket matches can be slow affairs, a sudden flurry of activity when the bowler delivers the ball to the batsman followed by a minute or so of inaction as the bowler prepares to bowl the next delivery.
- Much of the language used in cricket is arcane or just plain bizarre, see earlier in this chapter for more.

The truth is that you either love or loathe cricket and the fact that you have picked up this book means that you are at least inclined to join those that love it.

Many cricket watchers suggest that there has never been a more exciting time to be a cricket fan. The advent of one-day cricket – where a result has to be achieved in a single day – and aggressive batting by the great Australian side has helped quicken the pace of run-scoring in cricket matches.

Scorebooks, Scoreboards and Scorecards

Cricket matches can be long affairs – up to five days – and someone has to keep track of what's going on, delivery after delivery. This is called *scoring* and the people who keep score are called the *scorers*. The scorers' job is to note down what happens during each delivery – whether, for example, the batsman has scored a run or the bowler managed to dismiss a batsman.

These scorers note down all this information in a scorebook. To the untrained eye the marks made in the scorebook can look like a giant game of noughts and crosses is being played out. However, each tiny mark made in the scorebook records an event in the match. See Chapter 2 for the ins and outs of marks used in scorebooks, and Chapter 13 for the low-down on interpreting a scorecard.

Equipping Yourself as a Fan

Not every fan of cricket wants to play the game. From a playing perspective, cricket can be very time-consuming and equipment isn't cheap. What's more, some people just don't feel that their skills are up to playing the game. Instead they would rather just be a fan. And boy, does cricket offer a lot to its fans.

Nearly every day of the year a test or one-day international match takes place somewhere. During the summer months, 18 county sides in England compete in a plethora of competitions from the County Championship through to the quick-fire excitement of twenty20 cricket. Check out Chapter 3 for more on the different formats of the game, and Chapter 10 on savouring international cricket.

Don't forget that a thriving women's game exists, with county teams competing and the England teamclaiming the world cup in 2009. What's more, go to your local park during the summer months and you're likely to see two teams of players in whites indulging their love for the game.

Cricket fans are spoiled, and not just as spectators. A mountain of coverage exists in the press, online, and through books and magazines. Check out Chapter 13 for more on building up your cricket knowledge bank and following the game as an armchair fan.

Showing off your cricket knowledge

Cricket fans in particular love a list. Get a group of cricket fans together and quicker than you can say 'mine's a pint' they're gabbing away about the great players and matches from the past. Part IV of this book is full of lists and the inside track on the greater figures of cricket; check it out so that you can show off your cricket know-how.

Coaching and cricket tactics

Cricket coaching has come a long way in the past couple of generations. Players used to rely largely on natural ability and would practise their skills sporadically. Teams didn't have coaches. Instead, players relied on each other to impart technical tips on playing the game. But in the modern era players have all sorts of professional backroom staff to call on. The top professional teams such as those representing counties and nations now have fitness trainers, dieticians, sports psychologists and specialist coaches who are experts in one facet of the game such as fielding, batting or bowling. Chapter 9 gives you the inside track on training and practising for cricket.

Cricket coaching may be a relatively modern phenomenon but tactics have always played a big role in the game. The team captain has to decide the tactics, and the challenges facing the captain differ according to whether the team is batting or in the field. See Chapter 8 for more on the arts and crafts of captaincy.

Getting to Grips with the Laws of the Game

Cricket as a sport takes itself a bit seriously. Instead of simply just having rules, cricket has *laws*. Cricket administrators see themselves as protectors of the laws of the game. Cricket has more laws than you can shake a stick at. Full explanations in print of the laws of cricket can run to way over 10,000 words. Compare this to football which only has a few rules and mostly involves two teams kicking a bag of wind between posts. However, don't get the impression that because cricket has lots of different laws that somehow the game is impossible to pick up. The basics of the game are relatively easy to comprehend.

The first printed version of the laws of cricket can be traced way back to 1744. They were drawn up . . . guess where? A bar! The Star and Garter in Pall Mall, London, to be precise. But cricket laws haven't stood still, they have evolved and been changed on many occasions.

Cricket, despite its sometimes stuffy image, is always evolving. The game's governing body, the International Cricket Council (ICC), meets regularly to review the laws of cricket. The ICC often makes changes and is willing to experiment. Some law changes work and they remain, others don't and are, usually, ditched in double-quick time.

Gauging the Importance of the Umpire

Umpires are present to apply the laws of the game to the match situation. They decide, for example, whether a batsman has been dismissed by the bowling side, whether the bowler is bowling legally, and when play stops to take lunch and tea breaks. Their role is a crucial one: Without an umpire, a proper game of cricket can't be played.

See Chapter 2 for more on the role of the umpire and some of the signals he uses to alert the scorers, players and crowd to what is going on in the match.

Chapter 2

Getting to Grips with the Basics

. . . .

In This Chapter

▶ Checking out what the players do

▶ Taking a look at the cricket pitch

▶ Considering aspects of the pitch

▶ Appreciating the role and powers of the cricket umpire

▶ Acquainting yourself with the scoring system

▶ Getting the batsman out

. . . .

*I*f you want the low-down on how cricket works – from the scoring system, the pitch, through to the role of the players – this is the chapter for you.

Introducing the Players

Cricket is a game where two teams of 11 players square-off against each other.

Every player gets the chance to bat and to field, and, in theory, the team captain can call on everyone to bowl. But players tend to specialise in one of three roles: As *batsmen*, *bowlers* or *wicket-keepers*:

✔ **Batsmen:** These players are adept at defending their stumps from being hit by the cricket ball and at hitting the ball with their bat to score runs. Everyone in the team has to bat – though not every player can call himself a batsman! See Chapter 5 for the full low-down on batting.

✔ **Bowlers:** These players deliver the ball in the direction of the stumps and their raison d'être is to dismiss the batsman. The team captain decides which players get to bowl. See Chapter 6 for the ins and outs of bowling.

✔ **Wicket-keepers:** A wicket-keeper stands behind the batsman's stumps when the bowler delivers the ball. Clad in a giant pair of gloves, this player's main jobs are to catch the ball when it comes in his direction – as most balls will – and to gather the ball when it has been thrown by fielders. Each team has only one wicket-keeper, but he is the hub of the team when in the field. See Chapter 7 for more on wicket-keeping.

✔ **Fielders:** Everyone gets to field. Fielders are there to support the bowlers in their quest to dismiss the batsmen. They do this by taking catches and running out the batsmen. See the section 'Dismissing the Batsmen' later in this chapter for more on modes of dismissal. Fielders also have to chase, gather and return the ball to the bowler or wicket-keeper should the batsman hit it with his bat. See Chapter 7 for the inside track on mastering the art of fielding.

Some players are good at multi-tasking; they can bat and bowl, or bat and keep wicket to a decent standard. In cricket speak these players are called *all rounders* and, no, that's not because they have enjoyed too many sumptuous cricket teas and developed a bit of girth.

In cricket matches involving professional teams – such as national, county or state sides – there will be a twelfth man selected. Now the twelfth man doesn't get to bat or bowl in the game but if one of his side has to leave the field injured or just needing to go to the toilet, then the twelfth man will come on and field in his place until the missing player returns. The twelfth man will also help carry the drinks onto the field. Basically, the twelfth man acts as a bit of a dogsbody for his team.

Remembering Cricket Helpers

A cricket match isn't just a case of two teams of 11 players. You need the help of others to make it all happen. These cricket helpers include:

✔ **Umpires:** These people apply the laws of the game to match situations. They decide whether batsmen have been dismissed and they signal to the scorers. Someone has to be an umpire, and every game needs two. The umpire's role is key to the game of cricket. See the section 'Umpiring: The Men in White Coats' later in this chapter for more on umpiring.

✔ **Scorers:** These people sit on the sidelines, keeping a log of all the runs scored by the batsmen and the wickets taken by the bowlers. See 'Understanding the Scoring System' later in this chapter for more on scoring.

✔ **Groundsmen:** These hardy souls prepare the cricket pitch. They can expend huge amounts of energy ensuring that the condition of the wicket will provide a good contest between the batters and the bowlers. See 'Understanding the importance of the wicket' later in this chapter for more on preparing the cricket pitch.

✔ **Tea helpers:** A club cricket match is as much about food as about runs and catches. During breaks in play – outlined later in the 'Looking at Breaks in Play' section in this chapter – the players feast on sandwiches, cake and the ubiquitous sausages on a stick. I have avoided using the phrase tea ladies here but in my experience of 20 years of club cricket, 99.9 per cent of the people preparing the teas are mothers, wives or aunties of the players.

In club cricket sometimes you find it hard to persuade people to give up their Saturday or Sunday to act as umpire or scorer. Therefore, teams tend to improvise, with players waiting for their turn to bat, or those who have already been dismissed, taking on the job of umpiring or scoring.

Taking in the Field of Play

Unlike most other sports, no rule governs the exact size or shape of a cricket field (although strict rules exist for the pitch portion of the field where the bowler delivers the ball to the batsmen: See 'Understanding the importance of the pitch' later in this chapter).

Roughly speaking most cricket fields are oval, but some can be more like circles or even squares. The size can vary dramatically. Some cricket grounds like the Oval in London, UK, or Melbourne Cricket Ground in Australia are huge expanses of turf stretching in all directions for a hundred metres or more. Other grounds are much more diddy affairs, with the boundary merely a stone's throw away from the pitch.

The *boundary* is the line marking the limit of the cricket field. If the ball is hit over this line without it bouncing then six runs are scored. If the ball does bounce on its way to crossing the boundary then four runs are scored. See 'Understanding the Scoring System' later in this chapter for more on scoring in cricket.

The boundary is normally indicated by a white line with markers spaced along it or, in professional cricket, and some club cricket, by a rope. The advantage of using a rope to mark the boundary is that the size of the playing area can be altered between matches. Sometimes the rope can be located far away from the pitch; other times closer in. The boundary rope is often pulled in towards the pitch in one-day matches to heighten the chances of batsmen scoring boundaries.

The playing area of a cricket ground can be divided into three parts:

- ✔ **The *pitch*, often referred to as the *wicket:*** The *pitch* is the strip of turf where the stumps are located and on which the bowler delivers the ball to the batsmen. Confusingly, the pitch is often referred to as the *wicket*, a term also used for the collection of stumps and bails which the batsman is trying to defend, and which the bowler is trying to hit. Refer to Chapter 1 for more on cricket's maddening use of one term for several items.

- ✔ **The infield:** The *infield* is the part of the field where the wicket-keeper and close fielders stand when the ball is being delivered. In *first class* one-day matches – the ones played by professionals – the edge of the infield is marked by a circle of white discs placed thirty yards away from the wicket. Check out Chapters 7 and 8 for more on fielding positions and restrictions.

- ✔ **The outfield:** The *outfield* is everything else from the infield to the boundary rope. If the batsman hits the ball into the outfield he will usually try and attempt a run: See 'Understanding the Scoring System' later in this chapter for more on scoring.

You can tell the different parts of the cricket field by how close-cut the grass is. Groundsmen spend most of their time tending to the condition of the wicket, ensuring that the grass is cut very short. The grass in the infield is usually allowed to grow a little more and the outfield can be quite green and lush.

Understanding the importance of the pitch

The pitch is at the centre of the playing area and is where most of the action takes place (see Figure 2-1). The pitch is where the ball is delivered by the bowler to the batsman , who then tries to defend the stumps from being hit by the ball or executes aggressive scoring shots: See Chapter 5 for the ins and outs of batting.

Relative to the playing area as a whole, the pitch is relatively small, only 22 yards (20.12 metres) long and 10 feet (three metres) wide.

The condition of the pitch – how much grass it has, how many bumps or cracks exist, and so on – has a huge impact on the outcome of the game. This impact relates to the dynamics of a cricket ball. A cricket ball has a pronounced stitched seam running around its circumference. This seam acts as a ridge, and when the ball hits the pitch it will carry on straight or deviate in towards or away from where the batsman stands. In addition, the ball can either bounce high – even above head high – or keep low.

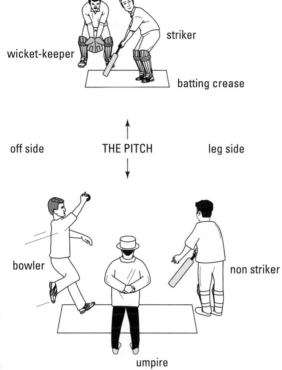

striker

wicket-keeper

batting crease

off side   THE PITCH   leg side

bowler   non striker

Figure 2-1:
The pitch.

umpire

The condition of the pitch can influence what happens to the cricket ball on bouncing. For example:

- ✔ If the pitch is grassy and even, the cricket ball will move towards or away from where the batsman is standing, but the bounce will be regular.

- ✔ If the pitch is grassy and uneven, then the ball is likely to move but the batsman has the added headache of uneven bounce.

- ✔ If the pitch lacks grass and is even, then it's usually happy days for the batsman. The ball is unlikely to move towards or away from where the batsman is standing and the bounce will be regular.

- ✔ If the pitch lacks grass and is uneven, don't expect to see much movement towards or away from the batsman, but when the ball bounces it may keep very low or steeple high.

Batsmen hate uneven bounce because they can never be quite sure at what height the cricket ball delivered by the bowler is going to reach them.

Sowing the seeds of a great pitch

A good groundsman is like a head gardener, carefully nurturing the pitch. In England, at the test match venues, the groundsmen plant grass seeds in the pitch around eight months before the test match is scheduled to take place. The pitch will then be rolled with a heavy roller in April, at the start of the season, and regularly watered. A couple of weeks before the test match the pitch will be covered from the elements, only being uncovered to be rolled at regular intervals. The idea is to produce a pitch which leads to an even contest between bat and ball. After all, a test match is supposed to last anything up to five days!

If the turf of the cricket pitch has large cracks in it then the turf will most likely produce uneven bounce. In addition, if a bowler lands the ball on a crack in the pitch then he can expect the ball to turn towards or away from the batsman.

Whether or not a pitch is moist can have a huge influence on the movement of the ball on bouncing. Generally, a moist pitch leads to the ball moving towards or away from the batsman a great deal, slowing sharply on contact with the pitch.

Bowlers, through a combination of wrist and finger movement, can cause a cricket ball to deviate in the air or off the pitch after it hits the ground. Bowlers aim to bounce the ball off parts of the pitch which they believe helps it move towards or away from where the batsman is standing. See Chapter 6 for details on mastering the art of bowling.

Because county cricket matches are also played at test match venues, the groundsmen prepare several cricket pitches side-by-side for use throughout the season. The area of the cricket pitch encompassing all these pitches is referred to as a *cricket square*. See Chapter 12 for more on county cricket.

Taking in the creases

Stumps come in two sets – which the bowlers try to hit and batsmen try to defend – at either end of the cricket pitch. Rather confusingly, these stumps are sometimes called wickets but I'll avoid that usage in this book, to keep things simple.

The batsman stands at one end of the pitch in front of one set of stumps and the bowler at the opposite end.

Each end of the cricket pitch has two sets of identically spaced white lines. One line dissects where the stumps are located; the other white line is 4 feet (1.1 metres) in front of this. The space between these white lines is called the *bowling crease* (see Figure 2-2).

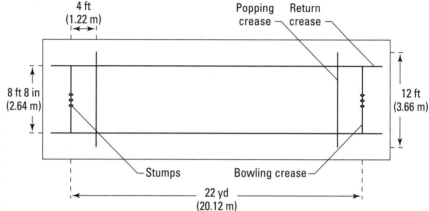

Figure 2-2: The creases of the cricket pitch.

The bowling crease is further marked by two white lines. These two white lines are approximately 8 feet 8 inches (2.64 metres) apart. These lines together are called the *return crease* but in the cut and thrust of a game they are of little consequence. The two bowling creases, however, play a key role in the game:

- The white line four feet in front of the line dissecting the stumps – also called at times a *popping crease* – is the marker from which the bowler is allowed to deliver the ball. If the whole of the bowler's front foot strays beyond this line while delivering the ball, then the umpire will call 'no-ball'. See Chapter 6 for more on the no-ball rule.

- The white line on which the stumps are placed is also a marker for the bowler. The bowler is not allowed to deliver the ball until his foot is planted beyond this line.

- The white line 4 feet in front of the line passing through the stumps is the marker for the batsman to complete a run. In order to complete a run both players have to run between the two creases and touch their bats down beyond the bowling crease line. If they don't do this then a run isn't complete.

- The gap between the two bowling creases is 22 yards (20.12 metres).

The length and width of the cricket pitch are strictly laid down in the laws of the game but the field of play can vary enormously in size.

Changing ends explained

The batsman stands at one end of the pitch and the bowler delivers the ball from the other end. Simple.

Now, after the bowler has delivered six balls, he has completed an *over*. At this point the bowling side *changes ends*. Put simply, the next set of six deliveries is bowled from the opposite end of the pitch to the previous set, by a different member of the bowling side.

The bowling team then changes ends again and the play goes on in this way until the batting side has completed its *innings* – in other words, when all the players in the team have taken their turns to bat.

Unlike the bowlers, the two batsmen don't change ends. If they have run an odd number of runs – 1, 3 or 5 runs – they will end up at different ends, and the batsman who faced the bowler at the end of the last over again faces the new bowler.

The batsman who is at the opposite end from where the bowler delivers the ball has to face the bowler until the over is complete, or he completes a run, and the bowling team change ends.

The batsman who is playing the deliveries from the bowler is said to be *taking strike*. The batsman at the opposite end of the pitch – the end the bowler is delivering the ball from – is said to be the *non-striker*.

Bowlers don't usually deliver one over and give up. The captain will usually ask a bowler to deliver several overs or more from one end of the pitch in succession, alternating overs with a bowler at the other end. The period of play during which a bowler is bowling is called a *bowling spell*. The idea is that the bowler has time to get into the rhythm of delivering the ball and, hopefully, to spot and exploit weaknesses in the batsman's technique. Check out Chapter 6 for more on the art of bowling.

If the player who is taking strike hits the ball in the air and is *caught* by a fielder then he is *out*, or *dismissed*; see the section 'Dismissing the Batsmen' later in this chapter for more on getting out. If, while the ball is in the air, prior to being caught, the batsman runs towards the other end of the pitch, crossing with the non-striking player, then the non-striking player faces the next delivery bowled and not the new player coming to the pitch on the dismissal of the player who has given the catch. The only exception to this law is if the ball that the batsman has been caught off is the final ball of the over in which case the bowling team changes ends and the new batsman will be taking strike.

Protecting the pitch

The condition of the pitch can have a crucial impact on the result of the match. If conditions favour the bowlers – lots of grass or uneven bounce – then the match may be over quickly because the batting side find it hard to score runs and stop the ball hitting their stumps. On the other hand, if the condition of the pitch favours the batting side – not much grass and even bounce – then plenty of runs will be scored and the game may take a long time to be won by one side or could even end in a drawn. Check out Chapter 3 for how a cricket match can be won, lost or drawn.

Groundsmen work to get their pitches just right. They try to make sure that any pitch offers a little something for both the batting and bowling sides. To achieve this they sometimes use a covering over the pitch area, keeping the elements off the pitch. The groundsmen may remove the covering now and then to roll the pitch or to water it.

At important cricket grounds where high profile matches are played (see Chapter 13 for more details on these) you may find that the run-up area of the pitch used by the bowlers to deliver the ball are also covered when not in use. The use of a cover prevents bowlers from slipping when delivering the ball and potentially injuring themselves. See Chapter 6 for more on the bowler's run-up.

Some small club grounds, though, don't have covers. The pitch is left open to the elements, as are the bowler's run-ups. Some cricket grounds even avoid grass pitches altogether, preferring artificial turf.

In matches lasting more than one day, such as test and first class matches, the pitch is covered at the end of each day's play. The pitches are then uncovered again in the morning about half-an-hour before play is due to start. The only exception is if it is raining, when the covers remain in place until the shower stops.

Throughout this book you'll read about batsmen playing shots or bowlers aiming their deliveries to either the *off side* or the *leg side*. This bit of cricket jargon helps players, commentators and spectators divide the cricket pitch into two.

- ✔ The offside is the side of the pitch facing the batsman in his stance at the wicket.
- ✔ The leg side is the side of the pitch behind a batsman's legs in his stance at the wicket.

What constitutes the off and leg side depends on whether the batsman is right-handed or left-handed. For example, the leg side of a right-handed batsman is the off side for a left-hander.

Sometimes you'll hear the leg side also called the *on side*.

Talking Stumps and Bails

The stumps and bails are essential pieces of cricket kit, a bit like goalposts in soccer. Without stumps and bails you can't have a proper match.

A *stump* is a long straight piece of wood which is hammered into the ground.

Stumps come in two sets of three, located at opposite ends of the cricket pitch. On top of each set of stumps rest two bails. Bails are little pieces of wood which sit in the grooves at the top end of stumps, and for small objects, their role in a cricket match is surprisingly large.

In order for a player to be bowled, run-out or stumped – see 'Dismissing the Batsmen' later in this chapter for more on modes of dismissal – the bails have to be dislodged from the top of the stumps, by contact with the ball. If the ball makes contact with the stumps and the bails are not knocked off then no dismissal takes place. However, if just one bail is dislodged then the batsman is dismissed.

A correctly erected set of stumps and bails should be no higher than 28½ inches in height and 9 inches wide. Stumps and bails must be made of wood. Books on umpiring and the laws of cricket dedicate pages and pages to talking stumps and bails. After all, the umpire's job is to look after the stumps and bails, and ensure that they are the correct height and width. Getting the width right is particularly important, because the umpire doesn't want the cricket ball to pass through a gap between the stumps.

Each of the three stumps has its own name. The stump on the leg side of the batsman's stance is called, funnily enough, the leg stump. The next stump along is called the middle stump and the one furthest away from the leg stump, on the batsman's off side, is called the off stump.

Umpiring: The Men in White Coats

The role of the two umpires is crucial. Without them you can't have a game. The umpires adjudge all of the following:

- Whether a batsman has been dismissed.
- Whether the players have completed a run.
- Whether the ball hit by the batsman has crossed the boundary and thereby scored four or six runs.

   ✔ Whether or not the bowler has bowled a legal delivery.

   ✔ When six balls have been bowled and the over completed.

   ✔ When the game should start and finish and whether the players go off the field during a rain shower.

   ✔ Whether to take the players off the field when the light is so poor that it is deemed potentially dangerous to the batsman to continue to play.

As you've probably worked out by now, the umpires have a lot on their plate during a match. The umpire has to make decisions all the time, often in a split-second. In short, being an umpire isn't easy; they have to concentrate on every ball bowled.

Making the big calls

When the bowling team believe that a batsman may be dismissed they appeal to the umpire. Usually they shout 'How is that?' Shortened, often, to 'Howzat!'

The umpire then adjudges whether the player is out or not out.

When the umpire decides that the player is out, he raises a finger and points it at the batsman (see Figure 2-3) – a bit like Alan Sugar when saying 'You're fired' in BBC TV's *The Apprentice* programme.

However, when the umpire decides to turn down the bowling side's appeal he will call 'Not out!'

If the umpire has any doubt over whether the player is out, he is supposed to give the benefit of the doubt to the batsman and give a 'not out' decision.

Working together as a team

One umpire stands behind the stumps at the end of the pitch from which the bowler delivers the ball. This gives the umpire the best view to judge *leg before wicket* (LBW) appeals – see 'Comprehending the LBW law' later in this chapter – and whether catches have been properly taken by fielders. In addition, the umpire has a bird's eye view of the bowling crease, able to spot whether the bowler's foot has landed beyond it, requiring a 'no-ball' call.

The other umpire stands at the square leg position, on an invisible line parallel with the bowling crease, roughly in a line with where the batsman taking strike stands. See Chapter 7 for where precisely the square leg umpire stands.

The square leg umpire adjudges appeals for run-outs and stumpings from the bowling side. More later in this chapter about these modes of dismissal in the section 'Dismissing the Batsmen'.

When the bowling team changes ends after the completion of an over, the umpire who was standing at square leg moves behind the stumps at the end of the pitch from which the bowler is now delivering the ball. The other umpire moves out to square leg.

Respecting the umpire

The umpire's job is to interpret the laws of the game of cricket and apply them to the match situation.

Thankfully, soccer-style histrionics are rare in cricket. Players don't surround the umpires, shoving and pushing and swearing at them, trying to get them to change their minds. Players accepting the umpire's decision as final is a long and welcome tradition in the game. However in recent years, with the march of new technology, in test and some one day international cricket it has become the practice for the umpires' decisions to be reviewed by an off-field umpire – known as the third umpire – with the use of video technology. But which decisions can be reviewed in this way, and the frequency of reviews, are the subject of strict rules. See the later section 'Embracing new technology: the Decision Review System' for more on the how umpires use technology.

The world's best umpires are employed in test match cricket. The International Cricket Council (ICC), the game's governing body, draws up a panel of umpires who travel the globe umpiring test matches and one-day international games.

In international cricket, the players' on-pitch behaviour is monitored very closely by the match referee. This referee, normally an ex-test player, is there to keep discipline and ensure that the umpire's decisions are accepted without question. Referees have sweeping powers, able to fine and even ban players who break the laws of the game or show dissent to the umpire.

Looking at umpiring signals

One of the main jobs of the umpire is to let the scorer know what is going on in the match. The umpire does this through a series of signals, which are interpreted by the scorer (see Figure 2-3).

Wide   No ball   Byes & Start of play   Leg byes

Out   Four runs   Six runs   Five runs, not penalties

Dead ball   Short runs   Last hour   New ball

Figure 2-3:
Umpiring
signals.

Third umpire   Revoke the last signals   5 penalty runs to the batting team   5 penalty runs to the fielding team

Some of these signals look bizarre – a little like a cross between semaphore and something performed by the freemasons. But get your head around the umpiring signals laid out here and you will have an A1 chance of keeping track of what's going on in a cricket match.

✔ **Right arm outstretched:** No-ball. This signal indicates that the bowler's foot has landed over the front line of the bowling crease and the delivery is deemed a *no-ball*.

✔ **Both arms outstretched:** Wide. This signal shows that the ball was out of reach of the batsman and has been adjudged a *wide*, see 'Understanding the Scoring System' later in this chapter for more on wides.

✔ **Right leg raised and clasped by the right hand:** This signal indicates that the ball hit the pads of the batsman , not the bat, and that the runs completed are adjudged to be *leg byes*. These runs are not credited to the individual player's score but to the team's, as *extras*. See 'Understanding the Scoring System' later in this chapter for more.

✔ **Right arm raised skywards:** Byes. Indicates that the ball has been missed by both the batsman and the wicket-keeper. Any runs scored are deemed to be *byes*. Byes, like leg byes, are counted as extras.

✔ **Right hand and arm swept across the body:** Four runs. This signal shows that the ball has been hit all the way to the boundary. The ball has bounced on its way to the boundary and four runs have been scored.

✔ **Both arms held above the head and index fingers outstretched:** Six runs. The ball has been hit over the boundary, without the ball bouncing. Six runs are awarded for this fab feat.

✔ **Index finger raised towards the batsman:** Out. The umpire has given the batsman *out* and he has to leave the crease and take the long lonely walk back to the pavilion.

✔ **Right arm held out horizontally then flexed back to touch the shoulder:** Short run. One of the batsmen has failed to touch their bat down beyond the front line of the bowling crease when going for a run. This is deemed a *short run* and the scorer is being told to take that run off the score.

Embracing new technology: The Decision Review System

Time stands still for no man, not even for a cricket umpire. The advance of new technology such as Hawkeye and Hotspot – see Chapter 13 for more on these wizard new inventions – makes it relatively easy to adjudicate key umpiring decisions with the use of video technology.

But cricket has a fine balancing act to carry off. The International Cricket Council don't want too many delays to the game caused by frivolous calls to use new technology, nor do they want the decisions of on-field umpires to be called into constant doubt. The idea is to use technology as a complement to the decision made on the field, rather than as a replacement for it. As a result there is a strict code of rules which govern how video technology can be used. The umpires may only refer decisions in the following circumstances:

- **In the case of a run out or a stumping decision:** In this case it is entirely up to the on-field umpire to refer to the third umpire, who sits in a room with a bank of video screens watching the action. The third umpire will then review slow-motion footage of the run out or stumping incident and then contact the on field umpire – who has a snazzy earpiece in place – his opinion on whether the batsman should be given out or not out. The on-field umpire will the, take this information into account, make his decision and adjudge the batsman out or not out and that's it – no arguing from the batsman or fielding team allowed.

- **To decide whether or not a bowler has bowled a no ball:** Again it is entirely the call of the on-filed umpire as to whether to have the third umpire look at footage of the bowler's delivery stride to see whether he has committed the offence. As with run outs and stumpings the views of the third umpire are relayed and it's up to the on-field umpire then to decide whether or not to call no ball.

- **To decide whether a boundary has been scored or not:** When a fielder has chased the ball down to the boundary, but the umpire is unsure whether the ball, or the fielder whilst holding the ball, has made contact with the boundary, he can refer the decision. If contact was made then the third umpire will tell the umpire on the pitch that he should award four runs.

- **When a catch is disputed:** This referral can occur when the bowling side claims a catch but the umpires on the field are unsure whether the ball has _carried_ – that the fielder caught the ball before it hit the ground. If it has carried then the batsman is out. If not then he will be given not out.

- **In the case of leg before wicket and caught out decisions:** Things get even more complex with the batsman and fielding side involved in the process. The on-field umpire gives his verdict on whether the batsman is out or not out. Depending on which way the decision goes, the batsman (if given out) or the captain of the fielding side (if the batsman is given not out) can refer the decision to the third umpire who will then look at the footage and tell the on-field umpire whether or not he concurs with the original decision. The on field umpire will then either change his original decision or stay with it. This is called the Decision Review System (DRS).

Protecting the umpires: Decision review system safeguards

Respect for the umpire and his decisions has been a key component of cricket for the past century and a half. Instances of players calling into question the integrity of the umpire are fortunately rare: see Chapter 17 for the furore that followed just such an incident – the Shakoor Rana affair. So for the ICC to allow players – the batsman or fielding captain – to appeal a decision made by the on-field umpire through the decision review system (DRS) is a pretty major step.

Safeguards had to be put in place to ensure that the DRS doesn't lead to an erosion of the umpire's authority. These are:

✔ The video footage is reviewed by a third umpire who is part of the ICC's panel so in effect it is still part of the umpiring team of three that come to the final decision.

✔ The third umpire can only advise the on-field umpire of his findings. Ultimately it is still the decision of the on-field umpire that matters. However if the third umpire says the original decision was mistaken, only a very intransigent on-filed umpire would ignore that opinion.

✔ The fielding and batting teams are limited to two unsuccessful appeals per innings. Once these are exhausted then the call automatically goes with the on-filed umpire, so no review takes place.

✔ The fielding captain or the batsman who has been given out have only fifteen seconds after the decision has been made to ask for a review by the third umpire.

✔ If the third umpire cannot see conclusive evidence that the decision made by the on-field umpire was incorrect then he will say so, and the on-field call stands.

The decision review system has been operable since 2009 and to date it has shown that on-field umpires get their calls right most of the time – in fact only about one in four reviews are successful. The remainder stay with the original decision.

Not all cricketing nations are fans of the decision review system. The Indian Cricket Board, for example, has expressed doubts over Hawkeye technology and its effectiveness. This has led to them insisting that this technology is not used in series they participate in. However, these objections are gradually subsiding and most test series are now played with full video technology deployed. See Chapter 13 for more on Hawkeye and the other aspects of video technology.

Video technology is only deployed in international cricket and some major games between county teams in England and state teams in Australia. 99.9 per cent of all cricket matches which are played around the globe – whether professional or amateur – the old ideal that the on-field umpires' decisions are final still stands.

Understanding the Scoring System

Generally, in the game of cricket, whichever team scores the most runs wins. Therefore, nailing down exactly how runs are scored is important. In the main the batsmen score the runs, but runs can be awarded by the umpires should the bowler bowl a delivery they deem contrary to the laws of the game (more on this later in this section). In addition, the umpires are free to award penalty runs to the batting side in some unusual instances.

Understanding runs and boundaries

A batsman scores *runs* by using the bat to make contact with the ball. The two batsmen – the one who has hit the ball (the *striker*) and the other at the opposite end of the pitch (the *non-striker*) – then run between the wickets, touching their bats down at the ends of the pitch, to register runs.

Off a single contact of the bat with ball – called a *stroke* or *shot* – the batsman can, in theory, score an unlimited number of runs. In reality the bowling team will gather and throw the ball to the bowler or wicket-keeper to stop the player from scoring more than four runs from any one hit.

Generally, you find that players will run one, two, three, or occasionally four runs after making contact with the ball.

If the player hits the ball all the way to the boundary then the umpire will award runs without the batsmen having to run between the wickets. If the ball bounces before reaching the boundary, four runs will be awarded: if not then six runs are scored.

Pretty simple so far? Sadly, cricket's scoring system doesn't stay easy-peasy for long.

Totting up the extras

The umpires may also award runs in circumstances other than the batsman striking the ball. These runs are referred to as *extras*.

- ✔ **No-ball:** The bowler's front foot has landed in its entirety over the bowling crease; see the section 'Taking in the creases' earlier in this chapter for more. The umpire shouts 'no-ball' and a run is automatically added to the batting team's total in addition to any runs the batsmen may score. In other respects, the delivery doesn't count. A batsman cannot be dismissed off a no-ball unless run-out, and the bowler has to bowl the ball again.

- ✔ **Wide:** Should the bowler deliver the ball so far wide of where the batsman is standing that he has no prospect of making contact the umpire can call *wide*. Again an extra run is added to the batting teams score, the delivery doesn't count, and the bowler has to deliver the ball again.

- ✔ **Leg bye:** Should the ball strike the batsman's leg guards – also called *pads* – or any part of the anatomy, without touching the bat then he is free to attempt to run a leg bye. Any runs scored are added to the batting teams total but not to that of the individual player. Unlike a wide or a no-ball delivery the ball counts, and the bowler doesn't have to repeat the delivery. The umpire will not allow a leg bye if in his judgment the batsman has not attempted to play a shot. Perhaps the player has simply let the ball hit his pads or anatomy on purpose.

- ✔ **Bye:** If the ball is missed by the batsman, fails to hit the stumps, and is then fumbled or missed altogether by the wicket-keeper, then the batsmen are entitled to run. Like a leg-bye the ball is added to the batting team's total but not the individual player's score.

Should the umpire shout 'no-ball' and the batsman hits the ball to a fielder in the air to be caught or misses it altogether and the ball hits the stumps, the player is not out. Players can hit the no-ball delivery to score extra runs. They can do this with wild abandon as they can only be dismissed by a run-out, when a no-ball has been bowled.

Extras are very common. On average you can find that around 5–10 per cent of a team's total runs scored are extras.

Incurring penalty runs

Umpires can also award penalty runs to the batting team. Penalty runs are awarded for offences committed by the bowling team. For example, should the ball hit a protective helmet or piece of clothing, discarded by the bowling team (the mind boggles), then the batting side is awarded five penalty runs. The law governing penalty runs is fiendishly complex and fortunately the incidences of penalty runs being awarded are few and far between. In the 2006 test series between England and Pakistan, when Pakistan were penalised five runs for supposedly altering the condition of the ball, was an extreme rarity. This decision caused such a furore that the Pakistan team refused to play on, and the match had to be abandoned. In fact, you could play cricket for decades and never see a penalty run awarded. For full details on penalty runs, check out the relevant sections of the Lords Web site `http://www.lords.org/laws-and-spirit/laws-of-cricket/`.

Keeping count: The role of the scorer

With so many different ways to score runs, someone needs to keep track of it all. This is where the scorer comes in. The scorer's job is to keep his eyes peeled for the number of times the batsmen run between the wickets, and to register signals from the umpire. See 'Looking at umpiring signals' earlier in this chapter for more on the signals given by umpires.

The scorer sits with a score book and keeps a tally of the following:

- ✔ The total runs scored by each team when batting.
- ✔ The runs scored by individual players.
- ✔ The extra runs awarded by the umpires.
- ✔ The mode of dismissal of each individual batsman: the identity of the bowler and catcher, or in the case of run-out, the fielder throwing the ball at the stumps.
- ✔ The team score when each player was dismissed.
- ✔ The number of overs bowled by the bowling team
- ✔ The number of overs bowled by individual players and how many runs have been scored during the overs.

As you can probably guess, this tally is an awful lot for one person to get his or her head around. But the key to scoring is to have a routine; after each delivery is bowled the scorer makes a note of what has just happened. Score books are printed allowing all this information to be jotted down in double-quick time using a type of scorer's code.

An over has six deliveries; therefore a mark is made relating to each delivery. The basics to help you crack the scorer's codes are:

- ✔ A dot mark indicates that nothing has happened off the delivery. No runs have been scored, and no player has been dismissed.
- ✔ A number indicates that runs have been scored off the delivery. For example, the number 4 indicates four runs scored.

✔ The letter W – standing for 'wicket' – indicates that a player has been dismissed by the bowler's delivery.

✔ A cross (+) indicates that the delivery has been adjudged wide by the umpire. An extra run is added to the batting team's total score and the delivery has to be repeated.

✔ A circle indicates that the delivery is a no-ball; an extra run is added to the batting team's total score and, what's more, the delivery has to be repeated. Sometimes you'll see a number inside the circle; this denotes how many runs have been scored by the batsman off the no-ball.

✔ A triangle indicates that the delivery has gone for byes. There will be dots in the triangle, and this denotes how many byes have been scored. Therefore, a triangle with four dots denotes that the ball has gone for four byes.

✔ An upside down triangle indicates leg byes; again the number of dots denotes the number of leg byes scored.

If you watch television coverage of a cricket match or go to a game, don't worry – you're not going to be bombarded by dots, Os and +s. The scoreboard gives you the low-down on the match situation: The total number of runs scored by the batting team, the number of batsmen dismissed and the number of overs bowled. In addition, the scoreboard shows you how many runs have been scored by the individual players as well as the runs conceded and players dismissed by the individual bowlers. Part of the scorer's job is to keep the scoreboard up to date.

You often hear the batting team's score referred to as being *for* something. For example England are 300 for 7. This simply means that 300 runs have been scored and seven of the team's batsmen have been dismissed. Just to confuse matters further, down under, in Australia, the number of players dismissed comes first and the runs scored last. In Australia, therefore, England's score would be referred to as 7 for 300.

If the batsman fails to score any runs in an over, the over is said to be a *maiden*. As far as bowlers are concerned maidens are great news; second only in the happiness-inducing stakes to dismissing a player. The best of all possible worlds for a bowler is a *wicket maiden*. This is when no runs have been scored off the over and a player has been dismissed. Sometimes you find that two players are dismissed and no runs are scored, and this over is called a *double wicket maiden*: Now the bowler is in fantasy land. In the score book a maiden is indicated by the joining of six dots into the letter M. A wicket or double wicket maiden is indicated in the score book by the six dots joined up to form the letter W.

Cricket boffins have come up with an incredibly complex scoring system for rain-affected one-day cricket matches. This system, known as the Duckworth/Lewis system means that a result can always be reached even in a match where weather interruptions mean that not all the scheduled overs are bowled. See Chapter 3 for the ins and outs of the Duckworth/Lewis scoring system.

Dismissing the Batsmen

The game of cricket is a tussle between the batters and the bowlers. The batsmen may initially hold the whip hand, creaming the bowler's deliveries to the boundary and getting the team score rattling along. But sooner or later the bowlers get their turn to enjoy the good life, namely dismissing the batsmen. Once 10 of the team's 11 batsmen have been dismissed the innings is at an end, and either the bowling team get to bat or the game ends. See Chapter 3 for more on different match formats in cricket.

Batsmen can be dismissed in ten different ways, but the most common are:

- ✔ **Bowled:** The bowler has managed to hit the player's stumps with a delivery and the bails have been dislodged. High fives all round for the bowler.

- ✔ **Caught:** The batsman has hit the ball in the air to a fielder who has held onto the catch.

- ✔ **Leg Before Wicket (LBW):** The ball has struck the batsman's leg guards – also called batting pads – and the umpire adjudges that the ball would have hit the stumps if the leg guards had not got in the way. The player is dismissed LBW. See 'Comprehending the LBW law' later in this section for the ins and outs of the complex LBW law.

- ✔ **Run-out:** The fielder has managed to dislodge the bails with the ball at the end the batsmen is running to before the player has completed a run. In other words, the player is still running between the wickets and hasn't yet managed to get the bat down beyond the line of the bowling crease, when the bails are taken off the stumps using the ball.

- ✔ **Stumped:** The batsman has strayed out of the crease in an attempt to play a shot and the bails have been removed by the wicket-keeper with the ball in his gloves.

When the bowler catches a ball hit by the batsman in the air, the bowler is said to have dismissed the player *caught and bowled*. The gloating rights in the bar after the game belong, well and truly, to the bowler.

Unusual dismissals

Ninety-nine per cent of dismissals are one of five types: bowled, caught, LBW, run-out or stumped. But, every now or then, a player is dismissed for one of the following five unusual transgressions:

- ✔ **Hit wicket.** The player hits his own stumps, dislodging the bails with the bat or pads. Why would a player do such a silly thing? Well, it would, undoubtedly, be an accident, usually caused by the player knocking the stumps while moving his feet to get into position to play a shot.

- ✔ **Handled the ball.** Sometimes, in a desperate attempt to stop the ball hitting the stumps, the player instinctively hits the ball with his hand.

- ✔ **Hit the ball twice.** The player has a brain-wave and decides to hit the ball not just once but twice with the bat. I'm afraid this means a long lonely walk back to the pavilion.

- ✔ **Obstructing the field.** The player uses the bat or body to stop a throw reaching the wicket-keeper.

- ✔ **Timed out.** When a player has been dismissed a new batsman is expected to take their place within three minutes. If the player fails to turn-up in the allotted time, they can be timed out. This mode of dismissal is the rarest of all.

If the bat, or hands holding the bat, makes contact with the ball and then ricochets off the leg guards to be caught by a fielder, then the player is dismissed caught *bat and pad*. Spin bowlers are particularly adept at getting batsmen caught bat and pad, see Chapter 6 for more.

Some cricket matches involve sides having to complete two innings, others just one. See Chapter 3 for more on the different formats of cricket matches.

Lots of phrases are used for describing a batsman's dismissal. The most simple refers to the player being given out. Other descriptions are more prosaic; such as a player being *given the dreaded finger* – which sounds really unpleasant – *taking the long walk back to the pavilion* or just *sent on his way*.

Comprehending the LBW law

The LBW law is a little like that governing offside in soccer or what constitutes a maul in rugby: Most people involved in the game claim to know it inside out but few actually do.

Put simply, a player is dismissed LBW when the ball hits him on the pads and the umpire adjudges that it would otherwise have hit the stumps (see Figure 2-4).

Simple, eh? But several provisos exist, including:

- ✔ If the ball has bounced – or *pitched*, in cricket lingo – outside the line of the player's leg stump, then the player can't be out LBW, period.

- ✔ Where the ball has bounced not in line with any of the player's stumps and the player has attempted to play a shot, he can't be dismissed LBW.

- ✔ If the ball hits the player's bat before striking the leg guards then, again, the player can't be out.

In addition, to all this stuff about the line of the ball the umpire has to adjudge whether the ball is likely to bounce over the stumps. If the ball strikes the batsmen high on the leg – say somewhere above the knee – then the ball is quite likely to be adjudged to be headed over the stumps. As a result, the umpire is likely to give the batsmen not out.

Whether a player is dismissed LBW or is adjudged to be not out is one of the most difficult calls an umpire has to make. Umpires are only human and they can get these calls wrong. Some bowling teams make life hard for the umpire by appealing nearly every time the ball strikes the batsman's pads.

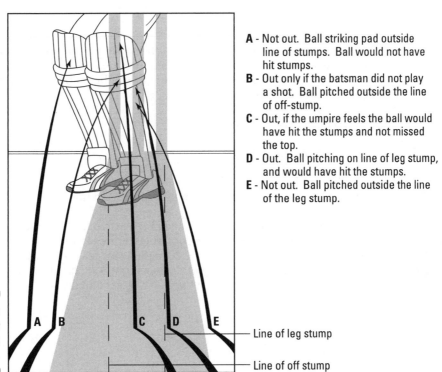

A - Not out. Ball striking pad outside line of stumps. Ball would not have hit stumps.

B - Out only if the batsman did not play a shot. Ball pitched outside the line of off-stump.

C - Out, if the umpire feels the ball would have hit the stumps and not missed the top.

D - Out. Ball pitching on line of leg stump, and would have hit the stumps.

E - Not out. Ball pitched outside the line of the leg stump.

Figure 2-4:
A summary
of the
LBW law.

Line of leg stump

Line of off stump

Understanding retirements

A batsman is allowed to *retire*. This doesn't mean that he suddenly ends up spending an inordinate amount of time in the garden. A player retiring simply means that he has had enough for that innings. He may want to rest or give another team member a chance to bat. A player who retires is deemed to be dismissed and is not allowed to return to bat again in that innings. However, a player who *retires hurt* – say after being struck by the ball or pulling a muscle – is allowed to return to bat at a later stage of the innings.

A batsman can't just be dismissed by the umpire. First the bowling side has to appeal to the umpire. However, when a player has been bowled or clearly caught, the player often just walks off towards the pavilion, without waiting for the umpire's decision.

Looking at Breaks in Play

Cricket is a long game. Even 'twenty20' matches, the shortest format of the game, take over three hours from start to finish. See Chapter 3 for more on twenty20 cricket.

Not surprisingly, therefore, cricket is littered with breaks in play. Some of these breaks in play are agreed between the sides before the match, or set down in competition rules; others, though, are the umpire's decision due to poor light or rain.

Pre-arranged breaks include:

- ✔ Taking lunch and tea.
- ✔ Changeover between innings.
- ✔ Drinks breaks, normally a minute or two each hour.

The number and length of pre-arranged breaks in play tend to vary between the match format and the competition rules. For example, in a test match breaks of 40 minutes for lunch and 20 minutes for tea are always taken. However, in most one-day competitions just one long break is taken between the changeover in innings, when teams get to eat and drink.

Going off the field for rain

As mentioned earlier in this chapter, moisture can have a profound effect on the condition of a cricket pitch. Therefore, to be fair to both sides, umpires tend to take players off the field during rain. At this stage the groundsmen cover the pitch and the bowlers' run-ups. Once the weather is better, the covers are removed, the players return, and the game recommences.

When the umpires take the players off the pitch because of rain, they continue to monitor the weather for improvement. When the umpires think that conditions are dry enough they bring the players back out of the pavilion to recommence play.

Going off the field for bad light

A bit more controversially, umpires can also take the players off the pitch when they think that the light is so poor that it constitutes a hazard to the batsmen. A cricket ball is a very hard object – particularly when propelled by the bowlers at up to 90 mph. The umpires figure that conditions aren't safe unless the batsmen can see the ball properly.

If the umpires feel the light is so bad that the fielders risk injury – as well as the batsmen – they can choose to take the players off regardless of whether the batsman want to stay on or not.

The controversial thing about the umpires' power to take players off for bad light is that some cricket watchers reckon umpires exercise this power too often. Such critics believe that umpires are too willing to take the players off the field and that with all the protective equipment available today, the players aren't at much risk anyway of being genuinely hurt.

Chapter 3

From 20 Overs to 5 Days: The Many Formats of Cricket

. . . .

In This Chapter

▶ Examining one and two innings formats

▶ Introducing test match cricket

▶ Looking at first class matches

▶ Getting a result: The joy of one-day cricket

▶ Taking a look at twenty20 cricket

▶ Explaining the unexplainable: The Duckworth/Lewis method

. . . .

C ricket matches can last days or just hours. They can be highly charged occasions with batsmen playing big shots or more sluggish and genteel affairs where not much seems to be going on to the untrained observer.

I can't think of any other sport where the viewing and playing experience alters so much according to the format.

Soccer is essentially the same whether played for nine minutes or ninety. In cricket, though, the format of the match has a huge influence on lots of things from team tactics through to the scoring system adopted to decide the winner.

In this chapter, I lay bare all the different formats from test cricket through to the crash, bang, and wallop of twenty20 cricket. Ultimately, though, something can be said for all of cricket's formats as each offers the spectator and player something different.

Looking at an Innings

Cricket matches are divided into *innings*. Each of the two sides has at least one innings, no matter what the format.

Here's how an innings works.

1. **The batting side sends in its first two batsmen.** They bat until the fielding team *dismisses* one of them. Being dismissed may sound like something from your schooldays but it actually refers to the batsman being got out by the bowling side, through being caught, run-out or bowled, for example. See Chapter 2 for more on modes of dismissal in cricket.

2. **The dismissed player's place is taken by another player.** This player is said to be batting at number three in the batting order.

3. **When one of the two players – the player who went out to bat at the start of the innings or the number three player – is dismissed then his place is taken by another player.** This player is batting at number four in the batting order.

4. **This process goes on and on until the 11th batsman comes in to bat.** When the number eleven batsman is dismissed – or his or her batting partner – then the batting side is *all out*. The batting team's innings is over.

5. **Once the batting side is all out, they swap places with the bowling side.** The side that has been fielding and bowling becomes the batting side.

The team whose turn it is to bat then goes through its innings, sending in its first two players to bat, and so on.

In very simple terms the winner of the game is the team that manages to score the most runs in its innings.

The bowling side needs to dismiss ten of the batting team's eleven batsmen to bring the innings to an end.

An over has six deliveries.

The players in a team who are the most capable at batting usually occupy high numbers in the batting order whereas those less able to score runs and defend their stumps bat lower in the batting order. See Chapter 5 for more on batting skills.

The team that gets to bat first is decided by whichever of the team captains wins the toss of a coin before the start of the match. Flip forward to Chapter 8 for more on the importance of the toss.

Every weekend, during the summer, thousands of people turn out for their local club teams. The players are amateurs, so club games are played at the weekend. Furthermore, the matches are usually over in a day with each side getting just one innings.

The number of allotted overs for the completion of innings in club matches varies according to the cup or league competition being contested. Generally, though, most club games involve teams having a single innings each, limited to between forty or fifty overs.

Throwing the second innings into the mix

Some cricket matches – such as test and first class – involve teams having not one but two innings.

This means that after the two sides have batted once they have to come out and bat again. Therefore, team A bats, team B bats, team A bats again and finally team B bats for the final time in the match.

The idea of having two innings, rather than just one, is that it provides a truer test of the abilities of the two teams. Sometimes, in a single-innings match, an inferior team can get lucky and score more runs than a better side, yet this is less likely to happen if teams have to bat twice!

The total runs scored in both innings are added together to decide which team wins.

For example, during the first innings team A scores 250 runs and team B scores 200. Now in a single-innings match team A would be the winner by 50 runs. However, this is a two-innings match and this gives team B the chance to fight back. In the second innings, team A scores 130 runs, giving them a total aggregate score of 380 (130 plus 250 from their first innings). Team B, therefore, needs to score 181 runs to beat team A's aggregate and win the match. This they promptly do, having five batsmen dismissed; so winning by 5 wickets.

Sometimes after the completion of both team's first innings, the team that has just batted may have scored far fewer runs than the bowling side managed. For example, team A may have scored 600 runs, while team B managed just 200 runs. When the gap is big enough, the captain of the bowling side is allowed to tell the batting side to bat again, or *follow on*. Telling the batting side to bat again is called *enforcing the follow-on*. See Chapter 8 for more on when this can happen.

Taking extra time to complete two innings

The fact that some matches involve teams having two innings means that more time is needed to establish a winner.

Finishing a two-innings match in a single day is nigh on impossible: The batsmen are too skilled to be dismissed by the bowlers in such a short time frame. As a result, two-innings matches are usually spread over four or five days.

Whether the match is scheduled to run for four or five days depends on whether it is contested by players representing their countries, or by those representing county clubs, state or provincial sides.

Two-innings contests between two teams representing their countries are given the most time to reach a finish. The reason is that players who represent their country are the cream of the professional game, and the skill levels are such that it takes longer for two innings to be completed. These two-innings matches between international teams are called *test matches* and they are scheduled to last for five days.

Two-innings matches between county, state, or provincial sides are usually scheduled to last for four days. This schedule is less time than for a test match because the skill level of the players is a little lower.

Just because a match is scheduled to last four or five days doesn't necessarily mean that it will go the distance. Often one team dominates the other or the condition of the wicket favours bowling over batting – see Chapter 2 for more on the condition of the wicket – and a result is reached prematurely.

However, having four or five days to finish a match doesn't always mean that one side can get to triumph over the other.

Bad weather can take time out of the match, the players on both sides may bat particularly well, and the time allotted to reach a result may be used up before both sides' innings are complete, in which case the match is a *draw*. The rules of some club cricket leagues also allow for single innings matches to end in a draw. What usually happens is that the team batting second in the match fails to reach the total of the team batting first, yet has still not been bowled out when the end of the days play has been reached.

Most club cricket matches are single innings and last for no more than one day.

Most two-innings matches last four or five days but you may find that some matches between women's teams or minor counties sides are allotted only three days. See Chapter 12 for more on these matches.

Captains can chivvy along a two-innings match to get a result in several ways. For example, the batting side can *declare* its innings at any time. By declaring, the captain of the batting side is saying to the opposition we have scored enough runs now, our innings is over and it's your turn to bat. The idea of a declaration is to leave enough time in the match to achieve a result. See Chapter 8 for the ins and out of declaring an innings and some instances of how this tactic can occasionally go horribly wrong.

Cricket aficionados can get excited about drawn matches, particularly when one of the teams comes very close to defeat but somehow manages to last the distance and draw the match. But most people, new to the game of cricket, find it very odd indeed that two teams can lock horns for four or five days with no clear winner emerging.

Two-innings matches between county and national teams are called *first class matches*.

First class status only applies to games played between teams of men – all rather sexist! Playing first class cricket is a big deal and close to the pinnacle of the sport, second only in fact to playing in a test match.

Whatever the format, when a side wins, the triumph is recorded in one of two ways. If the team winning the match does so while batting, the victory margin is said to be the number of wickets they have spare. For example, if team A scores 200 and team B scores 201 but only has one of its batsmen dismissed, the margin of victory in nine wickets. On the other hand, if the team winning the match does so in the field then the victory margin is said to be the total number of runs that side had to spare. For example, if team A scores 200 runs and team B scores 150, team A is said to have won by 50 runs.

Taking a Closer Look at Test Cricket

As far as keen cricket buffs are concerned test matches are 'where it's all at'.

Test matches see two national teams slug it out over five days. The results of these test matches are flashed around the world and great individual performances are recorded and pored over by cricket fans and historians alike.

Test matches started way, way, back in the 1870s and since then more than 2,000 tests have been played. See Chapter 11 for more on the history of test cricket.

Test matches are great set piece occasions. Great care is taken over the condition of the wicket used in a test match; see Chapter 2 for more. Ideally, a test match should last into its fifth day.

Test matches can be long drawn out affairs and very hard on the players' bodies. Nevertheless, unlike other major team sports such as soccer and rugby, players can't be substituted if they are performing poorly or are simply tired. However, if a player is injured during the match then a substitute can be used in the field but not to bat or bowl.

A total of ten nations play test cricket. These nations have joined the test-playing club over a long span of time. For example, the first two nations to play test matches were England and Australia in 1877 whilst Bangladesh became the tenth nation to start competing in test matches in 2000. See Chapters 10 and 11 for test cricket's major competitions and rivalries.

Four results are possible in test and first class cricket matches: win, lose, draw or tie. The first two are clear and how you achieve a draw is explained in the section 'Taking extra time to complete two innings' earlier in this chapter. A tie, though, occurs when both teams have completed their innings and the aggregate scores are level. Ties are extremely rare. In nearly 130 years of test cricket only two test matches have ever been tied.

Test matches haven't always been allotted five days. In the nineteenth century most tests played in England were only scheduled for just three or four days. Later, things went to the other extreme, with *timeless tests* being played. These 'winner takes all' tests were meant to be played to a finish, regardless of the number of days. The longest timeless test ever played was between England and South Africa in 1939, the match went on and on and on for ten days before it had to be called off or the England team would have missed its boat journey home! However, since the Second World War the norm for test matches has been five days.

Taking it slowly: Test and first class tactics

Two-innings matches tend to be quite slow-paced affairs. This mostly has to do with the attitude of the batsman.

Generally, when a batsman starts to bat their approach is cautious. They are focused on not being dismissed, which means they look to play defensive shots – or even no shots at all to some deliveries. The batsman wants to survive because they know that sooner or later they'll get used to the way that the ball is bouncing off the wicket and the tactics being deployed by the bowler. This process is called *playing yourself in* or *getting your eye in* and is looked at extensively in Chapter 5.

Of course, the batsman doesn't stay on the defensive forever. As confidence grows he or she starts to play more aggressive run-scoring shots. But because a test or first class match lasts four or five days, batsmen often take their time – an hour or more – before going on the attack.

These initially defensive tactics can mean that the rate of run scoring in first class and test matches is slow. Particularly when compared to one-day matches, where teams have a limited number of overs to bat.

As a general rule a full day's play in a test or first class match sees between 250 and 350 runs scored.

In one-day matches, however, you commonly see 500 or even 600 runs scored in a day.

Slower scoring doesn't spell boring. The crowd enjoys the tussle of batsman versus bowler. It can be quite thrilling to see a batsman work really hard to prevent dismissal against a top-quality bowler and then later in the day – after he has got his eye in – start to get on top and play aggressive shots.

The Australian team during the 1990s and 2000smade great efforts to up the rate of run scoring in test match cricket. They have some superb batsmen who are capable of playing aggressive shots from the start of their innings. Aussie batsmen of the time could commonly score 300 to 350 in a single day's play. Other teams, such as England and India, have also tried to emulate the Aussies fast scoring rate with some success.

More frequent breaks in play happen in a test or first class match than in a one-day game. The players tend to come off for lunch and tea breaks during four or five day games, whereas in one-day matches players just take a break in play between innings.

In one-day cricket the pace of run scoring is generally faster than in a test or first class match.

To ensure that spectators get value for money cricket's authorities have laid down a strict series of guidelines governing the minimum number of overs that must be bowled in a day's play. In test matches bowling sides are expected to bowl at least 90 overs a day, whereas in the County Championship the minimum is 100 overs. In test matches the hours of play can be extended to ensure the 90 overs are bowled and fielding teams fined for a slow over rate. In the County Championship the sanctions are even harder, with teams being docked points for failing to bowl their overs in the allotted time.

Teams compete in *series* of test matches. A series involves playing anything from two to five separate test matches. The team that wins the most tests is said to have won the test series. Over a five-year period test teams compete in something called the test world championship. Basically, all the ten test-playing nations play each other in series home and away, earning points for series won or drawn. The team with the highest points tally at the end of the five years is crowned world champions. See Chapter 10 for more on the test world championship.

Taking a Peek at English First Class Cricket

In essence, first class matches are the same as test matches, just played over a slightly shorter period of time. Matches in the English County Championship (see more on this in Chapter 12) are scheduled to last four days.

Teams try to get a little bit more of a move on in first class cricket than in a test match. In the County Championship competition the bowling side is supposed to bowl at least 100 overs for each day that the match lasts.

The general skill level of the players tends to be a little lower than in a test match but a lot higher than say a club cricket match.

First class cricket is a proving ground for players with ambitions to play test cricket. A player has to perform in first class cricket competitions before being selected for the national test side.

The County Championship is contested by 18 county sides – 17 from England, one from Wales – divided into two divisions of nine. Teams in each division play one another home and away in four-day matches during a season lasting from April to September. Points are awarded for winning and drawing games as well as for scoring runs and dismissing a specific number of the opposition's batsmen. See Chapter 12 for more on point scoring in the County Championship.

Ensuring a result: One-day cricket

About 40 years ago cricket's bigwigs woke up to the fact that many people like to see one team win the match and carry away the spoils. One-day cricket was born to try and quench this thirst for a winner.

In one-day cricket teams get just one innings.

But even in a single-innings match no guarantee exists that the game will be over in a day. Therefore, in single-innings matches the number of overs is limited.

This belt and braces approach ensures that a result is reached within a day, hence these matches are referred to as either one-day matches or limited overs innings.

No difference exists between a limited overs and a one-day cricket match.

Spectators love the one-day format because, unless the game is a complete wash-out – in other words it rains all day – they get to see a result. See Chapter 13 for more on what makes one-day cricket special from the fans' perspective.

Although in many ways one-day cricket is the fans' favourite the longer formats of the game – first class and test matches – are considered the more prestigious. Cricket purists believe that a two-innings match truly shows which teams are the most skilful. In fact, the longer a game of cricket is scheduled to last the more prestigious the game is.

One-day matches, even if played between national sides, are not given first class status.

Test and first class cricket matches involve two innings being completed. However, teams are allowed to *forfeit* an innings. This forfeit is sometimes applied when bad weather has taken a lot of time out of the game and the captains want to try to achieve a result.

Gauging the differences between one-day, test and first class matches

One-day matches differ from the longer formats of the game – first class and test matches – in several key ways.

- ✔ **Difference one**

    One-day match: Each side only has one innings.

    Test and first class match: Each side has two innings.

- ✔ **Difference two**

    One-day match: The match has a maximum set number of overs.

    Test and first class match: The match has to be finished in a pre-arranged number of days; no maximum limit exists on the number of overs that can be bowled in those days.

✔ **Difference three**

One-day match: Each bowler can only bowl a maximum set number of overs. For example, in a 50 overs a side match, an individual bowler is limited to ten overs.

Test and first class matches: Bowlers are free to bowl as many overs as they and their captain want. The record for any test match is a staggering 129 overs bowled by West Indian spin bowler Sonny Ramadhin against England at Edgbaston in 1957. I bet old Sonny needed a bit of a lie down after all that!

✔ **Difference four**

One-day match: For a proportion of the batting side's innings – anywhere from 6 to 20 overs – the bowling side has to have nine fielders, including the bowler and wicket-keeper, in a 30 yard circle of the batsmen.

Test and first class matches: Captains are free to place fielders wherever they want on the field (with one exception, discussed next) for as long as they want.

Captains are forbidden from placing more than two fielders backwards of the square leg umpire on the leg side – see Chapters 7 and 8 for more on fielding positions. This rule was introduced after the controversial bodyline tour of Australia by England in 1932–33. On this tour the England captain asked his bowlers to bowl at the Australian batsmen's bodies with the aim that they would fend the ball to a gaggle of fielders placed backwards of the square leg umpire. See Chapter 17 for more on this biggest ever cricket controversy.

The batting side can be credited runs, called *extras*, for minor bowling and fielding infringements. For example, if the whole of the bowler's front foot oversteps the bowling crease line then the delivery can be called as a no-ball. The batting side gets given a run and the bowler has to re-bowl the delivery. Likewise, if the direction of the bowler's delivery is way off target, so much so that the batsman doesn't have a chance of hitting it, then a wide can be called. Again, a run is added to the batting team's score and the bowler has to re-bowl the delivery. Refer to Chapter 2 for more on extras and where the crease lines are located on a cricket pitch.

In one-day matches, umpires tend to be very strict in their interpretation of what constitutes a wide delivery. They are strict because they want the batsman to have the best chance of playing a shot so that the crowd is entertained. The upshot is that any delivery directed down the batsman's leg side by the bowler is in serious jeopardy of being called wide, unless the player gets a touch on it.

Understanding the one-day trade-off

The key to winning a one-day cricket match is to score more runs than the opposing team. In one-day matches batsmen often go for more aggressive shots than they do in first class or test matches. However, the batting team has to balance the need to score runs with preventing the side from being dismissed by the bowlers.

If batsmen take too many risks – play too many aggressive shots – the danger is that all the team's batsmen will be dismissed and the innings brought to a premature end.

What you tend to find, therefore, is that the batting side keeps a few batsmen in reserve so that the team can go for its shots near the end of the innings.

As a result, the final few overs of a one-day innings can be really frenetic affairs with batsmen throwing all caution to the wind, going for aggressive shots, and bowlers having a better chance of dismissing them. All very exciting for the spectators!

 In one-day matches, if a team is dismissed before the allotted number of overs has been bowled, that's it, the innings is over. For example, if in a 50 overs a side match, team A scores 250 runs in 48 overs but 10 batsmen are dismissed, the innings is kaput and the two overs that were scheduled to be bowled are not bowled. Generally, batting teams really like to use all their overs.

 One-day matches are played by national, first class county, and club sides. However, you rarely find a national team playing a club side; the gap in skills would be so great as to make the contest a walkover for the big shot stars. What you tend to find is that national teams compete against each other in one-day international matches and tournaments such as the cricket world cup; see Chapter 11 for more on that. County teams in England and state teams in Australiacompete against one another in knock-out cup competitions or round robin leagues. Club sides tend to compete in season long one-day leagues with games taking place at the weekend, when the amateur players have time off work to play.

Day-night one-day cricket

One-day cricket is big business – particularly when matches are played between national sides. The television companies love one-day cricket for much the same reason as spectators; they get a result and the match is all over in a single day. No wonder that broadcasters, particularly in cricket mad India, pay a king's ransom for the broadcast rights.

What also appeals to the broadcasters is the colour of the one-day game. For starters teams wear coloured clothing and the ball used is white, rather than the traditional red. But what makes one-day cricket come alive from a visual point of view is the use of floodlighting. Day-night games, as they're called, start in the afternoon and conclude late in the evening, normally around 10 pm. They can be really atmospheric occasions full of razzmatazz and pizzazz, and other words with lots of Zs! For more on the spectacle of day-night games see Chapter 13.

Every four years the cricket World Cup is held. The ten test-playing nations plus six associate member countries of the International Cricket Council (ICC) take part in a month long tournament. Matches in the World Cup are 50 overs a side and many are day-night. See Chapter 11 for more on the World Cup and which teams take part.

Crash, Bang, Wallop: Twenty20 Is Born

In 2003 the twenty20 format was born and quickly became just about the most exciting thing to happen to cricket in a generation.

Whereas most traditional one-day matches consist of innings of 50 overs a side, in twenty20, as the name suggests, teams have just twenty overs to post a total.

The shorter format means that all the batsmen in a team are less likely to be dismissed. As a result, batsmen have carte blanche to go for aggressive shots – and boy, do they!

In addition, compared to test matches, twenty20 games are over in a flash. They take just over three hours from start to finish. See Chapter 13 for more on why twenty20 cricket has such wide appeal.

Twenty20 matches are very popular. If you fancy going along to a game you're best off booking a ticket in advance, otherwise you may not be able to get in. See Chapter 13 for full contact details on England's 18 county sides.

The twenty20 format is very spectator-friendly, with hold-ups in play kept to a minimum. For example, when a batsman is dismissed they have to be replaced by another player within 90 seconds. In addition strict penalties exist for fielding teams who fail to bowl their 20 overs within 75 minutes.

In test matches batting sides commonly score an average of between two and four runs an over. In one-day matches the scoring rate is a little faster, usually between four and six runs per over. But in twenty20 games the scoring rates can be higher still, seven, eight, nine even ten runs an over is the norm.

How one-day cricket rules the roost

The one-day cricket format started in England in the 1960s. Originally teams played in a 60 over a side cup competition, called the Gillette cup. Many of the early finals turned out to be very exciting – real close shaves with teams winning by a whisker!

Following on from the success of the Gillette Cup, the Sunday league was born. This shorter, 40 over a side, league competition was played on surprise, surprise, a Sunday! During the 1970s and 1980s the Sunday League enjoyed huge success and games were shown on national TV.

But during the 1990s the one-day game in England went through the doldrums as spectators got tired of the same old competitions. Then along came twenty20 and public interest was re-ignited in a big way!

On the international stage, the first limited over international match was played in 1971 between the old rivals England and Australia. However, it wasn't until the advent of the cricket World Cup in 1975 that one-day matches between national teams started to really pull in the punters.

Several World Cups later, and countless smaller competitions between national teams around the globe, and one-day international cricket is in fine fettle.

In fact, nowadays, in many parts of the cricket world, the one-day format rules the roost, even supplanting test cricket in the hearts of spectators. See Chapter 11 for more on how one-day cricket has captured the public imagination and on declining attendances at test matches. Strangely enough, in England, test cricket matches still enjoy bumper attendances. It seems England fans just love the tactical intensity of the longer test match format.

In one-day matches, the economy rate is often a key determinate of how well a bowler has performed. Put simply, the economy rate is how many runs the bowler has conceded from his bowling divided by the total number of overs he has bowled. Therefore, a bowler who has conceded 50 runs off 10 overs has an economy rate of five. As a rule a bowler is usually said to have done well in a 50-over match if he has an economy rate below four. In twenty20 matches the benchmark for what constitutes a good economy rate is higher still, as batsman are more inclined to play aggressive shots – an economy rate of less than six is considered top drawer in these games.

Twenty20 games started as contests between English county sides but the popularity has been such that in 2005 the first twenty20 match took place between national teams.

The marketing men and women took about a nanosecond to work out that people loved twenty20 matches between national teams. Games have been sold out around the globe and the number of fixtures has grown.

There have now been four twenty20 world cups, with the most recent tournament held in Sri Lanka in 2012.

Bringing in the Big Bucks: The Indian Premier League

Twenty20 may have started in England, but it is probably having the biggest impact in India. Indian cricket fans love their twenty20 and its advent has coincided with India becoming a global economic superpower. As a result, sponsors and rich private individuals have been falling over themselves to get involved in the most lucrative cricket competition in the world: The Indian Premier League (IPL).

Tycoons and multi-national businesses have been buying franchises, which give them the right to enter a team to play in the IPL. Teams are based in large cities dotted around India. The Indian Cricket Board, which runs the IPL, sells the franchises, and the last franchise auction brought in a massive £500 million.

Signing up the talent: The IPL player auction

On top of the expense of investing in a franchise, the owners of the IPL teams need to buy in big-name players, and they do this, again, through an annual auction where players offer their services to the highest bidder. Some big international names who are very good at twenty20 cricket can become millionaires overnight through an IPL contract. Other less high-profile cricketers can expect smaller sums, but the lowest paid players are still on £100,000 for a few weeks work – a very good wage for a cricketer and more than an Australian state team or English county team will pay its players for an entire season, which lasts for six months.

Auction day is a massive set-piece occasion in India, with franchises signing players for big money. Sometimes, though, players will enter the auction but find that their services are not required by the IPL teams, in which case – no cash!

The Indian premier League season only lasts around eight weeks and takes place in April and May. This means that most players can juggle playing in the IPL and representing their countries at test and one-day cricket. Some players have it written into their IPL contract that they can leave the season early if necessary to fulfil their national team duties.

Looking at the teams of the Indian Premier League

Nine franchises curently make up the IPL, each based in a major Indian city. These are:

- **Chennai Super Kings:** Based in – you guessed it– the City of Chennai, the Super Kings are coached by former New Zealand captain Stephen Fleming. A renowned captain, Fleming is showing great skills as a coach. In five years of the IPL the Super Kings have won it twice and finished runners-up twice. They are like the Manchester United of the IPL.

- **Delhi Daredevils:** Daredevils in name and daring by nature, this side is captained by Indian batting legend Virender Sehwag, who is noted for his hard hitting. But to date the best the Daredevils have done is a semi-final.

- **Kings XI Punjab:** A little less razzmatazz in the name and frankly the play as well. The Kings XI has never come close to winning an IPL but under the captaincy of Australian legend Adam Gilchrist and coach and fellow Aussie Michael Bevan, the idea is to change all that.

- **Kolkata Knight Riders:** Back to the snazzy names. The Knight Riders don't drive talking cars like in the 1980s TV series of the same name, but in 2012 they claimed their first IPL trophy, beating the super kings in the final. Under Indian batting star Gautam Gambhir they look like a team on the up.

- **Mumbai Indians:** Runners up in 2010 and semi-finalists in 2011are the highlights of the Mumbai Indians IPL history to date. But with clever off-spin bowler Harbhajan Singh in the captaincy role – a real star of Indian cricket – the Indians are always one of the biggest draws in the IPL.

- **Pune Warrior Indians:** Led by former Indian skipper Sourav Ganguly the Warrior Indians have never challenged for top honours in the IPL but they probably have the toughest sounding name in the competition – so probably best not to mess with them!

- **Rajasthan Royals:** Led by Indian batting great Rahul Dravid, the Jaipur based royals won the initial IPL tournament in 2008 but haven't come close since to claiming the top prize.

- **Royal Challengers:** IPL teams love a touch of royalty in their name and the Banglaore based charges grand name has sadly not been matched by performance. Over the history of the IP they are the worst perform-ing side, despite the clever captaincy of New Zealand all-rounder Daniel Vettori.

- **Sunrisers Hyderabad:** The newest franchise to date, based in the home city of the now-defunct Deccan Chargers, the Sunrisers make their IPL bow in 2013, coached by Australian Tom Moody.

There are currently nine franchises in the IPL but this may change soon. In 2012 Kochi Tuskers Kerala had their franchise removed and the Indian Cricket Board will be looking for a new team to step into their shoes. The Deccan Chargers, who folded in September 2012, have already been replaced by Sunrisers Hyderabad.

The teams in the IPL play each other home and away in a league format with the top four teams going through to a semi-final knockout game and the winners progressing to the final.

Aping the IPL: The Big Bash in Australia

Seeing the huge popularity of the IPL – and the money it raises – other countries have tried to ape its success. In England county teams compete in the twenty20 cup and there are versions in South Africa, New Zealand and the West Indies. But it is the Australian Big Bash league which has most successfully captured the excitement and razzmatazz of the IPL. Eight teams hailing from Australia's biggest cities compete in a round robin and then a final knockout tournament. As in the IPL, expensive star names are brought in from overseas and the competition is played between November and December, with Australian test team players able to juggle their international commitment with appearances in the Big Bash.

Sydney and Melbourne are Australia's biggest cities and they have not one but two teams each entered into the Big Bash.

Maths Geniuses Required: The Duckworth/Lewis Formula

Sadly cricket is a game that is constantly at the mercy of the weather. Either through rain or bad light, playing time can be lost. This isn't too much of a problem in two-innings matches; after all they are scheduled to last four or five days.

But one-day matches run to a very tight schedule and any breaks due to bad weather can mean that the full number of overs can't be bowled. Therefore, cricket boffins Frank Duckworth and Tony Lewis came up with a mathematical formula to ensure a result can always be reached in a reduced overs match.

The big idea behind the Duckworth/Lewis method, as it's catchily called, is to come up with an equation that determines by how much the winning runs target for the team batting second in the match should be altered if bad weather reduces the number of overs that can be bowled.

The method works on the principle of team resources. This relates to how many players out of the batting side have yet to be dismissed and the number of balls remaining to be bowled in the innings. The greater the remaining resources of the batting side when the game is interrupted, the higher that team's score is calculated to be under the Duckworth/Lewis method, or the lower their target number of runs to achieve victory.

For example, a batting side which has not had a batsman dismissed and 20 overs still to bat will be presumed to score a lot more runs in those final 20 overs than if they had had more batsmen dismissed.

If the innings of the team batting first is interrupted then that team's score will be adjusted according to the Duckworth/Lewis method. It will then be up to the fielding team to score enough runs to overhaul this adjusted total when it's their turn to bat.

However, if the innings of the team batting second is interrupted then the target the team is trying to reach in order to win the match is adjusted according to the calculations laid down under the Duckworth/Lewis method.

The match umpires and scorers are given spreadsheets which show clearly what the team's score or target to win should be under the Duckworth/Lewis method at any given point if weather intervenes and the number of overs is reduced.

Scorers will put this information on the scoreboard so that players and spectators know what would be the result should the heavens open and game be washed out.

The mathematics behind Duckworth/Lewis are fiendishly complex and are available – I kid you not – from the University of West of England in an academic pamphlet form at the bargain price of £29.99!

The Duckworth/Lewis method isn't very popular, mainly because it's so incredibly complex but no-one, as yet, has come up with a fairer system.

Umpires are a little less willing to take players off the pitch for a light shower in one-day cricket matches than in longer two-innings games. They are aware of the need to keep the big crowd and TV broadcasters happy – but they also don't want to have to rely on Duckworth/ Lewis to get a result.

Some matches are complete wash-outs and no amount of Duckworth/Lewis mathematics can produce a result in a game where a ball hasn't been bowled. But in knock-out cup competitions a result still has to be achieved, so something called a *bowl out* takes place. Put simply, bowlers from the two sides bowl at a set of stumps and the team that hits the stumps most often wins the tie. The bowl-out is a little like a penalty shoot-out in soccer.

French, beach and garden cricket

Not all cricket formats require umpires, scorers or ultra complex mathematical formulas applied in order to achieve a result. Some cricket games just need a few people kitted out with a bat and a tennis ball.

Often the first contact you have with the beautiful game is a playing French, beach or garden cricket – light on rules but long on fun!

The few rules these games have tend to be pretty quirky.

In garden cricket hit the ball into the neighbour's garden and you score six but you're also out – hence the phrase six and out! You also have the embarrassment of having to utter the infamous line 'Please can we have our ball back?'

In French cricket – which, oddly, has nothing to do with France – you can be caught out on the first bounce if the catch is taken one-handed.

In beach cricket – very popular in the Caribbean, where they have one or two nice sandy beaches – hit the ball into the sea and you're out!

Getting into Hot Water: Breaking Cricket Rules

Whatever the format of the game – one-day or two innings – certain cricketing no-no's exist which at the very least can put the umpires' backs-up and even, ultimately, lead to a ban from playing.

- **Conduct contrary to the spirit of the game:** This covers a whole range of misdemeanours from swearing at an opponent to deliberately looking to damage the condition of the pitch to give your side an advantage.

- **Tampering with the ball:** You're not allowed to apply creams or gouge the cricket ball. Such actions can have a marked effect on how much the trajectory of the ball deviates when flying through the air or bouncing off the wicket. Early in the 2005 County Championship season Surrey were docked eight points after the umpires deemed that they tampered with the ball while fielding. Ultimately, this cost Surrey its place in the top division as they were relegated by just one point.

- **Intimidation of an opponent:** Cricket can be a dangerous sport and being hit by a cricket ball at over 90 mph is no laughing matter. There have been cases of a bowler deliberately targeting the ball at the batsman's body or head. The idea is to intimidate – and it's against the laws of the game. When deciding if intimidation bowling is taking place the umpire makes an assessment of the batsman's skills. If, for example, a bowler is aiming the ball at the body of a low skilled opponent then he's more likely to be disciplined for intimidation.

✔ **Throwing the ball:** The arm holding, then releasing, the ball is not allowed to bend and then straighten significantly in a throwing motion. If it does the umpire standing in the square leg position, may call a no-ball. A bowler throwing the ball, or *chucking* in cricket slang, is a big no-no. Some bowlers' careers have been ended when they have been found to be throwing instead of bowling the ball.

Chapter 4

Grabbing the Right Gear:
Cricket Equipment

*T*ake a peek into any cricket dressing room and the room looks like a bomb's hit it. You're sure to see equipment everywhere: bats, pads, gloves and stumps – the list goes on and on.

In fact, I can't think of any team sport in which quite so much equipment is used as in cricket.

In this chapter I guide you through the cricket equipment universe. If you read this chapter start to finish you should have a good idea of what kit you need to buy or borrow to play cricket safely.

Most equipment in cricket is designed for the batsman. After all, he has to defend his stumps and body from a ball bowled at upwards of 90 miles per hour.

Getting It Together: The Essentials

Cricket equipment can be divided into two kinds.

- ✔ Items of basic equipment which everybody involved in a game uses.

- ✔ Items of personal equipment; essential for performance and for personal protection.

Most of this chapter relates to personal equipment but you do need some basic equipment to start the game.

The furniture: Understanding what the club supplies

The basic equipment for setting up a game of cricket is fairly straightforward. The gear used in common by all the players, and provided by the club, includes the essentials:

- ✔ **Two sets of three stumps and two bails:** These items are positioned at the two ends of the pitch, one set at each end. Flip back to Chapter 2 for more details on these.

- ✔ **A boundary rope or markers to indicate where the field of play ends:** Most clubs play on fields where the boundary is marked out in white by the groundsman, but boundary markers are still useful. The boundary determines not only when a ball is out-of-play, but also how many runs are scored when the ball reaches the boundary: that is, a four or a six.

Taking a peek at the cricket ball

The shape and size of a cricket ball is one of the few things in the game to be stuck in a time warp (see Figure 4-1). It has been virtually unchanged for well over a hundred years. Perhaps cricket's authorities figure that if it's not broken, don't fix it. The cricket ball is key to the game. The seam that runs around its circumference can make the ball bounce away and towards the batsman once it hits the wicket. See Chapter 6 for the low-down on the cricket ball.

A cricket ball is made of cork and latex and is covered by leather. This leather is held together by stitching which is called the *seam*. A cricket ball should weigh between 155.9 and 163 grams, the circumference should measure between 22.4 and 22.9 centimetres.

In test and first class cricket matches, players use a red ball. In one-day limited overs matches a white or occasionally a pink ball is used (head over to Chapter 3 for more on the different formats of the game). The shape and dimensions are the same but for some unknown reason – possibly to do with the protective lacquer used on the outside of the ball – the white cricket balls tends to 'swing' more in the air than red ones. Flick through to Chapter 6 for more on swing bowling.

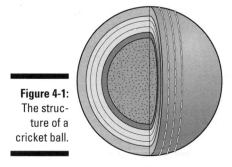

Figure 4-1:
The struc-
ture of a
cricket ball.

In club cricket red cricket balls are used. The club charges members an annual subscription fee, and part of this money is used to buy match balls. Players are expected to provide their own cricket ball for practice sessions.

Balls made by three different manufacturers – Readers, SG and Kookaburra – are used in test matches around the globe. Generally, Reader balls deviate more than Kookaburra balls when bouncing off the wicket; this happens because they have stitched seams which are raised higher than on the SG and Kookaburra balls. In club matches you find that a wider variety of ball manufacturers are used, such as Easton, Gray-Nicolls, Gunn & Moore and Woodworm. Often the decision on the type of ball to be used is at the whim of the home team captain. He may pick his favourite manufacturer or simply go for whichever ball is cheapest.

Getting Personal: Choosing a Bat

Whether your main job in the side is to bat, bowl or keep wicket you're going to need a cricket bat. You may never bowl a ball in anger, but every member of a cricket team gets to strut his stuff as a batsman.

Some club sides have a team kit-bag, normally with bats, pads and gloves for players to choose from. But, generally, you're best off buying your own bat to use.

Every cricket bat is unique. Bats come in all shapes and sizes, so choosing your own means you can decide on its weight and how it feels in your hands.

You get to choose the bat in the first place and are then able to maintain its condition; see the section later 'Preparing the bat for play' for more on bat maintenance.

Cricket bats are made from willow. This wood has the characteristics of being hard wearing, relatively light, and easy to sand and carve into shape.

Pricing up a cricket bat

You can pay anything from £50 up to nearly £300 ($80 to $500) for a cricket bat. At the lower end of the price scale, bats are made from low-grade willow – see more below – and are mass-produced. Pay full whack and you can get your hands on a prime example of the bat maker's art, made from the best quality willow and hand crafted to your own specification; see 'Buying a bat or having one made' later in this chapter for more on having a bat custom built.

In life you tend to get what you pay for, but you may still find a bat at the lower end of the price scale that suits you right down to the ground.

The quality of the willow used to make bats is normally given a star rating by manufacturers. Star ratings are from one to five, with one being the lowest quality and five the highest. You pay more for a five star bat than a three or one star bat. However, just because a bat has a high star rating doesn't mean it's going to be right for you.

The willow used in cricket bat manufacture hails from two main areas: England and Kashmir. The former is the traditional home of bat manufacture and the willow from England is often given a high star rating. Bats from Kashmir often get a low star rating but they're generally cheaper. In recent years, the quality of Kashmir willow cricket bats coming to the UK has improved and the bat-makers from the sub-continent have grabbed a fair chunk of the international market.

Manufacturers make bats especially for young children and teenagers. Junior bats are smaller and cheaper, see 'Kitting Out a Youngster for the Game' later in this chapter for more.

Deciding on the right bat

Even if you're on an economy drive and looking for a bat that simply does the job, rather than an expensive hand-carved piece of willow, you still need to consider three important points when making your bat selection:

> ✔ **The weight of the bat.** The weight can vary from just over 2 lbs to over 3 lbs. It may not sound like much of a difference but believe me when you go from lifting a light bat to heavy one you really notice the difference.

✔ **The length of the bat handle.** Bat manufacturers offer three types of handle sizes – short, normal, and long (see Figure 4-2). Which type you go for depends upon your grip on the bat and the size of your hands. If you have great big mitts and space them out on the handle when gripping it, you need a long handle. If you have dainty little paws and eave relatively little room on the handle, a short handle may be for you. Have a look at all three sizes: You'll soon feel which one is right for you.

✔ **Do you need full size?** Full-sized bats are too big for junior and – for want of a better word – short players. Fortunately, bats come in lots of different sizes below full size. Check out 'Kitting Out a Youngster for the Game' later in this chapter for more on smaller bats.

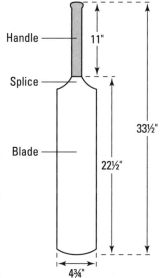

Figure 4-2:
The dimensions of a cricket bat.

The lighter the bat, the quicker you should be able to manoeuvre it in the air. On the other hand, the heavier a bat, the more impact it may have on the cricket ball. Most hard-hitting, powerful batsmen tend to use heavy bats. The great former England batsman Sir Len Hutton once described handling the bat used by fellow England great Ian Botham as 'like picking up a railway sleeper'. Botham was famed for hitting the ball high and far.

Cricketers describe how a bat feels in your hands when lifting it off the ground as the *pick up*. It has nothing to do with small trucks or dodgy one-liners. Generally, batsmen prefer bats to have a light pick up but still be weighty enough to give the ball a frightful tonk.

No two bats will feel exactly the same in your hands, even if they are of the same weight and handle length. Each piece of wood used in bat manufacture is unique.

Buying a bat or having it made

The vast majority of club cricketers buy their bats off the shelf: They hunt around the shops for one that feels just about right. Some cricketers, though, go the extra mile and pay for a manufacturer to make a bat to their own specifications.

One bat maker I know actually welcomes visitors into the workshop allowing them to pick the piece of wood to be used in the manufacture of the bat and introduces them to the person who will make it. However, such Hollywood treatment costs plenty of cash.

A specially made bat is normally as good as it gets, but buying off the shelf can be no bad thing: The standard of bat manufacture is high and you should be able to find a bat that is just right for you; see 'Shopping for cricket gear' sidebar later in this chapter for more on shopping for equipment.

If you're relatively new to the game, getting a bat specially made is pointless. Only with experience of playing matches will you become aware of what weight and handle size suits you. Often when buying a first bat, as an adult, it's best to go for one around a medium weight, say 2lb 8ozs, 2lb 9oz or 2lb 10ozs. Bat weights are always given in Imperial measure.

Well-known county and test match batsmen usually sign sponsorship deals with bat manufacturers. The players get paid to use and endorse the manufacturers' bats. What's more, the manufacturer will make the bats to order for free. The player gets A1 treatment, getting to visit the workshop and choosing the exact weight and specification of the bat. No queuing up down the local sports shop and buying bats off the shelf for top players!

If you join a cricket club, every so often you'll find that batsmen will sell one of their cricket bats – many have more than one. As long as the bat is in good condition – check for cracking of the wood or splintering of the handle – this can be a cheap way to get your hands on a good quality bat. What's more, the bat will be ready for play, *oiled* and *knocked-in*. See 'Preparing the bat for play' later in this chapter for more.

Some club sides have team kit-bags, which contain bats, batting gloves, pads and other pieces of equipment. These are fine to use when you're first starting out but if you're serious about getting good at the game then buy your own stuff and get used to it in both practice and playing in matches.

Space age science makes it in to cricket

Cricket may have the image of a fuddy-duddy, old fashioned, genteel kind of game, but in reality it is as open as anything else to the march of new technology. Super slow-motion video replays and hawkeye computer technology (a TV aid which can show with startling accuracy whether a ball hitting the batsman's pads would have gone on to hit the stumps) add a lot to the armchair spectator's enjoyment of cricket; see Chapter 13 for more.

And on the cricket pitch itself space age technology is having an impact. A few years ago, great Australian batsman Ricky Ponting courted controversy by using a bat strengthened with titanium. This metal has already turned the world of golf on its head by allowing golfers to hit the ball further than ever before and it seems that same thing could happen with cricket. Ponting's bat manufacturer Kookaburra has been delighted with the advance made through using titanium, but the game's governing body, the International Cricket Council (ICC), became concerned and asked Ponting to stop using the bat. Ponting, well-noted for his sportsmanship, agreed not to use the space age bat. But whether fancy material like titanium is used or not, bat technology has made a huge difference to weight and power delivery. Thicker edges to the bats as well as better weight distribution between the handle and the 'hitting zone' – the centre of the bat – means a modern cricket bat feels a lot lighter when you pick it up than an old one, but is actually the same weight. It's not a magic trick, just modern technology!

Even if your main job in the team is bowling or wicket-keeping the captain still expects you to be able to bat. In fact, one great way to get in the captain's good books is by being a bowler who is a bit of a dab hand at batting. After all, the more runs your team scores the better the chances are of it winning cricket matches.

Preparing the bat for play

A cricket ball is a very hard object, particularly when propelled at around 90 miles per hour. Bats have to go through a process of preparation before they are ready to be hit at high speed by a cricket ball.

Proper bat preparation includes:

- ✔ **Oiling with linseed oil.** The oil protects the wood. You should apply three coats of oil to the front of the bat, leaving it to dry properly each time you apply fresh oil.

- ✔ **Hit the bat with force.** You have to get the wood used to the impact of a cricket ball. Therefore you should spend several hours hitting it with a ball or a bat mallet. This process is called *knocking-in* and is essential, otherwise you'll find the bat cracks or shatters when you finally use it in a match. Knock the bat in gently at first and then gradually build up the force that you use.

Often you'll see that a manufacturer sells a bat as *ready to play*. This means that a machine has been used to knock the bat in and that a plastic protective facing has been fitted to the front of the bat. Generally, I have found that these bats could still do with being knocked in, particularly along the edges.

Some bats have something called a *toe guard* fitted. This toe guard is a piece of plastic fitted over the bottom – called the *toe* – of the bat. The idea is to prevent cracking at the toe of the bat, which is common. If your bat doesn't have a toe guard consider getting one fitted; your local cricket shop should be able to help.

A bat can be for life, not just one summer, if you maintain it properly. This means that before the start of each cricket season you should apply an extra coat of linseed oil. Over time, you'll probably find that the bat will change colour, turning a richer, darker colour, like that of the linseed oil.

Getting the Right Protection

Being hit on the torso, legs or head by a cricket ball is no laughing matter. Cricket may not be as dangerous a sport as motor racing, horse riding or rugby, but nevertheless people sustain serious injuries playing the game each year. Some poor unfortunates are even killed playing the game they love.

Fortunately, plenty of protection is available. In fact, name a part of the body and you can bet your last pound that someone has invented a form of padding to keep it nice and safe.

Starting from the top, the main types of personal protection are:

- The helmet
- The batting gloves and arm guards
- The box
- The thigh protector
- Batting pads – also called leg guards

I look at each in turn in this section.

Sadly these are litigious times: People are being egged-on by law firms to sue, even in circumstances which would once have been put down to bad luck. If you intend to play cricket seriously, you may be best to have insurance against being sued for any injury you may cause through hitting a fellow player or spectator with the ball. This is called liability insurance; talk to an insurance broker about this cover. Expect to pay a few pounds a month for liability insurance. Many cricket clubs are aware of the dangers and have a club-wide insurance policy, paid for through subscriptions. But going for the belt-and-braces approach and having personal insurance which covers the cost of being sued may be a smart play!

Using your head: Wearing a helmet

Wearing a cricket helmet when batting or standing in the field close to the batsmen can be a real life-saver (see Chapter 7 for more on fielding positions). If you have ever seen a player who was not wearing a helmet being struck on the head by a cricket ball, you'll know how sickening the sight is.

Against the faster seam and swing bowlers you really should wear a helmet. Some batsmen argue that they feel encumbered by a helmet but by practising in the nets while wearing one you get used to it. See Chapters 5 and 9 for more on net practice.

Expect to pay anything from £30 to £80 ($50 to $120) for a cricket helmet. Generally, the higher the price, the lighter the helmet and the better the quality of materials used to make it.

If you receive a hefty blow to your cricket helmet most manufacturers recommend that you should replace it.

Sometimes cricket sides in the field will have a helmet ready in case a fielder is told by the captain to stand close to the batsmen. When not in use, this helmet is usually placed directly behind where the wicket-keeper stands, by the fielding side. If the ball hits the helmet, while lying in the outfield, five runs are automatically credited to the batting side's score.

Protecting your hands and arms

Hand injuries are common in cricket. Some batsmen suffer broken fingers and blows to the arms with alarming regularity. All players, when their turn comes to bat, wear batting gloves – without them hand injuries would be even more commonplace.

The palm of a batting glove is made of leather, making it easy to grip the bat handle. The other side of the batting glove is encased in padding to cushion any blow received from the cricket ball.

Putting a lid on it

Batsmen started wearing helmets back in the 1970s. At first they were rudimentary affairs, resembling motor cycle crash helmets. Back then, visibility wasn't good from beneath the helmet's visor, but over time designs have improved. The modern generation of helmets are lightweight and offer the batsmen a good field of vision.

For some players just wearing gloves isn't enough. They choose to strap an *arm guard* on the arm closest to the bowler. The arm guard is a piece of thick padding that covers the forearm above the batsman's top hand on the bat handle. This is the left forearm for a right-handed batman, the right forearm for a leftie. Arm guards are less regularly used than other protective gear, but can prevent nasty injuries.

Expect to pay £15 to £60 ($25 to $100) for batting gloves and around £15 for an arm guard. Again, with batting gloves, you get what you pay for. The more expensive offer the most padding and best materials, helping to minimise injury.

Chest guards are also a protective option. A blow from a cricket ball in to the ribs can be very painful and can actually lead to breakages. Chest guards tend to be of most use on wickets where the ball is bouncing high and bowlers delivering the ball at high speed; see Chapter 6 for more.

Wicket-keepers also wear gloves when fielding. Wicket-keeping gloves are thicker and bigger than batting gloves; they are dual purpose, designed to protect the hands and make it easy for wicket-keepers to catch the cricket ball. Expect to pay £30 to £60 ($50 to $100) for a pair of wicket-keeping gloves; see Chapter 7 for more on the art of keeping wicket.

Looking after the rest of you

If a cricket ball makes contact with your genitals at speed the pain can be eye-watering. Therefore just about the first piece of protective equipment ever invented was the *box*.

Put simply, a box is a V-shaped hardened plastic protector which slips into the crotch area to protect your genitals. Never leave the pavilion to bat without wearing a box. Some fielders standing near the batsman and the wicket-keeper wear boxes too. In short, if you're at risk of being hit by the ball in the groin, wear a box! A box costs about a fiver – a small price to pay to prevent yourself from singing falsetto!

From tall hats to imperial stormtroopers

Over time, cricket gear has changed a huge amount. Early drawings and paintings of cricket matches depict players whose only protection seems to be a well-starched pair of trousers and a stove pipe hat. The bats, as well, were shaped differently back in the eighteenth and early nineteenth century, looking more akin to a hockey stick than a modern cricket bat.

Today, batsmen sometimes resemble American footballers – or Star Wars imperial stormtroopers – because they wear so much padding on legs, hands, chest, thigh and arm. The use of modern materials allows players to move freely, despite the excess of padding.

Bowlers' appearance has changed far less than the batters. After all, they are the ones potentially doing damage!

Stumps, as well, have evolved from two small wooden sticks with a single bail across the top to the current arrangement of three stumps and two bails. In some test and first class matches the TV broadcasters even build a miniature camera into one of the stumps, to give TV watchers an up-close and personal view of the action. See Chapter 13 for more.

Men and boys always need to wear a box to ensure the genitals are safe from being accidentally hit by the ball. The easiest way to wear a box is to slip it between two firmly fitting pairs of underpants to hold it in place.

Guarding your legs from injury

When going out to bat, every player wears batting pads – sometimes called leg guards – on each leg. These pads are meant to cushion the impact of the cricket ball and prevent bruising. In bygone times, batting pads were made of cane strips encased in hairy material, a bit like what's used to insulate a boiler. These days, though, pads are made of ultra modern man-made materials such as high-density foam and secured with a Velcro strap. The idea is that modern batting pads should be light to allow the batsmen to move in them freely.

Expect to pay £30–90 ($50 to $150) for a pair of batting pads.

If a batsman is struck on the batting pads by the cricket ball delivered by the bowler while standing in front of the stumps, the umpire may give him out Leg Before Wicket (LBW). Refer to Chapter 2 for more on the LBW law.

Wicket-keepers also wear leg guards. Unlike batting pads – which go above the knee – the leg guards sported by wicket-keepers only go up to around knee height so as not to interfere with the keeper's ability to take the ball.

One of the most popular forms of protection used by batsmen is the thigh pad. This protection covers the area above the pad – the leg guards – up to the waist. A thigh pad is worn on the player's front leg – the one facing the bowler. Therefore, a right-handed player would wear a thigh pad on his left leg. The reverse applies to lefties.

Getting Kitted Out Top-To-Toe

The clothing worn by club cricketers varies enormously, but the more serious players always try to adhere to the basic dress code of the sport.

Being whiter than white

When playing in matches, cricketers wear white clothing called, ingeniously, *whites*. The idea of diving around a field in white clothing may, at first, look a bit barmy. Fields are made of mud and dirt and a nice shiny set of cricket whites can look very dishevelled in double-quick time. But wearing white has practical purposes, mainly so the batsmen can more easily spot the red cricket ball. In short, wearing white is a courtesy to the batsmen – oh so very cricket!

If you play cricket you need to buy whites – trousers, shirt and sweater.

At the club you join you can buy a sweater, which will have piping in the club's colours. Expect to pay around £30– 50 ($50 to $80) for a decent, long-sleeved, thick sweater. You can buy cricket shirts and trousers off the peg at your local sports shop, through the Internet, or by telephone mail order. Expect to pay around £25 ($35) for trousers and the same for a shirt.

Shirts and trousers tend to be made of cotton and polyester mix and are machine washable; which is absolutely essential considering all the sliding around you do when fielding.

Buy more than one pair of trousers; with all the diving they don't tend to last very long. In fact, in my experience you're doing well if cricket trousers last more than a season.

When fielding, apply Vaseline to joints and wear knee pads under trousers to help prevent nasty and painful grass burns.

Professional cricketers dress in coloured clothing for one-day limited overs matches. See Chapter 3 for more on these types of matches.

Taking care of your feet

Having good footwear that allows you to grip the turf, is crucial to batting, bowling and fielding. Wear slippy or inappropriate footwear and you can come a cropper, perhaps even injuring yourself.

You need to wear a pair of cricket boots. Expect to pay £30–70 for a pair of boots. You have the choice of buying boots with metal spikes, rubber spikes and even a combination of both. Generally speaking, shoes with rubber spikes don't grip the turf as well as metal-spiked boots. However, many players prefer rubber spikes. This is because metal spikes can often stick in the turf and can actually become detached and lost. In short, there is no right or wrong boot: Use whichever you feel most comfortable with.

You can buy cricket boots specially designed for bowling. The main difference between bowling boots and standard cricket boots is that bowling boots offer more support to the ankle.

Some bowlers like to cut out the boot leather directly above where their big toe goes. This modification means that the big toe sticks out from the boot. This is to prevent rubbing of the big toe when the bowler runs up to the wicket to deliver the ball.

Choosing a Kit-Bag

After you have all the kit you can equip yourself with, you need to decide what you're going to carry it all around in. You're going to need a kit-bag. The more equipment you have the bigger the bag. Some players prefer to travel light – just the bare essentials of clothing, batting pads, gloves and helmet. Others, though, like to carry around an Aladdin's cave of cricketing goodies – a bit of strapping or special spray for every possible occasion.

The choice of kit-bags is huge. You can pay anything from £20 to nearly £100 for a bag or case alone. Here are some of the options:

- **A duffel bag with shoulder straps.** Very easy to carry but the smallest of all the bags, which means you're only able to transport the bare necessities. Prices vary from £20 to £50 ($30 to $80.

- **A standard over-the-shoulder kit-bag.** These are bigger than duffel bags and you can transport large amounts of equipment in them, not just the basics. They have separate pockets for boots and even, sometimes, bats. Some come with wheels and carry handles; expect to pay over £40 ($60).

✔ **A cricket coffin.** This rather gruesomely named item is the top of the pops. The coffin is a hard case – usually black – with wheels. Coffins are huge inside and very robust. Expect to pay more than £80 ($120) for a coffin.

The cricket club or the venue at which the game is being played supplies the stumps and bails.

Carry pain-relief sprays and plasters in case of injury. During a season you're certain at some stage to suffer a cut knee from diving in the outfield or a nasty bruise from being hit by the ball.

Don't forget to use plenty of sunscreen, even when the sky's cloudy overhead. Without sunscreen, not only are you risking the discomfort of being burned but also you're potentially putting your long-term health at risk. Cricketers are prime candidates for skin cancers.

You'll often see professional cricketers caked in zinc oxide cream. They don't just do this because they think it makes them look fierce. These guys play day-in, day-out. They know that as they are out in the sun far more regularly than most club cricketers, the cream offers them the very best protection from harmful ultraviolet rays.

You don't need to carry around every item of cricket equipment you possess to every game or net session. Think what you're likely to need for the occasion. For example, most club net sessions don't require whites to be worn or perhaps you're not planning to bowl in the nets session, so, therefore, you won't need to take bowling boots.

Shopping for cricket gear

Sadly, specialist cricket shops are getting rather thin on the ground. For example, only a handful survive in the London area, serving eight million people. But don't despair – tracking down the right cricket equipment isn't hard. You can buy clothing from most high street sports retailers and some may even have a selection of bats to choose from. Some department stores also stock cricket equipment. In addition, all the major county grounds have cricket shops – see Chapter 13 for more on county cricket grounds. By far the biggest trade is now done through the Internet and by mail order. You can pick up any item of cricket equipment this way.

Every April, *TheCricketer* magazine contains a guide to the very latest cricket equipment that's become available.

Here are some of the major UK cricket equipment manufacturers:

✔ Gunn and Moore

✔ Gray-Nicolls

✔ Hunts County

✔ Kookaburra

✔ Newberry

✔ Puma

✔ Slazenger

✔ Woodworm

Plenty of Internet cricket retailers exist; here's a selection of some of the most extensive Web sites:

✔ www.cricketdirect.co.uk

✔ www.bournesports.co.uk

✔ www.cricketsupplies.com

✔ www.owzat-cricket.co.uk

✔ www.cricket-hockey.co.uk

But if you want the personal service, and to pick up and feel the bat before you buy, you may be best taking time and going to a specialist cricket retailer or even to the manufacturers direct.

Kitting Out a Youngster for the Game

If your little treasure wants to take up the game, then here are some things to bear in mind when kitting them out:

✔ **Be careful not to buy too big a bat.** Having a bat that is too big can make it really hard to play shots. If anything, a bat that's too small is preferable to one that's too big. See the sidebar 'Cricket bat sizes' for some useful information.

✔ **Buying cricket equipment can be expensive.** Expect to pay a couple of hundred pounds to buy a kid a new bat and equipment essentials. And they are bound to grow out of clothes, shoes and bats in double-quick time.

✔ **Don't go overboard.** Your child has to carry their own equipment to practice, so be sensible and make sure they only have to lug around the essentials – bat, pads, gloves, helmet and boots.

Safety is paramount in youth cricket. It is now compulsory for all batsmen under the age of 16 to wear a helmet while batting. The only circumstance in which a player under 16 doesn't have to wear a helmet is when the parents sign a waiver.

You can usually find lots of cheap second-hand cricket equipment on eBay. Check out *eBay.co.uk For Dummies* by Marsha Collier and Jane Hoskyn (Wiley) for more help.

Cricket bat sizes

Cricket bats come in lots of different sizes. For younger children bat sizes progress from 1 up to 6. A special size for youths exists – sometimes referred to as Harrow size – which is just a touch smaller than full size. Table 4-1 contains a rough guide to cricket bat sizes.

Table 4-1	Bat Sizes	
Size	**Age range**	**Bat length**
1	4–5yrs	25¼ inches
2	6–7 yrs	27¾ inches
3	8 yrs	28¾ inches
4	9–11yrs	29¾ inches
5	10–12 yrs	30¾ inches
6	11–13 yrs	31¾ inches
Harrow/youth	12–14 yrs	32¾ inches
Men's full size	15yrs +	33½ inches (short handle)
Men's full size	15yrs +	34⅜ inches (long handle)

You'll notice that some of the ages in Table 4-1 overlap. This is because no two children grow the same. One child may be fine with a size 4 bat at age 11, while another has grown faster and needs a size 5 or even 6. Therefore, use the table only as a guide.

Part II
Playing the Game

Wide

No ball

Byes & Start of play

Leg byes

Out

Four runs

Six runs

Five runs, not penalties

Dead ball

Short runs

Last hour

New ball

Third umpire

Revoke the last signals

5 penalty runs to the batting team

5 penalty runs to the fielding team

Go to www.dummies.com/extras/cricket for online bonus content.

In this part . . .

✔ Wielding the willow: learning how to bat.

✔ Hitting the deck: sharpening your bowling skills.

✔ Fielding and catching: an outfield masterclass.

✔ Understanding the tactical side of the game.

✔ Training to play: fitness and practice.

✔ Go to www.dummies.com/extras/cricket for online bonus content, including an extra Part of Tens chapter: 'Ten Great Cricket Controversies'.

Chapter 5

Honing Your Batting Skills

· ·

In This Chapter

▶ Getting ready to bat

▶ Choosing a batting role

▶ Looking at the bowling

▶ Examining the scoring shots

▶ Taking control of the match

· ·

*A*h, batting! Easy-peasy. The thwack of leather on willow as you send another of the bowler's deliveries careering over the boundary rope.

That's the fantasy and this chapter is the reality. Batting is a bit of a war, with bowlers and fielders set full-pelt to grab your wicket. Your weapons in this war are your talent, determination, powers of concentration and team-mates. Harness all these and you can put the bowling to the sword and pile on those precious runs.

In this chapter, I examine everything you need to know about mastering the art of batting, from what judgement calls you need to make to how to play a scoring shot with aplomb.

Put simply the object of batting is to score as many runs as possible before being out, otherwise called *losing your wicket*, or *being dismissed* – which sounds like being asked to leave the headmaster's study.

Understanding What It Takes to be Good at Batting

Being a good batsman is not just about having the right equipment, or about how much zinc oxide cream you spread on your face to prevent it being burned by the sun.

Being an A1 batsman is about having all or most of the following characteristics:

- **Natural talent.** The very best players – test and first class cricketers here – all have good hand-eye co-ordination. But even if you don't have an abundance of natural talent – and few of us have – you can work on other aspects of the art of batting that I discuss in this chapter to become a run machine.

- **Excellent judgement.** Batting is all about making decisions, from split-second choices about which shot to play (or not to play), to tactical assessments of the match situation.

- **Concentration.** If you want to be a good at batting you have to be prepared to spend hours building an innings. As a batsman you have to concentrate intensely on each delivery – if you don't focus then you may find yourself being dismissed.

- **Physical fitness.** You don't have to be especially fit to play cricket, but being fit helps. Fitness aids concentration, enables you to move quickly when playing attacking shots as well as giving you the ability to run quickly between the stumps to register runs. See Chapter 9 for more on general cricket fitness.

One of the crucial things to understand about batting is that it only takes one mistake to end with dismissal. Being a batsman can breed a persecution complex, because nearly everyone else on the field is out to get you. The bowler is trying to knock over your stumps or trap you *leg before wicket* (LBW: refer to Chapter 2), the fielders are looking to take a catch or run you out and the umpires are poised to judge whether you should take the long, lonely walk back to the pavilion.

Any batsman will tell you bowlers have it easy; they bowl a bad ball which gets hit for four runs and then a minute or two later they get another delivery with which to grab a wicket.

But batting does have its upside. Batsmen enjoy most of the glory! When they're strutting their stuff on the field of play, the eyes of the crowd, teammates and opponents are on them. Those who execute scoring shots with particular panache – see the section 'Expanding Your Horizons: Playing Aggressive Shots' later in this chapter for a rundown of scoring shots – are often described as entertainers or artists and their approach as cavalier.

Gentlemen and Players

Back in the days when cricket was developing as a spectator sport – the nineteenth and early twentieth century – batsmen (and they were always men in those days) were usually assumed to be gentlemen, whereas bowlers were characterised as working-class. It used to be said that you could whistle down a coalmine in Yorkshire and a fast bowler would emerge (although they'd need a wash before putting on some cricket whites) but county and national sides were chock full of batsmen with double-barrel names, titles, and even the odd Indian prince playing for England!

All this isn't to say that the Gentlemen couldn't bowl – some were very adept at it, even without their butler on hand – it's just that bowling didn't have the same mystique as wielding the bat and dispatching the ball to all parts. A bit of this class divide still exists today.

Starting Out in the Middle

Even at the best of times, cricket is hardly a fast game. Arriving at the wicket, before facing the first delivery, you have to go through some preliminaries with the umpire standing at the bowler's end of the pitch. These goings on may all seem like a bit of a rigmarole but it's all done for good reasons.

Taking guard

When the umpire helps you line up your bat with the stumps the exercise is called *taking guard*.

You hold your bat vertically and ask the umpire which stump is covered. After hearing the answer you then tell the umpire which stump you want your bat to be in front of. The umpire then guides you to the position you requested by instructing you to move your bat towards you or away from you. This position is called your *guard*. Once you have been guided to your guard, you should make a dent on the crease by hitting it with the bat. The crease is the white line four feet in front of the line passing through the stumps (also the marker for the batsman to complete a run). See Chapter 2 for more on creases. Making a dent isn't about vandalising the pitch. You make a dent so you can easily return your bat to the same spot to take guard ball after ball and therefore not annoy the umpire by asking to retake your guard all the time.

You can take lots of different guards – from leg stump to off stump. But the two most popular guards are *middle and leg* – referred to sometimes by cricketers as 'two'; that is, both the middle and leg stump are covered – or a *middle stump* guard. Only a matter of inches difference exists between a middle and leg and middle stump guards.

The middle and leg guard is lined up on the gap between the middle and leg stumps.

Gripping stuff

You hold a cricket bat with both hands. If, like most players, you are right handed, your *top hand*, the hand nearest to the top of the handle, is your left hand. This means that when you stand in the side-on position that most batsmen use, your left shoulder faces the bowler. Your right hand is your *bottom hand* because it is closest to the bottom of the bat handle. The right side of your body faces the stumps and the wicket-keeper. The opposite applies for left-handers.

1 **Lay the bat down in front of you on the ground or floor with the handle pointing towards you and the flat side of the bat face down.**

   Put your arms out in front of you and spread your thumb and index finger on each hand so a natural 'V' forms between them.

2 **Now bend down and pick up the bat, grabbing the middle of the handle, with both 'Vs' pointing down the back of the bat.**

   Always pick up the bat with a dominant top hand and a relaxed bottom hand. If you're a right hander your right hand should fit comfortably into the 'V' of your left hand and your fingers should wrap around the front of the bat handle. Again, the opposite applies for a left hander.

3 **Stand with you feet comfortably apart, say about the width of your shoulders (about 15 centimetres or six inches is common) and bend your knees slightly so you can gently and comfortably rest the bat behind the toes on your right foot if you're a right hander, or left foot if you're a left hander.** This is called your batting stance, and I examine it in more detail later in the chapter.

The natural inclination standing in this initially somewhat unfamiliar position will be to let your 'top' or left hand, if you're a right hander, turn anti-clockwise away from you. Resist this. It is important that your 'bottom' or right hand remains in the 'V' of your top hand and both 'Vs' continue to face down the back of the bat. Some coaches recommend that the 'Vs' form a line pointing fractionally towards the front half of the bat but this is only a very minor change of direction.

This grip will naturally point a right hander's left or front elbow towards the bowler. This is vitally important to be able to play the majority of defensive and scoring shots examined later in this chapter. In most cases your front elbow will automatically become the pointer and guide of where you want to stroke the ball to score runs.

✔ Unless it feels completely unnatural to you, don't have a large gap between your hands on the handle. Keeping your hands together makes it easier to hit the ball straight.

✔ Do be comfortable in the way you hold the bat; it all has to feel natural.

✔ Don't grip the bat too hard; this will aid flexibility, as a less tight grip helps you direct the ball away from the fielders (see Figure 5-1).

Make sure you always hold the bat in the middle of the handle with your hands comfortably together and, as previously discussed, the 'V' created by the thumb and index finger on each hand pointing down the back of the bat. Some very good, very experienced players may vary their grip a little by moving it up or down the handle or leaving a small gap between the hands. However, holding the bat too low, or *choking* the bat as it is known, makes it difficult to play straight and drive properly. Likewise, holding the bat too high makes it difficult to control the strokes. See the section 'Expanding Your Horizons: Playing Aggressive Shots' later in this chapter for more on stroke play.

Generally, the bottom hand on the handle exerts the power in the shot while the top hand controls the direction in which the bat turns. When you want to go for a big six hit, you should bring more power to bear from your bottom hand: Get your timing right and you will loft the ball a long, long way.

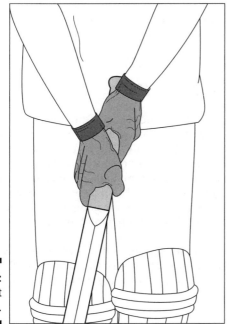

Figure 5-1:
The correct batting grip.

Listening to the umpire

Umpires try very hard to be fair and in the spirit of fair play, when you first come out to bat, they will offer you all sorts of useful nuggets of information, relating to the game situation and what the bowler is up to.

The umpire will tell you:

- ✔ The number of balls left to go in the over
- ✔ What hand the bowler will deliver the ball out of
- ✔ What side of the stumps, at the bowler's end, the ball will be delivered from

There are four combinations of ball and hand:

- ✔ Right arm over the wicket (the most common)
- ✔ Right arm round the wicket
- ✔ Left arm over the wicket
- ✔ Left arm round the wicket

A right-handed player bowling *over the wicket* delivers the ball from the umpire's left – the right-hand side of the stumps as the batsman looks at it. A right-handed player bowling *round the wicket* delivers the ball from the right hand side of the umpire and the stumps. For left-handed bowlers what constitutes over or round the wicket is reversed.

Setting the sight screens

Taking in all the above info, you should now check the position of the sight screens (if there are any). The sight screens are large wooden screens – a few metres high and wide, and painted white. The screens are mounted on wheels so they can be moved easily and are meant to be located directly behind where the bowler will be releasing the ball. If you are not happy with where the sight screens are you can ask for them to be moved so that they are directly behind where the bowler will be releasing the ball – and the fielding side will oblige by moving the sight screen, which is nice!

Once the umpire has helped you take guard, told you what the bowler is up to, and checked with you that you're happy with the position of the sight screens, he will shout 'Play' and it's time to face your first delivery.

What are they clapping for?

As you walk from the pavilion don't be taken aback if the fielding team break into spontaneous applause. This applause is part of the tradition of the game and shows respect for the incoming batsman. These days batsmen aren't applauded to the wicket in test, first class or serious club league matches, even when it's their birthday! But in many club-friendly matches new batsmen are still applauded: all very polite and oh so very cricket!

Facing up to the bowler: Stance

In order to score runs or defend his stumps from being hit by the ball, the batsman plays a *shot*, also called a *stroke*.

Many different shots can be played but they can be broken down into two clear types:

 ✔ **Aggressive shots.** The aim of these is always to score runs but it can mean risking dismissal.

 ✔ **Defensive shots.** The main aim of these shots is to prevent dismissal (it doesn't always work) and runs scored from a defensive shot are a bonus!

The batsman's stance tells you instantly whether he is a left or right hander. Quite simply, a right hander will be facing the bowler with his legs to the right of the bat and vice versa for a left hander.

The stance is all about maintaining good balance (see Figure 5-2). It should be relaxed and comfortable so the batsman finds it easy to stay in the middle and bat for hours scoring runs. At least that's the aim!

The idea is that the batsman's body and hands should be in the best possible position to execute a shot once the ball has been delivered. The best batsmen like to have their weight evenly distributed in the stance between their right and left leg. Keeping the head still is also considered key in the stance as this allows both eyes to point directly down the wicket at the bowler – allowing the optimum field of vision. Don't tilt your head – make sure your eyes are level.

The batsman also has to consider where he stands in relation to the stumps. The umpire will help the batsman align himself with the line of the stumps, see the earlier 'Taking Guard' section. But the batsman has to decide how close to the stumps he stands. If the batsman stands close to the stumps the risk is he will step on them when attempting to play a back foot shot, such as a pull or cut. Flip forward to 'Expanding Your Horizons: Playing Aggressive Shots' later in this chapter for more on these types of shot.

The default position for most batsmen is to place their feet either side of the line of the crease. This should give the batsman plenty of room to play back foot shots if needed.

The closer you stand to the bowler the less time you will have to move into position to play a shot before the ball arrives.

Some good batsmen stand with their feet outside the crease, effectively cutting the distance between them and the bowler. Why do they do this? Often it is to give them a better chance of meeting the ball on the half-volley or before it pitches – called hitting it *on the full* – giving the batsman even more chance to play aggressive front foot shots, such as the cover or straight drive.

Executing the shot: Backlift

The backlift is the movement made with the hands by the batsman to propel the bat towards the ball. In order to get power and timing into the shot the aim is to lift the bat behind the back – preferably in line with the off stump and perhaps even head-high – so that the bat comes back down in a pendulum motion to meet the ball when it arrives.

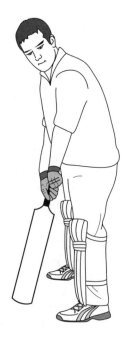

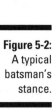

Figure 5-2:
A typical batsman's stance.

Cricketers talk about the batsman *timing a cricket ball* – which doesn't mean standing in the pitch measuring with a stopwatch how quickly the ball travels. A well-timed cricket shot is one where the bat makes contact with the ball at its most effective speed and the ball strikes the face of the bat around the middle. When a cricket shot is well timed, the ball often races away towards the boundary at a very quick pace. All batsmen like to have good timing.

The bat should always be taken virtually straight back towards the wicket-keeper. At the top of the backlift the end or 'toe' of the bat should be a little above the horizontal line running through your wrists. The bat should be pointing somewhere between the wicket-keeper and second slip. If it is any wider, say towards gully, or too far behind your body pointing towards fine leg, this will make it much harder to bring the bat down straight. See below for more on playing straight and Chapter 7 for fielding positions.

Some shots require a higher backlift than others to execute. As a general rule, the more aggressive a shot, the higher and faster the backlift – because the batsman is trying to generate extra power. Defensive shots, usually, involve a short backlift, which has the advantage that they can be executed with great speed.

Always start off with a short backlift, which makes the bat easier to control, particularly for defensive shots. As you spend time in the middle building an innings and becoming more confident, you may increase your backlift as you become more aggressive and the range of your shots increases.

Judging 'Line and Length'

When the ball leaves the bowler's hand you have to make a judgment over where the ball will land on the wicket. You need to assess:

- The direction the ball is moving in.
- How near to you the ball is going to land.

This assessment is called judging the *line and length* of the delivery. Everything should stem from this split-second judgement including what shot is going to be played and where the feet should be placed in order to get as close as possible to the ball to execute a correct scoring shot.

Looking at the line of the ball

Take guard in front of the stumps – usually in line with middle or leg stump – and as the ball is delivered try to assess the line that the ball is travelling down the pitch. The line that the ball takes falls into three clear subgroups:

✔ **Ball missing the stumps on the off side.** In this case, if the ball were to be left alone it would miss the stumps and head towards the wicket-keeper's position.

✔ **Ball missing the stumps on the leg side.** If the ball were left alone it would miss the leg stump. It would be up to the wicket-keeper to dive to stop the ball.

✔ **Ball heading towards the stumps.** In all probability if the ball were left it would strike the wicket and you would be dismissed. To prevent this situation you need to hit the ball with the bat.

When playing a shot try to *get into line*. This means ensuring your head is in line with the direction of the ball when striking it with the bat. Getting into line helps you retain your balance through the shot.

A ball that is set on a line missing the stumps can provide a good opportunity to score runs; particularly, if it's headed down the leg side – fewer fielders are usually on that side of the wicket to take a catch.

Good batsmen can play scoring shots off deliveries, regardless of whether they are set to hit the stumps or not. England's Kevin Pietersen and South African Graeme Smith are two top-class batsmen who are noted for their ability to hit balls out to the boundary that at directed at their middle stump. See Chapter 11 for more on these two stalwarts of modern day international cricket.

If the ball hits your pads – also called leg guards – and the umpire believes that the line of delivery would have taken the ball onto the stumps, then you are given out, leg before wicket (LBW). See Chapter 2 for more on the LBW laws.

Looking at the length of the delivery

At the same time as judging the line of the ball – whether it will hit the stumps or not if left alone – you must gauge where it will hit the pitch. From this estimate you can start to assess how high the ball will bounce.

When assessing how high the ball will bounce, you must take the following into account:

✔ **The pace of the bowler.** The faster the ball hits the pitch, the higher it bounces and the quicker a decision has to be made about which shot to play.

✔ **Angle of descent.** Taller bowlers should get a higher bounce than shorter ones.

✔ **How wet or dry the pitch is.** Usually, the damper the wicket the more slowly the ball comes off the surface once it hits the pitch.

✔ **How old the ball is.** The newer the ball, the higher it bounces and the faster it travels through the air.

Because new balls bounce higher and move more quickly through the air, teams generally give them to their meanest, fastest bowlers. On the flip-side, batting sides often send out the opening players who're adept at playing shots off the back foot to face the fast bowlers. Crucially, playing shots off the back foot gives you more time before the ball arrives. See the section 'Expanding Your Horizons: Playing Aggressive Shots' later in this chapter for more on scoring shots.

In test matches a new ball is used every 80 overs. Generally, in club cricket, each team innings begins with a new ball in use.

You can break down the length of a delivery into four categories.

✔ **A full length.** The ball *pitches* – hits the pitch – close to where you are standing in the crease. The response is, generally, to move onto your front foot, pressing the weight forwards. A ball of this length is also called a *half volley* and can be an easy length to hit a scoring shot.

✔ **On a good length.** If the bowler is fast, the ball pitches five or six yards in front of you. With slow bowlers, a good length delivery lands about two yards in front of the batsman's front foot. This length can be a tricky one to judge as to whether to play a back- or front-foot shot.

✔ **Short of a length.** The ball pitches around eight yards in front of you. The best response to this type of delivery is normally to play off the back foot.

✔ **A bouncer.** This delivery lands around halfway down the pitch and, depending on its pace, direction and bounce can either go safely over your head or home in on your face.

Later in this chapter, I look at the basic batting shots and the lengths of delivery for which they are appropriate. See Chapter 6 for more on length of delivery.

Standing up to seam and swing bowling

Seam and swing bowlers are the heavy artillery of the game. Their job is to blast batsmen out with a combination of pace, bounce and a little guile (see Chapter 6 for further exploration about both types of bowling).

Here are some clues as to what you should do to get that scoreboard rattling along:

- ✔ **Be brave.** Fast bowlers will try to intimidate you – often by directing their deliveries into your ribs. Get onto the back foot with short pitch and bouncer bowling as quickly as you can and decide early if you are going to play an attacking shot, such as a pull or a back-foot defensive, or simply leave the ball.

- ✔ **Wherever possible use the pace of the ball to boost your run total.** You don't need to use brute strength to hit a fast ball: Merely make sure your bat makes contact with the ball and direct it – using a turn of the wrists at the split second of impact – wide of the fielders. You'll soon find the runs piling up.

- ✔ **Try to watch the ball as it leaves the bowler's hand.** This should give you an idea of the direction in which it is likely to swing. See Chapter 6 for more.

- ✔ **Play the survival game.** Bowling fast is very tiring and generally pace bowlers can only bowl five or six overs in one go. What's more, the longer you last the more you get use to the pace of the bowling and the bounce of the ball.

Playing spin bowling

Spin bowling is a mysterious art and newcomers to batting can be bamboozled by it.

The ins and outs of spin bowling are examined in Chapter 6 but here are some pointers on playing spin bowling:

- ✔ **When playing a spin bowler off the front foot, try to keep your bat and pad close together but aim to strike the ball slightly forward of the front pad.** If you don't keep them close together then the ball could spin between them and bowl you out.

- ✔ **Advance down the wicket to where the ball pitches.** This action allows you to play it on the full, or as it bounces, so that the ball doesn't have a chance to spin and change direction before you hit it.

- ✔ **Try and hit the ball in the direction the spin is taking it.** For example, a bowler who is spinning the ball from the leg stump towards the off stump is easier to hit into the off side than the leg side. Hitting across the line of a delivery from a spinner can heighten the chances of offering a catch to a fielder. See Chapter 2 for an explanation of 'off side' and 'leg side'.

> ✔ **Be patient and wait for the bad ball.** Spinning a ball is hard and bowlers can get it horribly wrong, dropping the ball really short or *over-pitching* it – bowling too full a length – on occasions. When this happens you have a great opportunity to go for a boundary or a six hit!

Pulling Up the Drawbridge: Defensive Shots

You should consider playing a defensive shot when

> ✔ A ball is heading towards your stumps – if you don't make contact with the ball, you will be bowled out.
>
> ✔ You have only recently started your innings – often referred to as *arriving at the crease* – and you are getting used to the extent of the bounce of the ball off the pitch. See 'Getting your eye in' later in this chapter.

If you want to be good at batting you must master defensive shots: They get you out of trouble many, many times.

You can break defensive shots down into two different types:

> ✔ Front-foot defensive shots
> ✔ Back-foot defensive shots

Playing a front-foot defensive shot

The idea of the front-foot defensive shot, commonly called the *forward defensive*, is to get forward and smother the ball (see Figure 5-3). Put your weight onto the front foot and then take a stride down the wicket; the bat is then pushed beside the pad, with the face of the bat angled downwards towards the ground. The front leg should be bent at the knee and the bat held at an angle of 45 degrees or less. Executed well, a front-foot defensive shot will stop the ball in its tracks, sending it from the bat into the ground directly in front of you, leaving no chance of a fielder standing close to the bat taking a catch.

For a right handed player, the front foot is the left foot – the reverse is true for a left handed player.

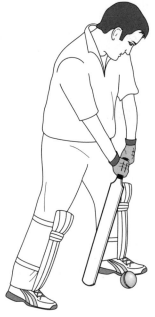

Figure 5-3:
The forward
defensive
shot.

Front-foot defensive shots are best played to deliveries landing on a good or full length.

If you play forward to a ball landing short of a length, or a bouncer length, you risk being hit in the face – called in cricketing circles *wearing one on the chin*.

Playing a back-foot defensive shot

As with the front-foot defensive shot, the idea is to smother. This time, though, you transfer your weight onto your back foot, moving back towards your stumps – although not too far, or you risk hitting your stumps and being given out *hit wicket*. Refer to Chapter 2 for more on modes of dismissal.

By moving back you have more time before the ball arrives and, as you are standing up tall, you are more able to cope with a ball that is bouncing high off the wicket (see Figure 5-4).

Back-foot defensive shots are best played to deliveries landing on a good length, short of a length or bouncer length.

Figure 5-4:
The back-foot defensive shot.

 Without mastering the defensive shots your innings won't last very long. Even the best, most aggressive batsmen in the world work on their defensive shots. They know that all good batting techniques are built on a solid defence.

Expanding Your Horizons: Playing Aggressive Shots

This is the fun part, when you get to (hopefully) see the ball rocketing into or over the boundary rope as you pile on the runs.

Here is the low-down on aggressive shots: How to play them, what length and line of delivery they are suitable for and where the ball should go if you execute the shot properly.

In order to appreciate this section fully you may want to familiarise yourself with the illustration outlining field placing in Chapter 7. The areas of the field are usually described in terms of the field placings that are, or may be, in position.

Cover drive

The cover drive is a front-foot attacking shot played through the offside.

- ✔ **Type of delivery:** Usually played off the front foot to a full length delivery pitching outside the off stump. A back-foot variant is played to short of a length bowling.

- ✔ **How to do it:** Move your front foot forwards to where the ball pitches and bring the bat down straight. Always keep your head over the ball as this helps you keep the shot down. Back-foot cover drives work on the same principle except in that case your weight is initially on the back foot as the ball arrives, but transfers forwards as you make contact with the ball (See Figure 5-5).

- ✔ **Direction the ball should go:** The cover drive should go through the cover region, which is located between the fielders at point and mid off. When executed well this is widely recognised as one of the most artistic of cricket shots.

Figure 5-5:
The cover
drive.

Straight drive

As the name suggests, the straight drive is a drive straight back past the bowler.

- ✔ **Type of delivery:** Ball pitches on off or middle stump, usually of a full length.

- ✔ **How to do it**: Basically the same as a cover drive, except aimed back past the bowler. Move your front foot forward to where the ball pitches and bring the bat down straight. Always keep your head over the line of the ball as this helps you keep the shot down.

- ✔ **Direction the ball should go:** Straight down the ground between mid off and the bowler. There is a leg side variant, played in the same way but with the ball pitching on leg stump which is then directed between the bowler and mid on. This is called an on drive.

Lots of different types of drive exist. They are all the same in principle, the only difference being where the batsman directs the ball. For example, a drive shot played in the area of point – opposite the square leg umpire – is called a square drive.

Leg glance

The leg glance is a shot by which the batsman uses the pace of the ball to score behind the wicket on the leg side.

- ✔ **Type of delivery:** Best played to full or good length deliveries pitching on or outside leg stump.

- ✔ **How to do it:** The key is to turn the wrists holding the bat in the direction of the field on the leg side when making contact with the ball. Make sure that at the moment of impact you have your head over the ball and your weight moving forwards into the shot (see Figure 5-6).

- ✔ **Direction the ball should go:** This depends on how far you allow the ball to come towards you before playing the shot. If you move onto your front foot, playing the ball early, then it should head in the direction of mid wicket or even mid on. Play the ball later, when it is closer to your stumps, and the ball should go towards the square leg fielding position or even behind the square leg umpire.

Figure 5-6:
The leg glance played off the front foot.

The pull shot

The pull shot is a spectacular cross-batted stroke played when the ball is short of a length and bouncing reliably.

- ✔ **Type of delivery:** Just short of a length or bouncer length delivery, pitching on your middle or leg stump or just outside.

- ✔ **How to do it:** This shot is usually played off the back foot to a rising delivery. It is a cross batted shot with the bat moving from off to leg stump, in a swatting type motion. The key is to roll your wrists over the ball on impact, this action plays the shot into the ground, minimising the chances of being caught by a fielder (See Figure 5-7). You roll the wrists in the same way as you would if playing a top spin shot in tennis or turning a door knob from right to left, assuming a right handed batsman.

- ✔ **Direction the ball should go:** Again it depends on how near to your stumps you are when you play it. Pull shots played early, when the ball still has someway to go to the stumps, can end up at mid wicket or even slightly in front of mid wicket. Shots played late can end up heading towards the square leg umpire or just behind.

Figure 5-7:
The pull
shot.

Hook shots are like pull shots except that the ball is bouncing higher and is played later and further back in the crease. If played well, hook shots head between square leg and fine leg fielding positions.

The sweep

One for the slow bowlers only, the sweep depends on the ball bouncing reliably.

- ✔ **Type of delivery:** A full length delivery from a spin bowler which pitches on or outside your leg stump.

- ✔ **How to do it:** Move your front foot forwards to get in line with where the ball is likely to pitch, at the same time bending your back leg towards the ground. This back leg movement helps transfer your weight onto the front foot. With your head over the ball, move your bat in a sweeping motion – hence the name of the shot – from the off to leg side. Again, you need to roll your wrists over the ball at impact therefore hitting the ball into the ground (see Figure 5-8).

Figure 5-8:
The sweep
shot.

✔ **Direction the ball should go:** Sweeps are played to full length deliveries and usually head behind the square leg umpire. This can be a very productive scoring shot.

The cut shot

The cut shot is a back-foot attacking shot played square of the wicket, or just behind square, on the off side.

✔ **Type of delivery:** A short of length delivery pitching well outside your off stump.

✔ **How to do it:** Transfer your weight onto the back foot and then bring the bat in a chopping motion from behind your ears towards the offside. Imagine a woodsman chopping a tree with an axe and you have the basic set-up of a cut shot. Again, the safety-first strategy is to roll the wrists over the ball on contact (see Figure 5-9).

✔ **Direction the ball should go:** The ball should head either just in front or behind the fielder in the point position on the off side.

This section is just a taster of the aggressive shots you can play. As you develop your skills further you will discover how to play more shots.

When no shot is the right shot

If anything proves how bizarre a game cricket is, it's the fact that sometimes you're far better playing no shot and letting the ball sail harmlessly past the stumps into the gloves of the waiting keeper. This 'shot' is called a *leave* and it involves the batsman raising his bat and hands above his shoulder, to avoid contact with the ball. The batsman leaves the ball when he feels that to play a scoring shot such as a drive or pull holds the definite possibility of a catching chance being offered to the wicket-keeper or slip fielders. In the first few overs of a test match, opening batsmen often leave as many deliveries as possible. Leaving the ball allows them time to gauge the pace of the bowling and the bounce and movement of the ball off the wicket.

Strange as it sounds, cricket watchers love a good leave. Leaving the ball shows that the batsman is being selective in the shots that he is making and it frustrates the bowler as he has gone to all the effort of delivering the ball only to see it harmlessly glide into the hands of the wicket-keeper. Batsmen are also keen to leave deliveries at the start of their innings as usually they are looking to take fewer risks, see 'Getting your eye in' later in this chapter.

But the leave is not always greeted with applause. If you're talking about a limited overs match the batsman is expected to get on with the business of scoring runs, while bowlers are trying to take wickets or deliver a ball from which no runs are scored. Therefore, if a lot of deliveries are left then the bowler is chuffed as it means the scoring rate is slowing and the fielding team will have to make fewer runs to win the match when they bat.

What's more, sometimes a leave is misjudged. Sometimes the player judges that the ball is going past the stumps but in reality the ball ends up hitting the stumps, therefore dismissing the batsman. If you leave a delivery which subsequently hits the stumps you end up feeling a right proper charley.

Figure 5-9: The cut shot.

Taking wrist movements into account

For a batsman, having a supple wrist is a real plus. Turning the wrist on impact helps open or close the face of the bat which can work the ball into gaps in the field – a sure fire way of scoring runs!

 Rolling the wrists over the ball when making contact will send it into the ground and minimise the chances of being caught by a fielder. However, if you're going for a six hit – clearing the boundary without bouncing – you won't want to roll your wrists over the ball because you want it to fly in the air.

Taking Control in the Middle

When you bat you have to be the person with a plan. After all, the team is depending upon you scoring runs which will help it win the game.

To be successful at batting you have to build an innings – your own and the team's!

This section covers how to go about building a big score which can help your team to victory and make you a hero in the bar after the game – when you get the chance to bore everyone rigid with a recounting of your legendary knock!

Getting off the mark

No one likes to be dismissed without scoring. Therefore, many players look to try and score a run off one of the first few deliveries that they face. One of the best tactics can be to go for a quick single run at the earliest opportunity. However, if conditions are difficult, don't be in too much of a rush.

Getting your eye in

Batting is about hand-eye co-ordination and good footwork. But even the best players take time for their eyes to adjust to the light and the pace, movement and bounce of the ball off the wicket. No matter what level of cricket you play you would benefit from playing low-risk defensive shots early in your innings rather than expansive aggressive ones.

Judging a run

When you play a shot you should let your batting partner know whether or not you want to go for a run.

You have to make a split-second decision on whether you run or not based on

- ✔ How far you have hit the ball and the pace that the ball is travelling.
- ✔ How near to the ball the fielders are.

The key question you have to ask yourself is can my partner and I complete the run before the fielder has collected the ball and thrown it at the stumps?

Throughout, you're relying on your batting partner. He has to be alert and should be *backing up*. This means that he should be on the verge of leaving his crease as the bowler bowls. Likewise, when your batting partner is facing the bowling and you are at the other end of the wicket – called the *non-striker's end* – you should be *backing up* too.

Good backing up can help you take more quick singles, which boosts the team's score and annoys the bowlers no end.

A degree of etiquette is involved in calling for a run, which doesn't just mean you have to enquire politely of your batting partner if they would care to run. Good run calling involves listening to whoever of the two batsmen – the striker and non-striker – is in the best position to judge whether or not a run is on.

If the ball is heading in front of square on the leg or off side, the striker is in the best position to judge whether a run is on and it is his call. But if the ball heads behind square on the off or leg side, the non-striker is in the best position to judge as the striker would have to turn around to look where the ball has gone – because in effect the ball has gone behind him.

Front or backwards of square on a cricket pitch is roughly either side of an invisible line across the entire playing field following the line of the batsman's crease. See Chapter 2 for more on the creases.

Don't forget to take into account the physical condition of your batting partner when calling for a run. If he is unfit or has been batting for a long time, he may be less likely to complete a quick single before the fielders are able to throw down the stumps.

Canny players like to avoid the call 'No', because it sounds awfully similar to the word 'Go'. Instead, common calls you hear are 'Yes' for 'Yes, let's run' and 'Wait' or 'Waiting' for let's stay our ground.

Putting your foot on the accelerator

Once you have got off the mark and got your eye in, and your confidence is up, you're ready to start looking to play some aggressive shots.

Judging when to take a few more risks and quicken the pace of scoring very much depends on the match situation.

Players are more aggressive earlier in their innings in one-day cricket than in test or first class cricket. In fact, when your team only has a few balls to make runs to win a game, you may have to bypass getting your eye in and go straight for your shots.

Whatever the scenario, at some time in your innings you should look to be more aggressive. After all, that is the fun part of batting.

Reaching personal landmarks

Every time a batsman makes 50 runs, he gets a polite round of applause from the crowd, team-mates and even sometimes the opposition. A player scoring 100 runs is a pretty big deal and so the round of applause is generally louder, with the player usually waving his bat above his head to say thanks for the applause. Batting isn't easy and some players can go through their whole careers without once reaching a hundred runs in one innings.

A player who scores 100 runs in a single innings is said to have scored a *century*.

Don't be a selfish player, concerned purely about protecting yourself from being dismissed when the team needs to make runs fast. Selfish batsmen who don't take risks when the match situation requires rub their team-mates up the wrong way and can spoil the fun of a good contest.

In two-innings matches, a player who is dismissed twice without scoring is said to have made a *pair*. Any batsman managing the very rare boob of being out twice in the same match without scoring, and both times off the first delivery faced, is said to have made a *king pair*.

Pairs, king pairs and cartoon ducks!

Being dismissed without scoring is called being out for a *duck*. Being dismissed for a duck from your first delivery is called being out for a *golden duck*. When batsmen are dismissed for a duck in test matches played in Australia, the local TV station heaps on the misery by showing a cartoon duck at the bottom of the screen as the disconsolate batsman is filmed trudging back to the pavilion. Cruel but very funny!

Preparing to Do Battle

Successful batting is as much about preparation as perspiration. Rock up with bat in hand and trusting purely to talent, and you may find yourself taking the long walk back to the pavilion pretty quickly.

Put in the long yards before play and reap the rewards out in the *middle* – cricket jargon for the grassy strip on which the teams square off. See Chapter 9 for more on smart training.

Remembering practice makes perfect

One mistake is all it takes for a batsman to be dismissed. This tightrope existence makes practice crucial. The best way to practise is in the *nets*. The nets are fenced-off areas, indoors or on a specially prepared outdoor wicket, where bowlers try to hone their skills of bowling wicket-taking deliveries, and batsmen look to defend their stumps from being hit and execute shots which, if they were replicated in a game situation, could yield them runs – and hopefully lots of them. They are called nets simply because they are pitches, usually artificial, surrounded by netting to contain the ball. See Chapter 9 for more on nets.

Some batsmen treat nets very seriously. In the same way that some golfers need to spend time on a driving range before a big tournament, these players like to hit deliveries in the nets. On the other hand some players hate nets. They see the whole scenario as artificial, and they prefer to hone their skills in a match situation, when the adrenalin is pumping.

Exercising for successful batting

People sometimes scoff when they are told that being a batsman requires physical fitness. But think about it. The object of batting is to score runs and in order to score sufficient runs to help your team win you may well have to bat for several hours, sometimes in high temperatures. See Chapter 9 for more on getting match fit.

Unfit batsmen tire more easily which in turn makes them more prone to making a mistake which can lead to their dismissal.

Before leaving the pavilion to bat you should spend a minute or two doing some rigorous stretching exercise. Stretching can stop you pulling a muscle while batting. See Chapter 9 for more on stretching prior to play.

Taking care of the mental side

Like all great sports cricket is as much about the mind as the physique. Good batsmen concentrate intensely. Once the ball leaves the bowler's hand you have a fraction of a second to decide which shot to play and to move your feet into position in line with the ball to play the right stroke.

But that's not all your grey matter has to cope with. You have to take into account:

- **The match situation.** Is it the right time to be playing attacking or defensive strokes? If the team has lost wickets it may be wise for you to take fewer risks and aim primarily not to be dismissed.

- **Playing conditions.** You have to assess what will happen to the ball once it leaves the bowler's hand. For example, will the ball swing in the air? If so, will it swing inwards towards the stumps or out towards the slip fielders. If the ball hits the pitch, is it likely to move off the seam? See Chapter 6 for what happens to the ball when it moves off the seam.

- **Personal form.** You are expected to score runs; if you don't you can be left out of the team for future games. If your place is under pressure you may be less likely to take risks and play aggressive shots.

- **Ability limits.** You should try and work out which shots you are good at and which ones you aren't so hot at playing. The plan should be to stick to shots you can do well. Remember, only the best batsmen are good at all the shots.

A cricket ball has a stitched seam on it. When this hits the pitch it acts like a ridge causing the ball to move towards or away from the batsman. This phenomenon is called *seam movement* and is explored in Chapter 6.

You can score runs from defensive shots, as long as you steer the ball away from a fielder and are prepared to run between the wickets at pace. In cricketing circles this tactic is called *taking a quick single*.

Mike Atherton, the former England opening batsman, would spend several minutes at the wicket before the match began, familiarising himself with the surroundings and visualising how he planned to bat. His approach seemed to work: He was England's most successful opening batsman of the 1990s.

Choosing a Batting Role

During a team's innings eleven batsmen get an opportunity to strut their stuff out in the middle. This procession of players is called a *batting order*.

Teams put their best batsmen near the top of the batting order for several reasons:

- ✔ **To negate the new ball**. A cricket ball is most capable of moving off the seam and swinging in the air when it is new or nearly new. Therefore, you need your best batsmen fronting up and using all their skills and good judgement to score runs and prevent the team losing wickets. See Chapter 6 for more on swing and seam bowling.

- ✔ **To tire the bowlers**. If all goes to plan, players at the top of the order should be there for a long time and this can frustrate the opposition's best bowlers – who are getting more tired all the time.

- ✔ **Longer time at the crease.** The sooner the best batsmen get to face the bowling then the longer, potentially, they have to build a really big innings. Having your best batsmen at the bottom of the order risks them running out of batting partners.

Many of the best players in the modern game, such as South Africa's Jacques Kallis, Sri Lanka's Mahela Jayawardene, England's Kevin Pietersen and Australia's Ricky Ponting, bat at numbers 3 or 4. The idea is that the opening players, numbers 1 and 2, face up to the new ball and tire the bowlers a bit. Once the openers are out the best shot makers in the team take full advantage of an older, softer cricket ball and fatigued bowlers. Go to Chapter 6 for more on how the changing condition of the ball affects the game.

If you are batting and all your team-mates have been dismissed you are deemed to be not out. Sadly you don't get to carry on making hay, as under the laws of the game you need a batting partner to complete a run. However, you do have the bragging rights over your team-mate: You can remind them in the bar later that you were not out!

When an opener – the player who bats at number 1 or 2 in the batting order – is not out after all their team-mates have been dismissed he is said to have *carried his bat*. This is a pretty rare feat and openers tend to get very big-headed when they manage to pull it off.

Dividing up the batting order

The batting order can be divided into three definite categories:

- **The top of the order.** Numbers 1 and 2. These are the two opening players. These guys have it hard, as they take on the new ball while it is still hard and bouncy: Stopping the bowlers dismissing them can be a real battle. Usually, the players with the best defensive techniques open the batting.

- **Middle order.** Numbers 3, 4, 5, 6 and 7. These are good players who are usually famed for their shot-making ability. All going well, these players arrive once the bowlers are tiring and the ball is old, piling on the agony for the fielding side. However, they have to have a sound defensive technique just in case the top order batsmen are dismissed early and they have to face the new ball and the bowlers at their freshest.

- **Lower order.** Numbers 8 through to 11. These players are not in the team for their batting; they will be bowlers or possibly a wicket-keeper. However, they are still expected to do a job of scoring runs or at the very least being sound enough defensively to avoid dismissal. They often find themselves playing alongside a middle or top order batsman. In such circumstances, they are expected to stick around and give their more capable batting partner the chance to face as many deliveries as possible, by running quick singles.

Having bowlers and wicketkeepers who can score runs on a consistent basis can often be the difference between success and failure. In the 1990s and 2000s Australia was noted for having bowlers like Shane Warne and Brett Lee who could also make crucial contributions with the bat. More recently, England's lower order has blazed the trail, with bowlers Stuart Broad and Graeme Swann scoring vital 50s and 100s to help turn matches. Check out Chapter 11 for more on these current cricket stars..

It used to be the case that lower order batsmen – often called *tailenders* – were complete duffers when it came to batting. But in the modern game, coaches emphasise the importance of bowlers and wicket-keepers practising their batting skills.

In test match and first class cricket each side has two innings, so that if the end of the day's play is near and a top-order batsman is dismissed, the batting side will sometimes promote a lower-order player up the order. The idea is that the team captain prefers to risk a lower-order player being dismissed than a top-order one. A lower-order player facing the music like this is rather quaintly called a *nightwatchman* – but his job doesn't involve wandering the streets shouting out the time and announcing that 'all is well!'

Chapter 6

Making It Big as a Bowler

A good bowler is a bit like a magician, playing tricks to deceive the batsman. Clever bowlers can make the ball do strange and unexpected things, confusing and eventually dismissing the batsman.

In this chapter I examine the bowling arts – how to bowl fast, 'swing' a cricket ball in the air, and make it change direction off the wicket.

Looking at the Object of Bowling

Each over bowled consists of six balls, or *deliveries*. Every time the bowler runs into bowl a new contest begins with the batsman. When delivering the ball the bowler is trying to dismiss the batsman or limit the number of runs that he scores off each delivery.

Ideally the bowler would like to take a wicket off every delivery but, realistically, even the best in the world can't manage to get it right all the time.

In fact, top-class batsmen provide bowlers with formidable foes. The bowler has to think, observe what shots the batsman is good or bad at and vary the pace, line and length of the ball he bowls to expose any weaknesses in technique. Spin bowlers can also vary the *flight* – how high the ball flies in the air between being delivered and landing – and the direction that the ball spins after landing on the wicket. See the section 'Taking It to the Batsmen: Spin Bowling' later in this chapter for more.

A delivery that tests the batsman's technique is one that is also difficult for him to score runs off.

When it comes to achieving the twin objectives of dismissing the batsman and stopping him scoring runs, you won't find a better exponent than Pakistan spin bowler Saeed Ajmal. In a relatively short test career to date he has taken over 100 wickets while conceding very few runs. He has done this through clever, accurate spin bowling and by denying the batsmen scoring shots. In fact, he concedes on average around two and a half runs per over, making him one of the most miserly and dangerous bowlers in current test cricket.

Because a new cricket ball bounces higher and moves more quickly through the air, teams generally give it to their meanest, fastest bowlers.

In test cricket the bowling side is allowed to take a new ball at the start of the innings and every 80 overs bowled thereafter.

Getting to Grips with Bowling Basics

The act of bowling, or delivering the ball, can be broken down into three elements. Get these three elements right and you will take a big stride towards becoming a good bowler and a batsman's worst nightmare!

1. The approach to the bowling crease to deliver the ball, unsurprisingly called the *run-up*.

2. The position of the bowler's body, head and arms when propelling the ball out of the hand, called the bowler's *action*.

3. Coming to a halt after delivering the ball, called the bowler's *follow through*.

When many youngsters first begin to play cricket they want to emulate their heroes on television. This can mean charging in from a long way back like the exciting South African fast bowler Dale Steyn, and letting the ball go as fast as they can. This goal is great to have, but first you need to come to grips with the basics before you try to blast batsmen out. Seeing a fast bowler run at full pace can be one of the most thrilling sights in world sport.

Getting started

If you've never bowled before and are wondering how to do it, start by standing with a bit of space around you. If you're inside, make sure no fan or light fitting is dangling from the ceiling in case your bowling claims an unexpected victim when you bring your arm over.

If you're not sure whether you're a left- or right-arm bowler, decide which arm you would naturally throw with: that is your bowling arm. Stand comfortably, and if you're a right-hander turn your head 90 degrees and look along your left shoulder. Everything is the opposite if you're a left-armer. You're now facing the batsman, even though he may look more like a wall or fence.

Bring both hands comfortably up to your chest with your elbows loosely by your sides and put your left hand on your right hand. Imagine you're holding the ball in your right hand. Now raise your left arm up straight and slightly towards the batsman. At the same time step forward with your left foot, your 'front' foot – this is called the *delivery stride* – and bring your right arm down beside you.

A straight line should run down your raised left arm and through your right arm as it begins to rotate. Keep this straight line as your right arm comes over and your left arm tucks in beside your body. You are now at the point of release. Your weight will have transferred onto your left or 'front' foot and you want to have another straight line, this time running vertically from your right hand as you release the ball all the way through your body and left leg. Your left, or front, foot should be facing the batsman.

As the ball is released your right, or 'back', foot comes through with the momentum and lands in front of you. Once you can bowl an imaginary ball comfortably, you're ready to develop into a bowler who may one day end up on television.

The run-up

The run-up is sometimes called the bowler's *approach to the wicket*. The term covers the bowler's forward movement before releasing the ball, culminating in the *delivery stride* – the point at which the ball leaves the hand as he reaches the crease. Refer to Chapter 2 for more on the crease and other pitch markings.

The idea is to pick up enough momentum to be able to propel the ball at the speed the bowler wants. Fast bowlers need to run-up faster than spin bowlers. The very fastest bowlers run-up at top speed for 20 or 30 metres in order to build up the momentum they need. As a result, fast bowlers tire more quickly than their spin bowler colleagues whose run-ups are usually only a few metres long.

Taller bowlers often have longer run-ups than shorter bowlers. This is because their size means that they tend to take longer to build up speed.

In some forms of one-day cricket the length of the bowlers' run-ups are limited, to ensure the bowling side delivers all their overs within the allotted time.

The momentum created by the run-up is crucial to the delivery of the ball. All bowlers try to get the ball to leave the hand with their front foot on the line of the front crease (sometimes called the popping crease; See Chapter 2 for more on pitch markings) so that the ball has the least possible distance to travel to its target.

The bowler needs to get his run-up right. Many aspiring young fast bowlers make the fatal mistake of believing that the farther and faster they run, the faster they will bowl. This is not the case. Although a long run-up may look impressive, the most important function of a run-up for a fast bowler is to make sure that he not only has momentum but also is well balanced when delivering the ball. Don't run any farther than is necessary to achieve this aim. You waste your energy and are less effective as the day progresses because you tire more quickly.

A bowler's run-up should begin slowly and be smooth and comfortable. Avoid over-striding as it leaves you unbalanced at the point of delivery, reducing your pace and accuracy.

If the bowler's front foot lands beyond the popping crease and the umpire spots this, he calls a *no-ball*. The umpire sticks out his right arm and shouts 'No-ball' while the ball is in flight. A run is added to the batting team's total and furthermore any runs scored by the batsman off that ball count but the player cannot be out, unless run-out by a fielder. See Chapter 2 for more on modes of dismissal, and the no-ball rule. To cap it all the ball has to be re-bowled. Bowlers hate no-balling. On the other hand, if the bowler delivers the ball from too far back the ball has a greater distance to travel to the batsman, giving the batsman crucial extra time to decide which shot to play and to execute it properly.

The length of the run-up has to feel natural and repeatable time-after-time. Some bowlers retain the same style and pace of run-up throughout their career. Inexperienced fast bowlers often make the mistake of trying to run in as fast as possible, thinking this will simply generate pace. Bowling isn't as simple as that. A smooth, repeatable run-up takes lots of practice in the nets (refer to Chapter 9 for more on net practice).

The best way to work out a run-up is to stand next to the stumps at the bowler's end facing away from the batsman and run *away* from the pitch using the same run-up that you would to bowl the ball. Go through your bowling action (see the following section 'The action' for more) and put a mark where your front foot (left foot for a right-arm bowler) lands as you deliver an imaginary ball. This is the basis of your run-up. Once you have achieved a comfortable run-up at practice, pace it out from the bowling crease, which runs across the pitch either side of the stumps, back to where you want to start and remember the number of paces. Before bowling in a match, pace out your run-up with the same number of strides and make a mark with your shoe so you start from the same place every time. If you're really lucky the umpire will have a marker to put down as well so you can more easily see where to start. Have a practice run-up and if it doesn't feel right, pace it out again to be sure.

The action

Changing from your run-up into your bowling action involves slowing a little in the last couple of strides to be balanced going into the delivery stride. The bowler then jumps a little and brings his body side-on to the batsman to deliver the ball.

The direction of your *back foot*, the right foot for a right-arm bowler, on landing dictates what sort of an action you should develop. With our imaginary bowling earlier in the chapter the back foot was parallel to the bowling crease (see Chapter 2 for more on the creases) and at 90 degrees to the direction of the ball's trajectory down the pitch.

However, when bowlers jump into their bowling action after the run-up, their back foot can naturally land anywhere between 90 degrees to the direction of the pitch and straight down the pitch. Although the direction that the back foot faces may vary from bowler to bowler, a bowler with a natural, comfortable action should find his back foot landing in pretty much the same position and facing in the same direction time after time.

The direction of your back foot decides whether you bowl with an *open* or *closed* action. This is particularly true of fast bowlers. If your back foot naturally lands at 90 degrees to the direction of the pitch, the way it was placed during our imaginary bowling in the section 'Getting started' earlier in the chapter, then you have a closed action. This means your chest is closed to the batsman and facing the leg side. You need to get your body directly side-on to the batsman and look over your left shoulder, if you're a right-armer. You look past the outside of your left arm, which is raised high and slightly towards the batsman, creating a window to look through.

However, if your back foot is pointing down the pitch towards the batsman, then you will bowl with an open action (see Figure 6-1). This means your chest faces towards the batsman. Instead of getting side-on and looking over your left shoulder, if you are a right-armer, you look past the inside of your left arm.

The type of action you have also determines where your front foot lands as you deliver the ball. If your action is closed (side-on), the front foot lands almost directly in front of the back foot. But if your action is open (front-on), with your back foot pointing straight down the pitch, then your front foot should land a little to the left, if you're a right-armer.

Figure 6-1:
Bowling
with an
open action.

The reason for these slight variations, particularly in a fast bowler, is to ensure that a bowler's feet, hips and shoulders all line up. Experts have found that this is by far the safest way for a bowler to avoid injury.

Bowling, particularly fast bowling, is very taxing on the body. Unnecessary twisting and stress in the back is created when a bowler has his back foot facing straight down the pitch and then bowls with a closed, or side-on, action when they should be bowling with an open or front-on action.

Studies have found that if your hips and shoulders are more than 30 degrees out of line when delivering the ball your chances of injuries are increased dramatically. This is called *counter-rotation* and takes place in the delivery stride as weight is transferred from the back foot to the front foot. For example, a bowler's back foot may land with hips and shoulders front-on, but when the front foot lands the hips may stay front-on but the shoulders rotate to side-on putting strain on the lower back. Remember, if you're a fast bowler up to 10 times your body weight goes through your body with each ball you bowl. If imbalances are present, they lead to even more pressure on your body.

Dennis Lillee and Glenn McGrath have been Australia's two greatest fast bowlers, probably of all time yet their actions are very different. Lillee, with his powerful, athletic run-up, classical action, aggression and courage, was the hero of a generation. Every aspiring fast bowler growing up in the 1970s and early 1980s wanted to be Dennis Lillee. Yet even Lillee broke down with a serious back injury and was forced to remodel his action. Unfortunately, in the days before medical science caught up with cricket, many coaches instructed their fast bowlers to get classically side-on like Lillee, even though their back foot may have been facing down the pitch. This gave many young fast bowlers mixed actions and left them particularly susceptible to injury. A generation later Glenn McGrath, the most successful fast bowler of all time because of a high action that creates uncomfortable bounce and miserly accuracy, bowls with his back foot pointing down the pitch. He has a more open action that Lillee but still achieved deadly results.

Balance is just as important as brawn in a good bowling action and all the great bowlers have their heads upright and their eyes level, looking at where they want the ball to land on the pitch.

The follow through

After you have gone through the bowling action and released the ball you probably won't be able to come to a dead stop. The momentum you have built up to propel the ball at the pace and direction you want still carries you along. These extra strides you take are called the *follow through*.

All bowlers need to have a strong follow through, with all their momentum aimed at the batsman. This follow through ensures that fast bowlers generate the most pace and spinners impart as much spin on the ball as possible. Only when a bowler has followed through towards the batsman should they then start moving off the pitch and slowing down. Fast bowlers with a proper follow through can finish up half way down the pitch.

After you have released the ball, your follow through has no impact on how fast the ball will go. However, if your follow through is stopping short, say after just a couple of steps, or you veer too quickly sideways either way, that means something has gone wrong in your run-up or action and that you are not getting enough momentum. Generally if you can get your run-up and action right, your follow through should be straight and powerful.

Do not run straight down the pitch in your follow through. If you are playing on turf (see Chapter 2 for more on pitches) then you will run into what is known as the 'danger' area. This area is where bowlers, particularly spin bowlers delivering alternative overs from the other end, will be attempting to land the ball. The idea is to stop bowlers, fast bowlers in particular, from roughing up this important area with their spiked boots (see Chapter 4 for details on the right equipment) and making the pitch difficult to bat on. So after you have delivered the ball running towards the batsman, start heading towards the side of the pitch.

Umpires get very cross at bowlers whose feet stray onto what is called a *good length* in line with the stumps. What constitutes a good length is dealt with below. Umps get so twitchy about this because the spikes bowlers wear on their shoes can damage the wicket, making the ball bounce unevenly, and making it harder for batsmen to play shots and defend their stumps.

The danger area as listed in cricket's laws is an area contained in an imaginary box, with an imaginary line 1.22 metres, or 4 feet, down the pitch from the popping or front crease (see Chapter 2 for more details), and parallel to it, and within two imaginary and parallel lines drawn down the pitch 30.48 centimetres or 1 foot either side of the middle stump. If bowlers persist in going into this area the umpire will start to officially warn the bowler and his captain. Three official warnings and the bowler is banned from bowling for the remainder of the innings.

Examining the line and length of the delivery

When releasing the ball you want to have a good idea where you would like it to land. Aim for the part of the pitch that is going to give you the best chance of dismissing the batsman. The direction of the delivery – the *line* – and how close it bounces in front of the batsman – the *length* – are crucial to what happens next; whether the batsman scores runs off the delivery or whether he fails to score or is dismissed.

You can break down the length of a delivery into four categories.

- **A full length:** The ball *pitches* – lands – close to where the batsman stands in the crease. Generally, a batsman moves onto the front foot, pressing his weight forwards to hit full-length deliveries. A full-length ball is also called a half-volley and can be an easy length from which the batsman can hit a scoring shot. A delivery that is directed at the batsman's feet, in the hope that it will go under the bat and hit his stumps, is called a *yorker*.

- **A good length:** The ball pitches five or six yards in front of the batsman, if the bowler is of fast or medium pace. With spin bowlers, a good length delivery lands about two yards in front of the batsman. This is often a tricky length for the batsman as he's unsure whether to play a back-foot or front-foot shot. Refer to Chapter 5 for more on the different sorts of shot a batsman can play.

- **Short of a length:** A short delivery pitches around eight yards in front of the batsman. He is likely to play off the back foot to a ball landing short of a length. If the ball is bowled fast, bounces sharply and is directed at the player's ribs it can lead to the batsman fending a catch to any fielders close on the leg side. On the flip-side, a ball landing short of a length that is only slow pace and doesn't bounce high, can be easy to hit. Such balls are called *long hops*.

- **A bouncer:** A bouncer lands around halfway down the pitch and depending on its pace, direction and bounce can either go safely over the batsman's head or home in on the face. The idea of the bouncer is to cause discomfort to the batsman, and prevent him from scoring. If a scoring shot is attempted it will have to be a high-risk shot, such as a hook. See Chapter 5 for more on the hook shot.

As for the line of the delivery, the options are as follows:

- **Direct at the stumps**: The idea is if the batsman misses then you hit the stumps and dismiss him. Of course if the length of the delivery is a good length or shorter, the ball is likely to bounce too high to hit the wicket.

- **Down the leg side:** Bowling to miss leg stump sounds a bit daft. This sort of delivery doesn't tend to threaten taking a wicket – although you will find exceptions such as during the infamous bodyline Ashes series (refer to Chapter 17 for more), but leg side bowling can be very tricky to score runs off.

- **Down the off side:** The ball is heading down the off side towards the wicket-keeper and slip fielders. This line is the most common one for bowlers to take; see the sidebar 'Making use of the corridor of uncertainty'.

Making use of the 'corridor of uncertainty'

The *corridor of uncertainty* may sound a bit like a John Le Carré novel but it's nothing of the kind. A ball bowled by a fast or swing bowler on a good length and directed around 12 to 18 inches outside the off stump is said to be *in the corridor*. The batsman faces a quandary. He may not be sure whether to play a shot or to leave the ball. Playing a shot is high risk because the slip fielders and wicket-keeper are lined up behind waiting for the ball to hit the edge of the bat and give them the chance of a catch. Meanwhile, simply leaving the ball brings dangers; what if the ball moves in the air or deviates off the seam when it hits the wicket? It could move back to hit the stumps. No wonder most fast and swing bowlers aim for the corridor of uncertainty.

Deliver the ball too far away from the wicket at the batting end and the umpire may deem that the batsman had no chance of striking the ball. If that is the case the umpire may award a *wide* which gives the batting side an extra run and you have to re-bowl the delivery. Very annoying!

Try to bowl on the side of the wicket where most fielders are located; if that's the off side then bowl at or outside the off-stump.

The most common mode of dismissal in cricket is caught behind the wicket on the off side by the wicket-keeper or slip fielders.

Choosing between over or round the wicket

Before delivering his first ball the bowler has to tell the umpire:

- ✔ From which hand the ball will be released.
- ✔ From which side of the wicket the ball will be delivered.

The bowler has the choice of delivering the ball from over or round the wicket.

- ✔ A right-handed player bowling *over the wicket* delivers the ball from the left-hand side of the umpire and the stumps.
- ✔ A right-handed player bowling *round the wicket* delivers the ball from the right-hand side of the umpire and the stumps.
- ✔ For left-handed bowlers what constitutes over or round the wicket is reversed.

Put simply, whether you are left- or right-handed, over the wicket your bowling arm is closest to the umpire and round the wicket your bowling arm is on the side away from the umpire.

The side of the wicket from which the bowler delivers the ball can have a major influence on the direction the ball heads once released. For example, if a right-handed bowler delivers the ball from round the wicket to a right-handed batsman, the ball, because of the angle of the bowler's arm at the point of release, is directed from the batsman's leg side towards the off side (slanting across the body of the batsman) unless, of course, the bowler gets the ball to swing against this natural angle (see the section 'Swinging Your Way to Success' later in this chapter for more on swing bowling).

Most right-handed seam and swing bowlers will choose to bowl over the wicket to right-handed batsmen, because this is the same side of the wicket that the slip fielders and wicket-keeper stand.

Sometimes the bowler will switch the side of the wicket he bowls from in order to change the angle of the delivery.

The umpire tells the batsman which hand the bowler is going to release the ball from and whether he will be delivering from around or over the wicket. The umpire will tell the non-striking batsman to take up position on the opposite side to where the bowler is delivering – for example, if the bowler delivers from the right of the umpire the non-striker stands on the left – so as not to impede the bowler while he is delivering the ball.

All bowlers run-up to the wicket, go through a bowling action, aim for a particular line and length, and follow through once they have delivered the ball.

Checking Out the Different Bowling Types

The position in which a bowler holds his fingers along the seam that runs around the circumference of a cricket ball can make the ball bounce towards or away from the batsmen. The bowler can make the ball swing in the air merely by having the hand delivering the ball turn in a particular direction. Some bowlers even rotate the wrist of the hand holding the ball at the split-second of delivery with the aim of getting the ball to rotate in the air so that it has a better chance of spinning away or towards the batsmen when it bounces off the wicket.

In short through a combination of finger, hand and wrist movements bowlers can make the ball do the strangest of things – called in cricketing circles *making the ball talk*.

Types of bowlers can be divided into:

- ✔ Seam and swing bowlers
- ✔ Spin bowlers

Normally people find a type of bowling which suits them and stick to it but some players become multi-skilled – able to vary between seam, swing and even spin. Top-class fast bowlers will vary between relying on swing in the air and movement off the seam.

The most multi-skilled cricketer of all time was the great West Indian Sir Gary Sobers. He could bowl seam, swing and spin all to an incredibly high standard. Add to all this the fact that he was a fantastic hard hitting left-handed batsman and you can see why he features in this book's list of ten greatest ever cricketers in Chapter 14.

Seam and spin bowlers are striving for the same thing when delivering the cricket ball. They are both looking to move the ball off the straight, in order to trick the batsman into making a mistake that will lead to his dismissal.

Seamers do this through getting the ball to swing in the air and/or getting it to move off the wicket once the ball pitches. Confusingly, top-class seam bowlers look to achieve both movement off the seam and swing in the air.

Spinners try to get the ball to achieve exaggerated movement off the wicket, in an attempt to bamboozle the batsman.

How they try to achieve the aim of moving the ball off the straight differs markedly. A seam bowler tries to get the ball to move once, bouncing off the wicket through how they hold their fingers in relation to the seam of the cricket ball and occasionally a movement of the wrist at delivery. In addition, some seam bowlers look to coax the ball into a condition which aids swing movement in the air. They do this by shining one side of the ball, see the section 'Putting swing under the microscope' later in this chapter for how this aids swing movement.

Spinners aren't that bothered about the condition of the ball – apart from the fact they prefer the ball to be older, as it's less shiny and easier to grip.

Generally, seam bowlers like a new ball and the spinners an older one. The only exception is when the older ball is *reverse swinging*, in which case bowlers who are capable of swinging the ball can't wait to get their grubby paws on it. See the section 'Turning things on their head: Reverse swing' later in this chapter for more.

Understanding the Importance of the Ball's Seam

A cricket ball is made of cork and latex and is covered by leather. This leather is held together by stitching, called the *seam*. A cricket ball must weigh between 155.9 and 163 grams, and the circumference should measure between 22.4 and 22.9 centimetres.

The seam on a cricket ball creates a ball that has an effect on the game unlike that of any other type of ball used in competitive sports.

Used properly, the seam can alter the direction of travel of a cricket ball. A bowler, by positioning his fingers in different positions relative to the seam of the ball at release, can make the ball move in a particular direction through the air, and when it hits the wicket. Positioning the fingers along one part of the seam can send it *away* from the batsman and towards the slip fielders after it bounces, whereas locating the fingers along a different part of the seam can make the ball move in the opposite direction, *towards* the batsman even though the ball lands on exactly the same spot on the wicket. The position of the ball's seam also helps it swing in the air – in the same way a rudder helps direct a boat. See 'Swinging Your Way to Success' later in this chapter for more.

How far a cricket ball deviates on bouncing off the wicket depends not only on the skills of the bowler but also on the condition of the wicket. Cricket balls tend to move off the seam more on wickets that have a bit of green grass on them and are a little damp, caused by, say, early morning or evening dew. But if the wicket is hard and dry and grassless, the ball may not deviate much off the seam. In such circumstances, spin bowlers tend to pose the biggest threat to batsmen. Take a look at the section 'Taking It to the Batsmen: Spin Bowling' later in this chapter for more on spin bowling.

Mastering Seam Bowling

Often the first thing taught to a young bowler is to bowl the ball *seam up*. Seam up is probably the simplest type of delivery to bowl, but can still cause considerable problems for the batsman.

With seam up the ball is held between the middle and index finger of the bowler's hand with the seam pointed upwards towards the sky. The seam then acts a bit like a ridge sending the ball away or towards the batsman once it bounces off the wicket.

✔ A ball that jags away from the batsman towards the slip fielders is called a *leg cutter* (nothing to do with surgery!).

✔ A ball that jags from the slip fielders towards the body of the batsman is called an *off cutter*.

However, nothing guarantees that the ball will move to leg or to the off side, it may well just carry on straight.

Seam bowlers do try to add some spin to a cricket ball. However, they don't have the same variety of spinning deliveries as a spin bowler and they don't vary the flight of a ball as a spin bowler. Leg cutters and off cutters – spinning deliveries bowled by seam bowlers – are normally used as a surprise tactic to bamboozle the batsman. Generally, seamers use seam movement and swing to beat batsmen.

More experienced bowlers won't just trust to luck – they will use the following techniques to bowl off cutters and leg cutters.

The leg cutter

The middle finger is placed along the seam, and the index finger placed a couple of centimetres away. The ball is cradled by the thumb and third finger. As the ball is released, the index and middle fingers move down the left hand side of the ball and the thumb passes over the top of the ball. The ball rolls out of the bowler's hand over the little finger.

The off cutter

The index finger is placed along the seam with the middle finger a couple of centimetres away. The thumb is also underneath the ball cradling it and pointing along the seam.

As the ball is released, the index and middle fingers move down the right hand side of the ball and the thumb passes over the top of the ball

A bowler who relies primarily on his deliveries to move off the seam to attack the batsman is called a *seamer*. These types of bowlers particularly enjoy bowling with a new ball, which is hard and bouncy.

Sometimes you hear cricketers refer to a *jaffa* or a *peach*. They are not referring to the fruit salad they're going to have at the lunch break. They're talking about a delivery which swings into the batsman's body and then moves away off the seam after it lands on the pitch.

Seam and swing bowlers sometimes bowl what is called a *slower ball*. The run-up and delivery action are exactly the same for a slower ball as for a normal paced delivery but the bowler spreads his fingers to grip the ball farther apart, which has the effect of slowing the ball down in the air. The idea is to deceive the batsman into trying to play a shot as if the ball was bowled at full speed. The result could be a mis-timed shot and a greater chance of the batsman being dismissed.

Swinging Your Way to Success

What is the mysterious art of swing bowling? Put simply, swing bowling is bowling deliveries that deviate – sometimes dramatically – in the air. The batsman can spot a ball leaving a bowler's hand and work out its line, only for the ball to move suddenly in a different direction while still in the air, catching him off guard. Recent test match successes that England have enjoyed over the Australian cricket team in 2005, 2009 and 2011 have had a lot to do with well-executed swing bowling. In 2005 Matthew Hoggard and Andrew Flintoff spearheaded the attack, while in 2009 and 2011 it was the turn of James Anderson. However, good swing bowling is not the preserve of a single country. In recent times Australia has been picking handy swing bowlers like Ben Hilfenhaus and Ryan Harris with some notable success. Which team has the best swing bowlers will go a long way to deciding the winner of the 2013 back to back Ashes test series.

Putting swing under the microscope

The reason a ball swings is pure textbook physics. But here is the science behind swing bowling.

Whenever the ball hits the pitch and makes contact with the player's bat the lacquer protecting it gets rubbed off and the surface of the ball is scuffed. This process is pretty natural. However, this slow deterioration of the ball's condition gives the bowlers an opportunity. They know that if they polish one side of the ball – while leaving the other one untouched – then the polished side of the ball will get heavier than the unpolished side – offering less resistance to the air. This is why you see many cricketers with red patches on their trousers: These patches come from shining the ball!

And this is where the physics kicks in. The ball will swing in the direction of the unpolished, lighter side of the ball. The bowler, on releasing the ball, places his fingers along the seam to ensure the polished side faces in the direction he wants the ball to swing away from. This is called orthodox swing bowling and there are two types, as outlined in Table 6-1.

Not only old polished balls swing, but new balls can too. The extent of new ball swing depends on a number of factors such as overhead conditions – warm, cloudy days tend to aid swing movement – or the skill of the bowler who is particularly adept at bowling inswingers or outswingers, (see below for more). England's James Anderson, see chapter 11 for more on him, is a master at swinging the new ball.

Table 6-1	Types of Swing Bowling	
Type of delivery	*How it moves*	*How you do it*
The Inswinger	In the air from the off side of a right-handed batsman to the leg side.	The fingers should be on the seam, which is in a vertical position but angled towards the batsman's leg side. The thumb cradles the ball underneath the seam. The polished side of the ball should be pointed on the batsman's off side, assuming he is right-handed.
The Outswinger	In the air from the leg side of a right-handed batsman to the off side.	The seam of the ball should be angled towards the slips with the polished side of the ball towards the leg side of the batsman. The polished side of the ball should be on the batsman's leg side, presuming he is right-handed.

Swing bowling is very difficult to master. Some bowlers, no matter how hard they try, never quite get it. Some manage to master it one day but not the next. Give swing bowling a go in practice first before trying it out in a match situation. See Figure 6-2 for the correct grips used to bowl outswingers and inswingers.

Weather conditions seem to have an effect on how a cricket ball swings. In cloudy, muggy conditions the ball usually swings more than if the weather is cloudless and cold – no-one quite knows why, not even the Met office! What's more, white-coloured cricket balls – used in one-day matches – swing more than traditional red-coloured balls. Again, no-one quite knows why, for certain.

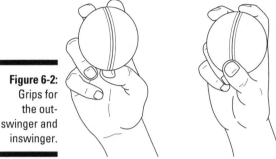

Figure 6-2:
Grips for
the out-
swinger and
inswinger.

Teams go out of their way to shine one side of the cricket ball more than another to help aid the swinging process. Some players have gone a bit too far in the past and have altered the condition of the ball by applying creams such as Vaseline to the ball; this is called *tampering with the ball* and is against the laws of the game.

Turning things on their head: Reverse swing

Reverse swing is one of the strangest phenomena in sport. Sometimes, after a ball has got old – say after 40 overs of use – one side gets badly scuffed from hitting the hard surface of the wicket and the ball can start to behave unconventionally (and I don't mean the ball gets lots of piercings and starts listening to Marilyn Manson).

Clever bowlers can start swinging deliveries in the opposite direction to orthodox swinging deliveries. Therefore balls delivered with the polished side facing the leg side and the seam angled towards the slips don't swing out from the right-handed batsman as happens with orthodox swing – they actually swing inwards. This is called *reverse swing*.

Reverse swing can create havoc for batsmen because one minute the ball behaves in line with orthodox swing but the next it starts reversing.

No-one quite knows why reverse swing happens – it sounds like a case worthy of Mulder and Scully from TV's *X Files*. One theory is that the rough side breaks up the air around the ball and actually creates less air pressure than the smooth side, allowing the rough side to travel through the air more quickly. Some bowlers seem more able to get a ball to reverse swing than others. England's 2005 Ashes triumph was in part due to two of England's bowlers, Simon Jones and Andrew 'Freddie' Flintoff, being able to reverse swing the cricket ball. Before these English heroes, the great Pakistan quick bowlers Waqar Younis and Wasim Akram were the kings of reverse swing.

Telling speedsters from slow coaches

Cricket anoraks have come up with a way to categorise who is a really quick bowler and who isn't. In test cricket working out the pace of a delivery is a cinch, as TV broadcasters measure the time it takes from a ball leaving the bowler's hand to reach the batsman. Sometimes you hear a bowler being described as fast, medium-fast or just medium pace. The divisions are

✔ **Fast bowler:** Delivers above 90 mph

✔ **Fast-medium bowler:** Delivers at 80–89 mph

✔ **Medium-fast bowler:** Delivers at 70–79 mph

✔ **Medium bowler:** Delivers at 60–69 mph

✔ **Medium-slow bowler:** Delivers at 50–59 mph

✔ **Slow-medium bowler:** Delivers at 40–49 mph

✔ **Slow bowler:** Delivers below 40 mph

In reality, only top-class professional cricketers have a shot at delivering a cricket ball at fast or fast-medium pace. The fastest bowlers playing in club cricket fall into the medium-fast bracket.

The pace at which a ball is delivered can make a huge difference. The quicker the ball, the less time the batsman has to react. Sometimes you hear that a batsman has been *beaten for pace*; this means that the player did not react quickly enough to execute a shot.

You won't find an easy route map to follow on how to bowl reverse swing. Whether reverse swing occurs is simply down to the condition of the ball.

Good batsmen are able to spot the polished side of the cricket ball as it leaves the bowler's hand. In an orthodox swing scenario this makes it easy to read which way the ball is going to swing but when deliveries are reverse swinging it puts the kibosh on this early warning system.

Taking It to the Batsmen: Spin Bowling

The aim of spin bowling is to bowl the cricket ball with rapid rotation so that when it bounces off the pitch it will change direction, either towards or away from the batsman.

Spin bowlers use wrist or finger motion to cause the ball to rotate.

Deviation – or spin – off the wicket can make it hard to hit the ball properly. The direction and the extent of the ball spin may be misjudged which could lead to the batsman missing the ball altogether and being bowled or dismissed *leg before wicket* (LBW: see Chapter 2 for more on the LBW law). Alternatively the batsman may only manage to hit the ball with the edge of the bat – rather than off the middle – so giving the chance of a catch to the wicket-keeper, bowler or fielder.

Few sights are better in cricket than a spin bowler in action. Cricket watchers just lap it up because the bowler is trying to outsmart the batsman. The spin bowler doesn't rely purely on pace to get his wickets, but on guile.

Spin bowlers prefer to bowl with an old, worn cricket ball because the older a ball, the rougher the seam, and the more it spins off the wicket. In longer matches, such as test and first class games, spin bowlers tend to be more effective in the later stages of the game because the wicket deteriorates. Cracks appear and the pitch crumbles, providing more purchase for the spinning ball.

Here are some of the ways that spin bowlers can trap batsmen in their wicket-taking webs:

- ✓ **Spin off the wicket.** Spin is the number one weapon in the armoury. See the later section 'Understanding the types of spin bowler' for an explanation of the different types of spin bowler and an outline of the types of delivery each specialises in.

- ✓ **Variation of pace.** The ability to bowl quicker or slower is not just the preserve of seam bowlers – spinners can do it too. With just a little effort, most good spinners can bowl a ball much quicker or slower than normal, hoping to catch the batsman unawares and cause a mistake.

- ✓ **Flight.** The higher the ball loops in the air on leaving the bowler's hand, the longer it takes to come down. A delivery that is in flight for a long time can trick the batsman into playing his shot too soon. On the flip-side, a ball that is the same pace on leaving the bowler's hand but headed on a lower trajectory can arrive at the batsman quite quickly, possibly hurrying the batsman into playing a poor shot.

A delivery bowled by a spinner is far slower than one from a fast bowler or a swing bowler. Sometimes you may hear spin bowlers referred to as *slow bowlers.*

A cricket ball bowled by a spinner can also deviate in the air. This deviation is called *drift.* When combined with spin off the wicket, flight and changes of pace batsmen can find it very hard to judge where the ball is headed and what is the best shot to play.

Understanding the types of spin bowler

A cricket ball can be made to spin through use of the fingers or the wrist, and spin bowlers are divided into these two categories.

- ✔ **Players using *finger spin* to rotate the ball:** The right-hander is called an *off spin bowler*, the left-hander a *left-arm orthodox* spinner.

- ✔ **Players using *wrist spin* to rotate the ball:** The right-hander is called a *leg spinner*, the left-hander a *left-arm unorthodox spinner*.

Each type of bowler has their own set of special deliveries. The execution of these special deliveries depends on different factors depending on the type of bowler:

- ✔ **Leg spin and left-arm unorthodox bowlers:** The position of the wrist of the bowling hand at delivery.

- ✔ **Off spin and left-arm orthodox bowlers:** the position of the fingers in relation to the seam of the cricket ball at delivery.

Wrist spinners have far more special deliveries than finger spinners, making them many batsmen's bogey men. But finger spin bowlers can still vary their pace and flight, as well as use drift in the air to take batsmen by surprise.

Looking at finger spin bowling

Finger spinning is far and away the most popular variety of spin bowling. Most club, first class and test teams will have a finger spinner in their ranks. The popularity of finger spinning is understandable as fewer special deliveries exist that need to be mastered. However the best exponents are able to bring all sorts of other weapons to bear such as varying flight, pace and drift in the air.

The off-break

An off-break turns from the off side to the leg on pitching, assuming the batsman is right-handed.

To bowl an off-break spread the middle joints of the index and middle fingers wide across the seam of the ball and rest the ball on the third finger of the hand (see Figure 6-3). The index finger turns on release of the ball aiding rotation. In cricket lingo this turning of the index finger is called giving the ball a *rip*. The more revolutions the bowler is able to put on the ball through the turning of the index finger, the better the chance the bowler has of getting the ball to deviate a considerable distance from the off to leg side, assuming a right-handed batsman is facing.

Figure 6-3:
The grip for
bowling an
off-break.

The arm ball

The idea of an *arm ball* is to surprise the batsman. The bowler's action should look no different to a standard off-break. However, the bowler will place the index finger along the seam of the ball. In essence, as a result the ball may spin towards the slip area – the opposite direction to a standard off-break delivery – or just carry on straight.

The doosra

Doosra means 'the other one' in the Urdu language. Put simply, a doosra is a delivery bowled with an off-break grip, but released from the back of the hand, so that it faces the batsman, rather than from the front. This sends the ball in the opposite direction – from leg to off – to a standard off-break. In addition, the doosra delivery tends to bounce a little higher than an off-break. Very few bowlers around the world have mastered the art of the doosra.

The doosra was named by Pakistani off spinner Saqlain Mushtaq, who perfected the delivery during the late 1990s. Although Saqlain was a master at it, very few off spinners can manage the doosra without illegally throwing the ball – called 'chucking' in cricket jargon. Indeed, off spinners must be careful because the natural action of flicking the ball with the index finger can result in a throw. Carrying on Pakistan's lineage of doosra bowlers of late has been Saeed Adjmal. His perfection of this delivery led to his nation's 3-0 series whitewash of the powerful England side in 2012.

Left-arm orthodox spinners are the left-handed mirror images of off spin bowlers. The fact that the ball is delivered from the left hand means that left-arm orthodox spin turns away from, rather than towards, a right-handed batsman. Left-arm orthodox bowlers often bowl from round the wicket rather than over with the aim of getting the ball to drift towards the bat in the air only for it to move away towards the slips on bouncing.

Not every ball bowled by a finger spin bowler will be an off-break. The bowler will try to mix things up, bowling the odd ball straight in a bid to surprise the batsman who maybe expecting an off-break delivery.

Focusing on wrist spin bowling

Wrist spinners have lots of special deliveries to choose from but wrist spin bowling is incredibly tricky to master. You may be able to bowl one or two of the special deliveries once in a while but to be considered top-class you have to be able to bowl most of the following deliveries consistently.

The leg-break

A leg-break will 'break' – change direction through spin – from leg side to off side (from the batsman's legs towards the slip fielders). This ball is often considered the easiest one for the wrist spinner to execute and as a result is the one bowled most often.

To bowl a leg-break, the top joints of the index and middle fingers are held across the seam of the ball (see Figure 6-4). The seam rests on the thumb and the third finger, which is bent. On release the third finger tweaks the ball in an anti-clockwise direction and the wrist rotates to finish facing downwards towards the floor.

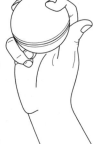

Figure 6-4:
The grip for
bowling a
leg-break.

The googly

From the batsman's perspective the wrist movement involved in a googly will look almost identical to that for a leg-break . However, the ball once delivered, should behave in the opposite way to a leg-break and turn towards a right-handed batsman – from off side to leg side – rather than away. A googly is also called a 'wrong-un' and is one of the hardest types of delivery to master.

The top joints of the index and middle fingers should be across the seam, with the ball resting between the thumb and the third finger, which is bent. At release the palm of the hand opens upwards, with the back of the hand facing the batsman. In addition, like a standard leg-break, the third finger tweaks the ball anti-clockwise at release.

The top spinner

A top-spinner, once it bounces off the pitch, should head towards the batsman – like a googly. However, a top spinner tends to bounce higher than a googly, increasing the chances of the ball striking the top of the bat or hitting the gloves and offering the chance of a catch to the fielders.

The top joints of the index and middle fingers are held across the seam of the cricket ball. The ball rests between the thumb and third finger, which is bent.

The ball is delivered with the back of the hand facing the sky at release. The ball is delivered out of the side of the hand in contrast to a googly where the wrist is 180 degrees relative to the floor. As with the googly, the third finger tweaks the ball in an anti-clockwise direction at release.

The flipper

The flipper straightens and keeps low on pitching. If directed at the stumps a flipper can be a deadly weapon as it often takes batsmen by surprise. The ball is held in the hand like a normal leg-break but doesn't actually spin as much or even, sometimes, at all.

The ball, like a standard leg-break, is held with the index and middle fingers across the seam of the ball. The ball rests between the thumb and third finger, which is bent. On release, though, the thumb tweaks the ball in a clockwise direction. In effect the bowler is clicking his fingers when releasing the ball; this motion is used to negate the natural spinning effects of the wrist spin action. If executed well the clicking motion and the position of the wrist at release should cancel one another out and the ball should straighten.

Only more mature cricketers should try the flipper, after they've mastered the basics of wrist spin. It takes a strong hand and wrist to bowl this delivery and puts a lot of strain on the bowling arm and shoulder. Wrist spinners can suffer injuries just like fast bowlers because of the stresses and strains they put on their bodies.

Generally, over their career, club-standard wrist spinners can get by with having only perfected one or two types of delivery. Bowlers who have ambitions to play at a higher level need to have more variety because the batsmen they face will be better. See Chapter 9 for coaching tips.

Focusing On What You're Good At

With very rare exceptions, bowlers become good at just one particular aspect of this sometimes difficult but rewarding craft. If you're just starting off bowling, experiment during practice. See what you're good at and most enjoy. It may be that you can bowl accurately for long periods and become a steady medium pacer, discovering how to move the ball in the air and off the pitch. You may have a strong wrist which allows you to bowl sharp-turning wrist spin, the patience to work on being an off spinner, or that rare ability to bowl really quickly and unsettle batsmen.

Whatever you decide, develop a 'stock ball', a delivery that you can bowl over and over again with great accuracy and control. This will probably be the leg-break for the wrist spinner, the off-break for the off spinner and depending on your action, may be the outswinger for the fast bowler or the off cutter for the medium pacer. Having lots of tricks is pointless if you can't bowl them accurately. Inaccurate bowling will just give the batsmen easy runs and your captain will soon take you out of the attack.

Discover how to bowl one delivery well and then add occasional variations to surprise the batsman in the hope of dismissing him. Use these variations sparingly or they lose the element of surprise.

Bowling with Your Brain

Bowling isn't just about brawn; it's also about brains. All bowlers try to judge what type of delivery will best give them a chance of taking a wicket. But sometimes a match situation develops that requires something other than all-out attack by the bowler. In such circumstances, the bowler has to use his noodle for the benefit of the team.

Teaming up with the captain

A good captain talks to his bowlers, outlining whereabouts on the wicket he would like them to bowl. Sometimes the captain asks a bowler to direct deliveries in a direction that leaves little opportunity to take wickets but has a wider tactical significance.

For example, during England's tour of India in 2001, Nasser Hussain (the England captain at the time) asked his bowlers to direct deliveries bowled to India' batting ace Sachin Tendulkar down the leg side. This line of attack made it hard to take Sachin's wicket – a line just outside off-stump takes the most wickets – but it was also hard for the batsman to execute scoring shots. The chief aim was to stifle Tendulkar in the hope that eventually he would get frustrated and play a rash ill-judged shot that would lead to his dismissal.

Remembering to bowl to the field

The captain sets the field and expects the bowler to direct deliveries to make the most of that set field. For example, when the ball is new the captain is likely to have lots of slip fielders in place in the hope that the bowler will direct deliveries around off stump, giving the best possible chance of finding the edge of the bat and a catch being taken.

Bowlers who fail to follow their captain's instruction on where to bowl often find that they are taken out of the attack. The captain decides who does and doesn't bowl; see Chapter 8 for more on the importance of the captain.

Winning with patience

A bowler can't possibly take a wicket every ball but it can be very costly to the team if the bowler continues an unsuccessful attack, allowing a free flow of runs. A bowler must assess the strengths and weakness of each new batsman quickly and have a plan. Much of the time in club cricket that may simply be bowling at or just outside the off stump with most of the fieldsmen on the off side to try and frustrate the batsman by restricting the scoring.

In assessing a batsman a bowler should ask questions like 'Does the batsman play short bowling badly?' 'Does he play with a gap between bat and pad so that an inswinger, off-break or googly could sneak through and bowl him?' 'Does he fail to get his front foot close enough to the ball when playing forward, offering the chance of a catch in front of the wicket?' Consult your captain if you think a batsman needs attacking in a particularly way or the field needs changing because of the way he is playing.

Thinking clearly

All bowlers need to assess the conditions and the match situation. An opening bowler with a new ball will often try and pitch the ball up on a full length to give it a better chance of swinging. Likewise, if a turf pitch is damp or has plenty of grass on it, more movement off the seam is possible, also tempting the bowler to pitch the ball up to take advantage of the movement. However, if the ball is not swinging, the conditions are good for batting and the batsmen are 'set' – they have been batting for a while and look comfortable – then pitching the ball right up consistently can simply give away easy runs. Instead you're better to bowl a good length or even short of a length, also known as back of a length, to try and restrict the scoring and frustrate the other side. Again, discuss the conditions and the match situation with your captain.

Being Fit for the Task

If a bowler is going to make a significant impact over the course of a match he should develop a reasonable level of fitness. This is particularly true for fast bowlers. A fast bowler is not much good to their team or captain if they rush in for their opening spell with the new ball but are then too tired or sore to bowl extra spells later in the day. Bowling at the end of a day can be very important. If the bowlers tire and cannot maintain line and length, and pace in the case of the faster bowlers, the batting side will cash in big time. Bowlers who are not fit are also more vulnerable to injury and may miss matches completely if unable to bowl properly. Fitness is developed by a combination of general exercise and bowling in the nets. See Chapter 9 for more details on training and fitness.

Modern day fast bowlers are more conscious of the need to have peak physical fitness for the job. Strength and conditioning training, core stability and maximising flexibility are all important. Running techniques and recovery sessions are helping modern fast bowlers stay in the field.

Of all the fuss made about stretching and preparing properly to play sport, never is it truer than for bowlers, particularly fast bowlers. Before a match have a few gentle run-throughs to warm up, then bowl some gentle deliveries off a couple of paces in the nets or to a team-mate on the outfield. Then have a good stretch ensuring the calves, hamstrings, groin and back are all loosened before doing some more serious pre-match bowling if you want. But don't get carried away. You need all your energy for a big day in the field.

Chapter 7

Fielding Made Easy

. . . .

. . . .

*I*n the past, plenty of cricketers – even some professionals – didn't take fielding seriously. They saw having to stand around in the field picking up a cricket ball, throwing it to the wicket-keeper, and taking the odd catch as nothing more than a distraction from the serious business of batting and bowling.

Those days are now long gone. Cricketers playing at all levels of the game – from test match down to club standard – take fielding far more seriously. Why? Because nowadays players understand that if they shine in the field they can help their team to win the match.

In this chapter I look at the ins and outs of the different fielding positions and how you can be a success at cricket's third major discipline.

Catching On to Why Fielding Matters

Great feats of batting and bowling usually hog the headlines but good fielding can make a crucial contribution to a team's success.

Being good at fielding means doing the following:

✔ **Taking catches**: One of the main jobs of a fielder is to take catches. A catching chance is given when the batsman hits the ball in the air within reach of the fielder. If the catch is taken then the player is dismissed – unless the bowler has bowled a no-ball. Refer to Chapter 2 for more on the no-ball law.

✔ **Stopping runs**: If you are batting you want to score runs. The bowler tries all out to prevent you from scoring runs. But to do this they need the help of the nine fielders and wicket-keeper. Fielders try to stop the ball in the outfield and throw it to the wicket-keeper – or bowler – standing by the stumps, before you and your fellow batsman run up and down the wicket to register a run.

✔ **Running out a batsman:** One of the objectives of a fielder is to try to achieve *run-outs*. A run-out occurs when a fielder throws a ball that hits the stumps with the batsman out of his crease while attempting a run. A run-out leads to the player's dismissal. Refer to Chapter 2 for more on modes of dismissal.

A cricket field is divided into three areas (Refer to Chapter 2 for more on the different parts of the cricket field):

✔ **The pitch, or wicket:** This area is the cut strip of turf on which the bowler delivers the cricket ball to the batsman who then tries to hit it.

✔ **The infield**: This area is where the wicket-keeper, slip fielders and close catching fielders stand poised to catch out the batsman.

✔ **The outfield**: This area is everything else and is where the remaining fielders are located. The outfield ends at the boundary. If the ball goes over the boundary without bouncing the batsman scores six runs. If it bounces before reaching the boundary then four runs are scored.

When a fielder fails to take a catching chance the batsman is said to have been *dropped*.

One of the most famous sayings in cricket is 'Catches win matches'. Quite often, the team that drops the fewest catches in a match is triumphant. Bowlers work very hard to get the batsmen to make a mistake by hitting the ball in the air rather than along the ground, and when they are successful they expect those catching chances to be taken.

Understanding Fielding Positions

Excluding the bowler and wicket-keeper – more about wicket-keepers later in this chapter – nine players field in a team. However, the outfield is a very large open space. In truth, only a few fielders cover a great big space, and the available fielders can fill only a few of the possible positions. See Figure 7-1 for the basic fielding positions.

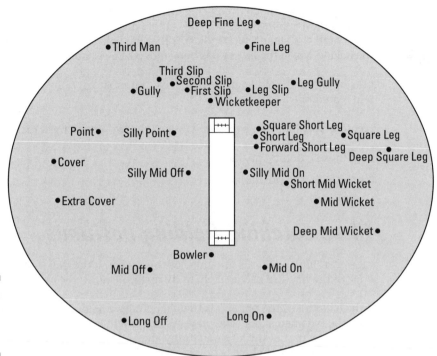

Therefore, over the years, captains and coaches have developed what are
called *fielding positions*. These fielding positions are locations in the outfield
where the fielders stand. The idea of fielding positions is to:

✔ Be in the best position to take catches

✔ Be in the best position to stop scoring shots

Some fielding positions try to do both, others just one.

Batsmen have a range of shots they can play – see Chapter 5 for more on
scoring shots – and once executed these shots will head into the outfield.

Shots from the batsmen don't always go where they are intended. Sometimes
the ball hits the edge rather than the middle of the bat, sending the ball in an
unintended direction and giving a catching opportunity to a fielder.

Far more potential fielding positions exist than fielders, see Figure 7-1. The
captain moves fielders to positions where he believes the batsmen may hit
the ball.

Nothing stops a captain from being inventive and asking a fielder to stand in a non-standard fielding position. The captain may spot something in the technique of the batsman which indicates that the ball is likely to go to the part of the field to which the fielder has been moved. See Chapter 8 for more on tactics.

Lots of different fielding positions exist, but most captains stick to a few tried and tested ones.

Fielding positions can be broken down into two distinct groups:

- ✔ Close catching positions
- ✔ Run-saving positions

Close catching fielding positions

Close catching positions are close to the wicket. If the ball is struck by the edge of the bat, the ball is likely to fly up in the air in these positions.

If the ball strikes the bat and is then caught by a fielder before it bounces, then the batsman is out. The player is out whether or not the ball hits gloves, pads or any part of the kit or anatomy after hitting the bat. If the ball strikes the glove while that glove is holding the bat and flies to a fielder and is then caught without bouncing, that too leads to a dismissal. However, if the ball hits the pads or any part of the anatomy, and does not make contact with the bat before or after doing so, then a catch should not be awarded by the umpire.

Close catching positions include:

- ✔ **Slip and gully fielders:** These fielders are located to the right side of the wicket-keeper for a right-handed batsman and the left side for a left-handed player. The fielders form a diagonal row, the idea being to catch any edged shots resulting from the batsman playing deliveries directed on or just outside the line of off stump. Refer to Chapter 6 for more on the best line to bowl to take wickets.

- ✔ **Leg slip**: The leg slip fielder is just like a standard slip fielder except that he stands on the leg side of the wicket. This is primarily a catching position and is usually deployed when the bowler is spinning or swinging the ball in towards the batsman from outside the line of off stump. The idea is that the player may hit the ball in the air to this position while attempting a leg side shot.

✔ **'Bat and pad' fielders**: These fielders are located close to where the batsman stands. In most cases they are used when a spin bowler is operating. Some of the fielding positions have laugh-out-loud names such as 'silly mid off', 'silly mid on' and 'short square leg' or even 'short backward point' – which sounds very painful! But disregard the comedy names, these fielders mean business. Their chief objective is to take catches which result from the batsman attempting to play a ball which is spinning after bouncing off the wicket. Sometimes the batsman gets the calculation of the direction and extent of the spinning ball wrong and it strikes the bat before hitting the pad or glove and looping into the air. This is where the bat and pad fielders do their work. Reacting with lightning speed, they fling themselves about in order to take a catch. Usually, bat and pad fielders stand no more than three or four metres from the batsmen. Refer to Figure 7-1 for where precisely these players stand.

The pace of the bowler determines how close the fielders in catching positions stand in relation to the batsman. The faster the bowler the farther the delivery should travel in the air, and the farther away the wicket-keeper, slip and gully fielders should stand.

When the fielding team puts on its meanest and fastest bowler and the cricket ball is new – which means it is more likely to deviate after bouncing off the wicket – you tend to find captains deploying more players at slip, because the likelihood of a batsmen edging the ball in that direction is quite high. Interestingly, in one-day matches, where saving runs is often just as important as dismissing the batting side, fewer slips – and sometimes no slips – are deployed. Refer to Chapter 3 for more on one-day cricket.

Usually, bat and pad fielders tend to be deployed when spin bowlers are bowling. On the flip-side, captains tend to deploy lots of fielders to stand at slip when seam and swing bowlers are in action.

Fielders have to be prepared, when instructed by the captain, to field in the slip area, bat and pad catching positions, or in run-saving positions.

Sometimes if the ball is bouncing high off the pitch the captain will place a fielder at 'short leg' position. Short legs stand a few metres from the batsman on the leg side just in front of the square leg umpire. The idea is that the batsman may fend off a bouncing delivery into the hands of the short leg fielder.

The word *square* indicates that the fielder is facing at right-angles to the direction in which the bowler is bowling, and is standing roughly in line with the batsman.

Run-saving fielding positions

Fielders in run-saving positions are there to stop the batting side from scoring runs. They usually stand around 20–25 metres from the batsman, giving them some time to move to their left or right to dive and stop the ball if it comes in their direction. If they are quick enough to the ball, they can deter the batsman from attempting a run.

The location of run-saving fielding positions has a lot to do with angles. Captains try to gauge how the batsman will see the field – finding the gaps into which the player may strike the ball. The captain attempts to plug those gaps by moving the fielders into those areas.

Some fielders are set far back. These *deep fielders* are placed near the boundary, and their main job is to prevent the ball going for four runs. However, because they are a long way from the batsman, by the time the ball reaches them the batsman will have completed a fairly easy single run. In essence, deep fielders are a trade-off; a run is being given up to have a good chance of stopping four.

The main run-saving positions you'll be expected to field at are:

- ✔ **Cover:** This part of the field is located on the off side, between the slips and mid off fielder. When you hear about someone being a demon in the covers the phrase isn't referring his love life! Instead, the player is likely to be quick to gather and collect the ball and to throw it back accurately. Cover fielding positions include point, cover point, cover, extra cover and short extra cover. Point is located on the opposite side of the batsman from the square leg umpire, cover point to the right hand side of point, extra cover farther to the right of cover point, and cover farther right still. Short extra cover is on the same line as extra cover just nearer the batsman, say 10–15 metres away as opposed to 25–30 metres. Cover fielders are there to stop the cover drive, off drive and cut shots outlined in Chapter 5.

- ✔ **Mid off and Mid on:** These fielders are the ones located immediately to the left and right of the bowler's run-up, about 30 metres from the batsman. They are there to field straight and on-drive shots. Most fielding teams have a mid off and mid on.

- ✔ **Mid wicket:** These fielders are on the leg side of the batsman – sometimes called the *on side* – between the mid on fielding position and the square leg umpire. Variations include mid wicket, and short and deep mid wicket. Generally, short mid wicket is an attacking position around 10– 15 metres from the batsman, mid wicket is located about 25–30 metres away, and deep mid wicket fielders often stand close to the boundary. All these three positions are meant to field the pull and leg glance shot.

✔ **'Behind square' fielders**: These fielders are located on the leg side of the batsman near the square leg umpire or behind the umpire in an arc to where the wicket-keeper stands. Typical fielding positions include: square leg, backwards square leg, fine leg, short fine leg and long leg. Generally, square leg stands parallel to the square leg umpire around 20–25 metres from the batsman; short square leg will be closer, say 10–15 metres. Backward square leg will stand 25–30 metres from the batsman, 5–10 metres to the right of the square leg umpire. Long leg is on a line equidistant between the square leg umpire and the wicket-keeper, but right back on the boundary. Deep fine leg will stand farther to the right of the square leg umpire near the boundary, and short fine leg will be closer to the batsman – around 20–25 metres but on the same line as fine leg. These fielders are in place for the hook shot, sweep, and some leg glance strokes: Refer to Chapter 5 for more on these batting strokes.

✔ **Third man**: This fielder stands roughly on the same line as the third and fourth slip fielders but right back near the boundary. The aim is for the fielder at this position to stop the ball if the batsman is *opening the face* of the bat in an attempt to direct the ball into a gap in the field, that is, twisting the face of the bat more towards the off side than towards the bowler. Third man is a run-saving position which is particularly popular with captains in one-day cricket.

The closer the fielder is to the batsman, the more likely he is to be concentrating primarily on taking a catch. But the closer the fielder the less time they have to react to the ball hit by the batsman.

Fielders in run-saving positions are also expected to take catching opportunities when they have the chance.

If you're fielding in a run-saving position, move a few paces towards the batsman when the bowler runs in to deliver the ball. Being on the move helps you to react more quickly if the ball is played in your direction. This moving forward is called *walking in* and all good cricket teams do it when they are in the field. The players excused from *walking in* are fielders in catching positions close to where the batsman is standing, such as the slips or short leg. These fielders stay still because their main job is to watch the ball and batsman closely and be ready to dive to take a catch. If you're fielding in these positions, you'll find it easier to dive quickly if you stay still.

Players fielding at short leg or silly mid off are not allowed to make substantial movements as the bowler runs in to deliver the ball. Unreasonable movement by these fielders is considered unfair to the batsman, as it can distract him as he tries to concentrate on playing the delivery.

Taking fielding restrictions into account

One-day matches played by international and first class teams are usually subject to fielding restrictions. These restrictions mean that the captain of the fielding side has to keep the majority of his fielders in a circle – marked out by white discs – for 6, 10, 15 or 20 overs (depending on the competition rules) of the batting sides' innings. This circle is usually no more than 30 metres from the stumps. The principle behind fielding restrictions is that the fielding captain is forced to have fielders in positions where they have the best possible chance of taking a catch, making the game more exciting for both the players and spectators. While the fielding restrictions are in place the batsmen tend to play attacking shots because they know that if they hit the ball past the fielders – in the 30 metre fielding circle – the ball is likely to go all the way to the boundary. If no fielding restrictions existed, captains would probably be more negative, placing fielders in mainly run-saving positions. See Chapter 8 for more on tactics used in one-day cricket.

Silly, short and deep fielding positions

If a fielder is asked to move from a standard run-saving position to one much closer to the batsman but on the same line, the new fielding position is normally prefixed with the words *silly* or *short*. For example, if mid off moves a few metres closer to the batsman he becomes 'short mid off': Closer still and the position is 'silly mid off'.

On the other hand, if the fielder is asked to keep the same line but go farther away from the batsman to near the boundary, the new fielding position is prefixed with the words deep or long. For example, mid off moves out to the boundary – but on the same line – the fielder is standing at deep mid off.

In the same way, if a fielder is asked to go 'finer' this means take a few strides in the direction of an imaginary line drawn from the wicket-keeper to the boundary behind him. Sometimes, though, a captain will ask a fielder to go 'squarer'; this means take a few strides in the direction of a line through the position of the square leg umpire.

As shown in Figure 7-1, this method of labelling applies to the vast majority of fielding positions.

Preparing Properly for Fielding

Fielding can be physically demanding. In test cricket, teams can spend days in the field, often in high temperatures. Even in club cricket, teams can spend half a day toiling away in the field.

Not only do you have to be physically fit for the long haul, but you also have to be prepared to explode into action. Think about it: If you have nine fielders – excluding the wicket-keeper and bowler – then a good chance exists of the ball heading in your direction, or close enough to you that you are expected to give chase.

In addition, you have to keep yourself supple and flexible so that you are fit to dive athletically to stop the ball, save runs or take a catch.

If you want to be good at fielding, you need to:

- ✔ **Warm up properly**: Stretch your hamstrings and muscles before play and during time spent in the field. This exercise prevents injury. See Chapter 9 on training for more on stretching exercises.

- ✔ **Practise catching**: Catching is one of your key jobs as a fielder but a cricket ball is hard and can deviate in the air. You need to get used to catching a ball hit at you at speed. Practice can be as easy as getting a team-mate to throw some balls in the air for you to catch.

- ✔ **Practise stopping then throwing the ball**: Basically the more efficient and accurate you are at stopping and throwing the ball, the more likely you are to minimise the number of runs scored by the batsmen and the greater the chances of executing a run-out.

See 'Getting Out on the Grass' later in this chapter for info on basic fielding techniques such as catching and throwing the ball.

Fielding can involve sudden sharp bursts of intense physical activity followed by relative inactivity. This pattern of activity is almost made to cause muscle tears and hamstring pulls. Hence the need to stretch intermittently: Playing a cricket match with a pulled or torn muscle is no laughing matter. Check out Chapter 9 for more on fitness training, pre-play warm-ups and fielding drills.

Even if you have no chance of stopping the ball going over the boundary, you're still expected to run to recover the ball.

Due to the structure of a cricket match – one side bats, while the other fields – you are bound to spend a long time in the field. Work on your fielding, practise and take it seriously. With each ball delivered you have the chance to make a difference by taking a catch, executing a run-out or simply stopping the batsmen from taking a run.

Getting Out on the Grass

So you want to be an ace fielder, helping turn the match in your team's favour through your athleticism and alertness? Great! But in order to be a top-class fielder, you have to master some skills, namely:

- ✔ Catching the ball
- ✔ Collecting the ball
- ✔ Throwing the ball

Taking the perfect catch

Taking a catch is the fielder's time to shine. The fielder plucks the ball out of the air, the team appeals to the umpire, and the umpire raises a finger to indicate that the batsman has been caught out.

However, as mentioned earlier a cricket ball is not soft, like a tennis ball, but hard; when propelled by the force of the batsman's bat it can be difficult to hold onto.

Here are things to bear in mind when trying to pull off a catch:

- ✔ **Watch the ball carefully**: If you don't watch the ball closely you won't catch it. Once you sight the ball in the air, tracking it with your eyes all the way into your hands is essential. Close fielders need to be watching the edge of the batsman's bat as the ball is delivered.

- ✔ **Make sure the ball's yours:** If the ball flies high into the air off the bat, probably more than one fielder will run for it. If you think that you are closest to where the ball is likely to land shout out 'mine', which tells your team-mates to stay away and allows you to concentrate on catching the ball.

- ✔ **Keep your balance:** Keeping your eye on the ball, run to the spot where you think it will land. As the ball arrives bend your knees and try to manoeuvre your body behind the ball, catching the ball and drawing it into the centre of your body. This is called the *set up*. Of course, quite often you won't have an opportunity to run to the ball and set yourself for the catch – you may have to dive forwards or backwards from a standing position in order to take the catch. If you want to be a good close catcher then you should set yourself in a comfortable, well-balanced position – crouched, with knees slightly bent.

  ✔ **Try to get two hands to the ball:** You know the phrase two heads are
  better than one, well in cricket two hands are better than one! If you
  have time before the ball arrives try to cup your hands to receive the
  catch, so that you can easily close your hands around the ball.

Fielders who stand close to the batsman – say in the slips or a bat and
pad position – have less time to move and set themselves to take a catch.
Therefore, as the bowler delivers they crouch and cup their hands together.
The idea is that they are already *set* for a catch when the ball is delivered. See
Figure 7-2 for how to take the perfect close catch.

When a catch is taken the fielding side will shout to the umpire 'How is that?'
or 'Howzat!' This is an *appeal*. If no-one appeals to the umpire then the umpire
cannot give the batsman out.

If when taking a catch the ball arrives below the height of your chest, have
the palms of your hands pointed upwards and fingers pointing forwards and
slightly down, in effect cupping the ball. If the ball is headed at the height of
your shoulders or above then reverse your hands; palms point down to the
floor while the fingers are directed back towards you. See Figure 7-3 for how to
take a high catch.

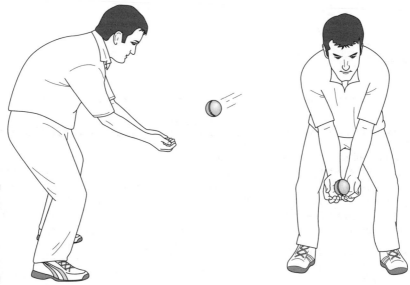

Figure 7-2:
Taking
a catch
close to the
wicket.

Figure 7-3:
Taking a
high catch.

The Australian versus English method of catching

When the ball is high in the air the English method is to take the dropping ball with the fingers pointed forwards and palms upwards – cupping the ball. At the same time the hands draw the ball towards the centre of the body to cushion its impact.

Australian cricketers go about catching a high ball differently. They prefer to take the dropping ball at head height with the fingers pointed skywards and the palms directed down; the feet are spread and the knees bent to cushion the impact of the falling ball.

One of the key differences between the two methods is that the Australian method ensures that the head is still and the eyes don't move. With the English method the fielder looks down, following the line of the ball, as the ball drops down past the face into the hands. No cut-and-dried answer exists as to which method is better. However, consider this fact – Since test cricket started in the nineteenth century Australia has won a far higher percentage of matches than England.

Collecting the ball

A cricket ball is not only hard, but also has a great big stitched seam running around its circumference which makes it deviate in all sorts of different directions when bouncing in the outfield. This makes retrieving a cricket ball a hard skill to master.

When the ball is hit into the outfield you need to:

- ✔ **Watch the ball:** Just like taking a catch, keep your eyes on the ball right up until the moment that you pick it up with your hands. Make sure you watch the ball because it can suddenly change direction – left or right – bouncing high or keeping low. Most mistakes in the outfield are made due to the fielder not keeping an eye on the ball.

- ✔ **Judge the speed of the ball:** When the batsman hits the ball it speeds into the outfield. At this moment you have to make a split-second decision as to which direction the ball is headed and where you should run in order to intercept it. Sometimes you may have to go in a slight arc in your run to the ball, picking it up as it loses momentum.

- ✔ **Attack the ball:** Chase the ball really hard. If the batsmen see you making a big effort it may put doubts in their minds over whether they can make it back to their ground before you are able to hit the stumps with the ball and run them out.

- ✔ **Collect the ball safely:** Once within reach of the ball, if you are right-handed make sure you approach the ball so that it is slightly to your right-hand side (reverse for the left-hander). Move your head and hands downward towards the ball, opening the palm and fingers to pick it up.

If the ball is hit in front of you, run as quickly as possible to it steadying yourself as you prepare to pick it up. Keep your head still as you pick it up and switch your gaze to where you want to direct the throw.

If you simply want to stop and collect the ball that has been hit to you in the outfield then you can deploy what's called the *long barrier*. Lower your left knee and left leg if you're right-handed – reverse for a left-handed fielder – onto the turf across the line the ball is travelling. This means that your body is behind the ball, so even if it bounces awkwardly little chance exists of it evading your grasp. Put your hands together – fingers pointed towards the turf – with the head pointing forward allowing you to follow the ball into your hands.

If you fail to collect the ball properly and it goes past you, the batsmen may take another run. This is called a *misfield*. Conceding runs on misfields is very embarrassing for you and damages the team's prospects of winning the match.

Throwing the ball

The throw is how you propel the ball from the outfield back at the stumps. Two types of throw are possible:

- ✔ The underarm throw
- ✔ The overarm throw

The underarm throw tends to be quite accurate and quick to execute, but you won't be able to generate much power so use the underarm throw only when you are close to the stumps and have a chance of a run-out.

The overarm throw gives you far more distance. Be sure to master this technique if you field in run-saving positions.

Getting the underarm throw right

With underarm throwing time is of the essence as you are usually looking to execute a run-out. Here's how to execute an underarm throw:

1 **Pick up the ball; the body should be stooped at collection.**

2 **Draw the arm back about half a metre, in line with the stumps you are aiming at.**

3 **Cock the wrist slightly to add power to the throw.**

4 **Bring the arm down in a pendulum motion.**

5 **When the hand holding the ball is 180 degrees to the head and the knuckle of the hand is pointing towards the floor, release the ball at the stumps.**

If you hit the stumps before the batsman reaches his crease you will have executed a run-out – high fives all round!

Getting the overarm throw right

The following presumes a right-handed thrower. If you're a leftie just reverse the procedure.

1 **When picking up the ball look directly at the target and turn your body towards it.**

2 **Point the hand or elbow of your left arm at the target. Draw back the hand holding the ball to around shoulder height, while extending it out behind you. This action should have the effect of transferring your weight onto the right-side of your body.**

3 Ensure that the arm holding the ball and your eyes are on a level plane and directed at the target; start transferring your weight from right to left and bring your arm through straight and at speed.

4 Release the ball at the target; you should find that the momentum carries your arm through from the right-hand side, across your torso. This is called the *follow through* and it should end with your head looking at the target over the throwing shoulder.

The description of throwing technique seems long and convoluted but experienced players can execute a throw in a fraction of a second. Practise your throwing so that it becomes second nature.

Try practising throwing with both your arms. Fielders who are able to throw accurately with both arms are the bees knees, as they don't waste time transferring the ball between their hands before executing the throw.

Most fielders aim to throw at the end of the wicket where the wicket-keeper stands because he has great big gloves to collect the ball in. However, sometimes a smart play is to aim at the end of the wicket the bowler stands at, as doing so may give you a better chance of a run-out. Once you have collected the ball glance and see whether you should be aiming towards the wicket-keeper or the bowler. This depends on which batsman is farthest from reaching the crease he is heading for.

If you don't direct your throw properly and the ball is missed by the wicket-keeper, bowler or other fielders standing close to the wicket, the batsman may decide to run again. This is called an *overthrow* and your team-mates are not going to be pleased if your throw leads to the batting team taking extra runs.

Currently England's best fielder is probably bowler James Anderson. He's an athletic fielder in one-day and test cricket , taking lots of catches and covering the ground quickly with effortless ease. He also has a startlingly accurate throw and is super fit. Internationally, most experts reckon that South Africa's AB De Villiers is the best around. He ticks all the same boxes as James Anderson, and is a superb slip catcher when in that position, and has even played a few test matches as a wicket keeper. All in all, he's a superb all-round cricketer and can change games with an array of flying catches or great run outs.

Making it Big as a Wicket-keeper

The most important fielder is the wicket-keeper. All sides have a player who specialises in wicket-keeping. He stands behind the stumps of the batsman and is kitted out with pads and a great big pair of leather gloves.

But the big gloves alone do not make being a wicket-keeper great; when the team are fielding you are always in the game. Here's why:

- ✔ If the batsman misses the ball and it doesn't hit the stumps, the wicket-keeper is responsible for stopping it flying through to the boundary.
- ✔ If the ball hits the edge of the player's bat, it often goes through to the wicket-keeper and it's up to him to take the catch.
- ✔ Fielders often throw the ball to the wicket-keeper, and it's his job to catch these throws.

If the batsman has not made it back to the crease the keeper can use the ball to dislodge the bails off the top of the stumps to execute a run-out.

The wicket-keeper can also stump the batsman; this can happen when the batsman attempts to play the ball and misses but in the attempt he leaves his crease. If the keeper is quick enough to gather the ball and use it to dislodge the bails off the top of the stumps before the batsman gets his feet back into the ground, the batsman will be out – stumped. Refer to Chapter 2 for more on this mode of dismissal.

As far as fielding goes the keeper is numero uno; he can have a huge influence on the success of the fielding team. If the keeper consistently does well at taking catches, collecting throws from the fielder, executing run-outs and stumping batsmen, he's a hero of the team.

If the batsman attempting a shot fails to make contact with the ball and the keeper subsequently fails to collect it, the batsman may run between the wickets. Any runs scored this way are called *byes*; keepers hate giving away byes.

In reality, the skills of wicket-keeping are not ones you can pick up overnight. In order to get to the top of the tree you have to start young and practise hard and even then you need the key requirements of talent, big match temperament and quicksilver reflexes.

The following sections give you some basics of wicket-keeping for you to reflect on.

Finding your stance

For those who have not experienced the joys of playing cricket, it can seem a strange game. Batsmen and bowlers get themselves into what can feel like quite unnatural positions to play strokes or deliver the ball, and it appears the same with wicket-keeping. But with practice, batting, bowling and keeping should all come relatively naturally and comfortably.

As with all sports, balance is one of the keys to success and wicket-keeping is no exception. Facing the bowler, wicket-keepers should stand with their feet about shoulder width apart and have their body weight evenly distributed on the balls of their feet as they crouch down (see Figure 7-4).

The knees will automatically spread in a crouching position, allowing the arms to fit comfortably between the legs so the fingers of the keeping gloves rest lightly on the ground below the keeper's chin. The gloves should be held together with the fingers and thumbs spread wide apart, presenting the largest possible target for the ball as the bowler delivers it.

Figure 7-4:
The wicket-keeper's stance.

The wicket-keeper should always crouch in a low position. Raising the body and hands to take a higher ball is much easier than going down to try and take a low one. A fundamental mistake of many keepers is to come up too early instead of remaining in their crouched position.

Getting into the right line

Most keepers take up their stance on an invisible line just outside the batsman's off stump. Standing just outside the off stump offers you two advantages:

- ✔ **Your view is not obscured by the batsman:** When batting, most players stand around their leg stump when the bowler delivers. See Chapter 5 for more on batting.

- ✔ **You can easily marshal the slip fielders:** Captains may be in charge of the team as a whole but wicket-keepers normally get to tell the slip fielders exactly where they want them to stand.

When you're keeping wicket try to collect and catch the ball with both hands together.

Gloving the ball

If 'staying down' is one golden rule of wicket-keeping, then never pointing the fingers at the ball is another. Apart from giving you less chance of taking the ball properly, it greatly enhances the possibility of suffering an injured finger should the ball hit the end of it.

The fingers of the gloves should always be pointing to the ground if the ball is coming at you below chest height; pointing to the sky if the ball is chest height or above; pointing to the right if the ball is coming to your right side and to the left if it is coming to your left side.

Keep the gloves together and out in front of the body but don't reach for the ball. Let the ball come to you so it settles comfortably into the cup you have created with the gloves, and let your arms give with the direction and momentum of the ball so the gloves automatically close around it.

Sometimes keeping the gloves together is simply not possible, but diving to take the ball, as spectacular as it may look on television, should be a last resort for the wicket-keeper. It greatly increases the chances of missing the ball, possibly costing your team a catch or valuable runs, or both. The best keepers can cover a lot of ground behind the stumps with good foot work. More about foot work later in the chapter.

Standing back . . . standing up

If you are a wicket-keeper, you want to give yourself the best chance of dismissing the batting side while minimising the risk of giving away byes.

The quicker the bowler is delivering the ball the more time you need to react to the movement of the ball. Distance equals reaction time, so it follows that for quicker paced bowling you should stand farther back from the batsman than for slower paced bowling.

In test matches, wicket-keepers often stand 20 metres or more behind the stumps – stand any closer and the fear is that they won't be fast enough to collect the ball or it will bounce over their heads. This is called *standing back*.

But against spin bowlers you should look to stand very close to the stumps, around a metre or so behind. Why so close? Well, the ball is delivered at a far slower pace and if the ball hits the edge of the bat it won't travel very far.

In addition, being so close means you have a greater chance of stumping the batsman. This is called *standing up*.

Standing back

Standing back, the wicket-keeper should be able to take the ball comfortably at about waist height from a fast bowler's good length delivery. See Chapter 6 for more on bowling lengths. As wicket-keeper, stand far enough back so that you take the ball just as it begins to drop. If the ball is still rising when it gets to you, stand farther back. However, if you're taking it at knee or ankle height, you need to move forward.

The wicket-keeper is a vital barometer to the slips, who form an arc next to him waiting for the batsman to make a mistake by edging the ball to them. If the keeper stands too far back, the ball is unlikely to carry to the slips. If the keeper is too close, the slips may not have time to react to a ball travelling quickly at them. See the section 'Close catching fielding positions' earlier in this chapter for more about slip fielding.

When catching a ball, taking it in front of you is natural. Ideally, wicket-keepers standing back do not. Instead, keepers standing back should always take the ball to the side of their body next to what is known as their 'inside' hip. This is the hip closest to the line of the stumps.

Not only does this allow greater give with a freer swing of the arms when taking the ball from a fast bowler, but it also means that the keeper is a little farther across to the off side and is able to cover greater ground for an out-side edge, the most common form of dismissal in cricket. See Chapter 2 for more on dismissals.

If the ball is heading down the leg side, the keeper should avoid diving unless absolutely necessary. Instead, he should almost skip across behind the stumps to the ball, eyes steady and gloves ready. This is done by bringing your outside foot, the foot closest to the off side, quickly across to meet your other foot, which pushes off towards the leg side. Do this several times until you can take the ball to the leg side of your body. If the ball is clearly too wide down the leg side and moving too quickly to take like this, dive in desperation. Stopping the ball is paramount.

Any ball that flies off the edge of the batsman's bat and is heading between the wicket-keeper and first slip is regarded as the keeper's catch and he must attempt to take it. First slip should never have to dive towards the keeper to take a catch. If the ball flies between the two, the keeper has failed to do his job properly. This is much worse than going for but dropping a difficult catch. Nobody can catch everything all the time and no-one ever means to drop a catch, in the same way that batsmen don't mean to get out and bowlers don't mean to bowl poorly. Dropping a difficult catch simply means a 'bad luck' pat on the back from the closest fielder and more work at training!

Standing up

Standing up is the toughest part of wicket-keeping. It requires great practice and skill because so little reaction time is available once the ball bounces off the pitch. Usually the wicket-keeper is standing up to a spinner who is trying to fool the batsman by flighting the ball in the air and spinning it off the pitch. When standing a little more than a metre behind the batsman, the wicket-keeper can also be fooled by these subtle and clever variations.

Therefore, a good idea is for a wicket-keeper to keep to his team's spinners in training so he discovers all their little tricks. This practice gives the bowler and keeper greater confidence in each other. See Chapter 6 for more on spin bowling.

As discussed earlier in this chapter, staying crouched down behind the stumps for as long as possible is important for keepers. Only when the ball has pitched, or bounced, should the keeper begin to come up, straightening the legs slightly until the gloves are level with the ball as it is about to be taken. If a keeper comes up too early then a ball that stays low, including edges that could result in a catch, may scoot past him. Few things are more embarrassing for a keeper than the ball flying between his legs.

If the ball is heading down the leg side, stay low but (if a right-hander is batting) push your left leg across until well outside leg stump and bring your right leg into line with leg stump. Always attempt to keep your body behind the ball when taking it. Ensuring that your right leg is in line with leg stump, for a right-hander, gives you a guide of where the stumps are should you attempt a leg side stumping.

Taking throws from the outfield

Not only does a wicket-keeper need to be fit and flexible to crouch every time the bowler delivers the ball, but keepers are also expected to run up to the stumps to take the ball from a fielder's throw every time the batsman plays the ball. This means a wicket-keeper standing back to a fast bowler can regularly run 20 metres, sometimes at full pace, to the stumps to take the ball.

Always call to the fielders, encouraging them to stop or chase the ball, and let them know if a possible run-out chance exists so that they can throw the ball back in as hard and quickly as possible.

Always make sure you are behind the stumps in a direct line with the fielder. This way, if a run-out chance is imminent, the throw may be good enough to hit the stumps without you needing to take it. Alternatively, taking the bails off once the ball has been gathered while facing the stumps is much easier rather than trying to turn around.

Bend over towards the stumps with the knees slightly bent. This makes it easier to gather a ball that is quite low when it reaches you. Again, coming up to gather a bouncing ball is easier than trying to reach down at the last minute if it scoots along the ground.

When you're keeping wicket, always try to collect and catch the ball with both hands together. This offers a much greater chance of taking the ball cleanly.

If the ball is being thrown in to the wicket-keeper but a run-out at the bowler's end is more likely, the keeper should flick off the glove on his throwing hand. Once the keeper has taken the ball, he should throw it at the stumps at the bowler's end. But make sure that you have a chance of dismissing the batsman, because if the ball misses the stumps it may go for extra runs, known as 'overthrows'.

Chapter 8

Talking Tactics: Captaining a Cricket Team

Cricket is chock full of tactics: Each delivery is a game within a game. The batsmen try to score runs while the bowlers and fielders try to stop them from doing so.

In this chapter I decipher cricket's tactics so that you can have more fun playing and watching this most fascinating of team games.

The info in this chapter will also come in handy should you have to captain a cricket team and be the person with a winning plan.

Understanding the Role of the Captain

I can't think of any other sport where the captain of the team plays such an important role as in cricket.

In sports like soccer and rugby the game is so fast-paced that the on-pitch captain has little time to breathe, never mind alter team tactics. In fact, in these quick-fire sports captains are often reduced to the role of cheerleader, imploring team-mates to *stick it* to the opposition. But the game of cricket is fundamentally different. A game is made up of hundreds – sometimes thousands – of set pieces, occurring every time the bowler delivers a ball to the batsman. These set pieces take only a few seconds to execute and then the batsmen, bowlers and fielders take 30, 40 even 50 seconds to prepare for the next delivery. In addition, matches are stopped for lunch and tea. In short, cricket captains have an inordinate amount of time on their hands to think about and change team tactics.

Some of the tactical decisions you, as captain, make during a match include:

- ✔ When the team bats:
  - Deciding on the *batting order* of the team.
  - Communicating with the batsmen to let them know whether you want them to play aggressively or defensively.
  - Choosing if and when to *declare* the innings if the team is not bowled out (or, in other words, stop batting and put the other side in to bat).
- ✔ When the team bowls:
  - Which bowlers should be given the new ball.
  - When to rest bowlers.
  - When to tell a fresh bowler to bowl.
  - Where approximately on the wicket you would like your bowlers to aim the ball.
  - Where to set and when to change the position of fielders to give them the best chance of dismissing the batsmen as well as stopping the flow of runs.
  - When to take the *new ball*, if playing a longer match – such as test and first class.

Being captain of the fielding side requires constant decision-making. The positions of fielders can be altered from ball-to-ball, and bowlers need to be rested every few overs. When the side is batting, however, the captain sitting in the pavilion can do much less. The batsmen playing the bowling need to decide personally whether to attack or defend each delivery. However, this doesn't stop a captain sending occasional messages out to his batsmen during breaks in play.

Even before the match begins, captains have decisions to make. Particularly in club cricket, captains often play the key role in team selection. See the next section for more on selecting a winning team.

On top of all this decision-making the captain has his own performance to take care of. Captains have to be worth their place in the team as players, not just as decision-makers. They have to bat, bowl or keep wicket well enough to merit selection. Captains who fail to maintain performance standards often lose the respect of team-mates – and without respect a captain is sunk!

Selecting the Right Team

Games of cricket can almost be lost before play even starts if the make-up of the team is wrong. When selecting a team you're looking for a mixture of talents. You should have enough batsmen to score runs and bowlers capable of dismissing the opposition. The ideal make-up of an 11-player cricket team is usually five or six batsmen and four or five bowlers as well as a wicket-keeper.

But selection doesn't stop there; captains also look to blend the individual talents to be found among their bowlers and batsmen.

When it comes to the team's specialist batsmen a captain wants two players who are adept at playing the new ball. These players are called *opening batsmen* and they need to be good at playing defensive shots. Then the captain looks for players who are more adept at playing attacking shots but can defend if needed. These players are called *middle order batsmen* or *strokemakers*. Refer to Chapter 5, on batting, for more on the different types of batsmen.

As for selecting the team's specialist bowlers, a captain usually wants a mixture of bowling styles: players who specialise in seam, swing and spin bowling. This gives the captain lots of options. Refer to Chapter 6 for more on how the different bowling styles can help win cricket matches.

The condition of the wicket can have a major effect on the selection of a team's bowlers, particularly in a test match. If the wicket has lots of grass on it, and some moisture on the surface, it will aid seam movement and a captain is likely to want to select pace bowlers. On the other hand, if the wicket is dry and grassless then spin bowlers are likely to come into their own.

A cricket ball has a pronounced stitched seam running across its circumference. When the ball bounces off the wicket, this seam can cause the ball's direction to alter towards or away from the batsman. This phenomenon is called *seam movement*.

The captain's influence on team selection tends to differ between professional and club cricket. In club cricket the captain is usually god, getting to decide on his own which players are in the side. But in professional cricket you may have a coach and a panel of selectors who want their say. Some test-playing nations such as Australia give their captains little say in who plays in the team; a panel of ex-test players meet under a chairman of selectors and vote on who should be in the team. In England the captain and coach of the test team sit on the selection panel under the chairman, currently Geoff Miller, a former test match spin bowler.

The twelfth man

In professional cricket, teams have 12 players; yet only 11 actually bat or bowl in the match. The twelfth man, as the extra player is called, spends the match carrying drinks out to fielders and relaying messages from the captain in the dressing room to the batsmen. If they are really lucky, they get to field as replacement for an injured team-mate or one merely wanting to go to the toilet – now there's glamour!

Having a team of 12 rather than of 11 gives the captain more tactical options in the run-up to the start of the match. The captain will look at the condition of the pitch and then decide which 11 players are actually going to bat and bowl and which unlucky player will be drinks-carrier-in-chief. If for example the pitch looks like it will aid seam or spin movement, the captain may decide to select an extra batsman, dropping a specialist bowler to twelfth man. Usually a captain will let the player know if he will be twelfth man the night before or the morning of the match.

Sometimes, you find players who are capable of both batting and bowling to a high standard. These players are called *all rounders* and are worth their weight in gold as far as selectors are concerned. One good example is England's Stuart Broad, a player good enough to be considered for selection both as a batsman and as a bowler but only occupying one place in the team. Likewise Jacques Kallis of South Africa is both a superb batsmen and a successful, wicket-taking bowler. Think of all rounders as akin to one of those two for the price of one offers you see in the supermarket. Chapter 11 has more on the modern game's great all rounders.

If you have to select a cricket team, you need to bear some other factors in mind as well as marrying up the skills of batsmen and bowlers into a winning unit. Here are some dos and don'ts of team selection:

- ✔ **Don't select a player just because you are friends**: Every player in a team has to earn his or her keep.

- ✔ **Do be honest with players who don't merit selection:** Tell them clearly why they aren't making the team on this occasion and indicate what they need to improve in their game to merit reselection.

- ✔ **Do monitor individual performance:** Cricket is a game of statistics – both team and individual – and by looking at these you can decide whether players merit selection. See Chapter 13 for more on cricket statistics.

- ✔ **Don't be too hasty in your selection**: Just because a player has a few bad games, doesn't mean he or she is a poor cricketer. Captains should try to think long term. A player's form is temporary but class is permanent. Players often respond well to a captain who shows them loyalty.

✔ **Do take fielding ability into account:** If two players are roughly of the same ability as a batsman or bowler, the deciding factor may well be fielding. In close call selections, best go for the player who is more adept at catching, collecting and throwing a cricket ball. Refer to Chapter 7 for more on sprucing up fielding skills.

If a captain chooses to leave out a player, that player is said to have been *dropped*. When a player is selected to play he or she is said to have been *given the nod*.

Calling Heads or Tails . . . the Toss of the Coin

Shortly before a cricket match starts the captains of both teams walk together to the wicket. The captain of the team playing at home tosses a coin in the air, and while the coin is in flight the captain of the team playing away from home calls 'heads' or 'tails'. If the away captain calls correctly then he has the choice of batting or fielding first. On the other hand, if the away captain calls incorrectly then the home captain gets the choice.

Whether a coin lands heads or tails is pure luck, of course, but the choice of whether to bat or field first is a big test of the captain's acumen.

The captain's decision on whether to bat or bowl first has a lot to do with his assessment of the state of the pitch, and the weather conditions.

If the pitch or the weather looks like it will favour pace and swing bowling then the captain winning the toss is likely to choose to bowl first.

Tell-tale signs of a pitch and weather conditions that favour bowling first include:

✔ **Grass on the pitch:** This factor could aid the bowlers in moving the ball off the seam.

✔ **A little moisture on the wicket:** Dampness in the pitch, perhaps caused by early morning dew, could also encourage seam movement.

✔ **Cloudy conditions overhead:** Cloud cover and a humid atmosphere can encourage the cricket ball to swing in the air, making play more difficult for the batsman.

However, on the flip-side, if the conditions look like they favour batting then the chances are the captain will decide to bat first; called in cricketing circles *having a knock!*

Tell-tale signs of a batting-friendly pitch and weather conditions include:

- ✔ **Dry and grassless pitch:** The ball is unlikely to deviate much off the seam – though if deterioration takes place later in the game then spin bowlers may have some success.
- ✔ **Sunny and dry overhead conditions:** The ball is less likely to swing, so making the opposition field on a hot day can be a sure-fire way to fatigue the bowlers and the fielders – cricket can be a cruel sport!

Just because a pitch starts out as a paradise for batsmen doesn't mean it will end the game like that. As the match progresses, dry pitches often deteriorate. The spikes used by bowlers and the impact of the ball on the pitch can make the turf crumble. This sort of surface can lead to uneven bounce, aid spin bowling and make the pitch harder to bat on successfully. Conversely, if the pitch starts off damp and green, a few days sunshine can soon turn it into a batting paradise – all dry and grassless!

The longer the format of the match the greater the role pitch conditions will play. For example, during the five days of a test match the condition of the wicket can change enormously, but in twenty20 games, which are over in a few hours, there really isn't much time for conditions to change much. However, this doesn't mean winning the toss isn't important in twenty20 and one-day matches: See 'Looking at One-Day Captaincy' later in the chapter for more on the leadership skills needed in shorter games of cricket.

A wicket with a lot of green grass is often called a *green top.*

In test match and first class matches each team has two innings. But in one-day matches each team only has one innings and the numbers of overs bowled to them are limited, usually to 20 or 50.

Captaining the Team in the Field

When the team is in the field the captain is out there calling the shots. Good captains earn the respect of their team-mates and their decisions are followed to the letter. Cricket is a complex game and the captain's role is to be in the firing line making the tough calls; never more so than when the team is fielding.

Deciding on the new ball bowlers

The captain has to choose which pair of bowlers will bowl first from the two ends of the pitch. These bowlers are called the *opening bowlers*. The ball will be new so the captain will usually choose players who can deliver the ball at a fast pace but also make the ball deviate off the seam. But other things enter the equation when a captain decides on the opening bowlers. The captain may want bowlers who attack the batsmen from differing angles – for example one bowler who delivers the ball with the right hand, and the other who bowls with the left. One bowler may deliver the ball faster than the other or make it bounce more. James Anderson and Stuart Braod have proved successful opening bowlers for England in recent years. Anderson is good at swinging the ball, while Broad is taller and faster and so generates more bounce. Anderson and Broad's styles of bowling complement one another. Each new ball bowler should pose different questions to the batting side.

In test match cricket a new ball is given to the fielding team at the start of each innings and then one is offered by the umpires every subsequent 80 overs of the innings. The captain can decline their offer if he chooses. Flick forward to 'Handling bowlers with care' later in this chapter for more. In club and one-day cricket things are lot simpler: A new ball is made available at the start of each innings.

A new ball tends to deviate off the pitch more than an old ball and flies through the air faster.

Choosing when to change the bowlers

Bowling is physically draining and you can find that some seam and swing bowlers, in particular, soon tire. Some bowlers may not bowl well at all. Lots of reasons exist for a captain to order a change in the bowling including:

- ✔ **The bowler needs to rest:** The bowler goes and fields for a while before returning to the fray.
- ✔ **The batsmen may be playing the bowler well**: If the batting side are scoring lots of runs, then a new approach is needed.
- ✔ **The captain wants to try something different:** Sometimes a different type of bowler may find it easier to dismiss the batsmen.
- ✔ **The conditions change:** The captain may see that the ball has started to reverse swing and so brings on a bowler who is good at getting a ball to reverse. See Chapter 6 for full details on reverse swing.

In one-day matches the number of overs an individual bowler can bowl in an innings is limited. Therefore at some point in the innings the fielding captain may decide he wants the bowler to stop, so he has some overs left and can return later in the innings and bowl; see 'Looking at One-day Captaincy' later in this chapter for more on one-day tactics.

When a captain is thinking about a change in the bowling – known as *bringing on* a new bowler – he tells the new bowler to warm up. The player should then do some stretching exercises to help ensure that he doesn't pull a muscle or hamstring when he starts bowling. See Chapter 9 for more on stretching.

Seam and swing bowlers tire more quickly than spinners. As a general rule, seam and swing bowlers show signs of tiredness after completing five or six overs, though some can breeze through eight or nine with relative ease. Spin bowling is less about physical exertion and more about guile, so spinners can usually bowl for far longer. Eventually a spin bowler tires, however. Generally, when a bowler tires, he loses accuracy making it easier for the batting side to execute scoring shots.

One of the best captains of the past couple of decades was Australia's Steve Waugh, who retired in 2004. Not only was he one of the best batsmen in the world, therefore earning his place in the team on merit, he was also superb at getting the timing of bowling changes right. One tactic Waugh was famous for was introducing a less able bowler – often himself – when two batsmen were batting well together, just before a break in play, or at the end of a day's play. Waugh was playing mind games. The idea was that the batsmen would underestimate the bowler and play some big attacking shots. Time and again the batsman (usually English!) would be dismissed playing aggressively. Some bright captains change the bowling just to unsettle the concentration of the batsmen, asking them different questions.

Handling bowlers with care

Bowlers are the team's strike weapons and captains have to handle them with care. The key to handling bowlers is a combination of the following:

✔ **Making sure that the bowlers are well rested:** This involves taking the bowlers out of the attack when they get tired and putting them in places in the field where they won't be expected to run around a lot after the ball. Traditionally bowlers are asked to field at long leg or third man fielding positions rather than in the covers where they would be expected to stop the ball or chase after it if it gets past them.

✔ **Listening to the bowler's opinion:** A captain would be well advised to listen to what the bowler has to say. By this I don't mean have a natter about politics or the merits of the euro. Bowlers will have their views on where fielders should go and the technical batting weaknesses of the opposition. A captain who doesn't listen to the bowlers but treats them in a high-handed 'do what I say' manner is bound not to get the best from them.

A good captain should listen to the views of his bowlers, but must not let himself be bossed around by them. A captain has to be his own man. When it comes to captaincy, success has many fathers but failure just the one. And when the team fails guess who ends up holding the baby? Yes, you guessed it, the captain.

After 80 overs of a test innings the fielding captain is given the option of switching the old cricket ball for a brand new one. Sometimes a captain chooses not to take a new ball when offered it by the umpire. This decision is usually taken because the captain believes that the old ball is more likely to spin when bouncing off the wicket or reverse swing in the air. Refer to Chapter 6 for more on this.

It used to be the case that the umpire's word was final, but no longer. New thermal imaging, computer and camera technology now means that some umpiring decisions can be scrutinised to see whether they are correct. Cricket, in fact, has been a pioneer sport in allowing captains and batsmen to ask for decisions made by the on-field officials to be checked by an off field official using new technology. At present this *Decision Review System* (DRS) is only used in test cricket and some one-day international matches but it is an extra tactical dimension to be taken into account, see Chapter 3 for the lowdown on how DRS works.

Setting the field

The captain decides where the fielders should stand. This is called *setting the field*. You can divide field positions into two main sorts:

- ✔ **Close catching positions:** These fielders are placed close to where the batsman receives the ball. Their main purpose is to take a catch should the player hit it in the air, usually off the edge of the bat.

- ✔ **Run saving positions:** These fielders are located farther away from the batsman. Their job is to stop the ball and prevent the batsmen from taking a run. However, if the ball flies to them in the air off the bat they are also expected to take the catch.

Refer to Chapter 7 for greater detail on the main fielding positions.

Close catching positions are sometimes referred to as the *close in fielders* whereas players in run saving positions are said to be standing in the *outfield*.

If the captain tells most of his fielders to stand in close catching positions then that's an aggressive field setting. If more of the fielders are in run saving positions, that's a defensive field setting. The main object of an aggressive field setting is to increase the chances of taking catches and dismissing batsmen. With defensive fields the main object is to reduce the number of runs the player can score.

The danger of having aggressive field settings is that lots of gaps exist between fielders into which batsmen can hit the ball and score runs. Generally, when teams are on the attack with aggressive fields you find that the batting side score runs at a fast rate – although at a greater risk of being dismissed.

Going for the jugular: Using aggressive field settings

Match situations in which the fielding captain should go on the attack include:

- ✔ **At the start of the innings:** This is when the bowlers are freshest, and the batsmen have not adjusted to the bounce of the ball. The start of the innings also means a new ball, which is more likely to fly through the air quickly and deviate before and after bouncing off the pitch.

- ✔ **When a new ball has just been taken:** In test matches a new ball is offered to the fielding side after 80 overs of an innings. This is a good time to attack.

- ✔ **When a batsman has just been dismissed and a new player is at the wicket:** Even the best batsmen take time to be able to judge the pace of the bowling and bounce off the wicket. Refer to Chapter 5 for more on the frailty of batsmen early in their innings.

- ✔ **When the batsman is not very good:** The batsman may be in the team for his bowling and hasn't really mastered the art of batting. Such players are called *tailenders*, or *late-order batsmen*.

A typical aggressive field setting, which may be used early in an innings, is shown in Figure 8-1.

Cricketers refer to a new cricket ball as a *new cherry*, because a new ball is very shiny and red.

Aggressive fields are set when the fielding team feels that the condition of the ball and wicket as well as the inexperience or lack of ability of the batsman gives them a better chance of claiming a dismissal.

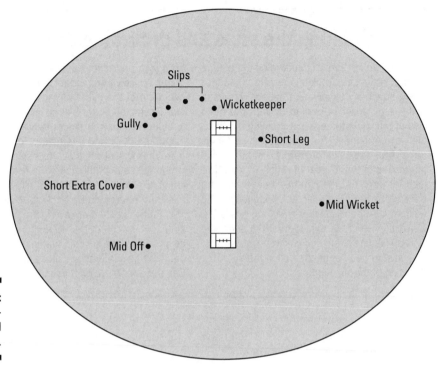

Figure 8-1:
An aggres-
sive field
setting.

You often find in cricket that captains who are confident and used to winning are more aggressive in their field settings and set aggressive fields for longer periods. These captains are confident that bowlers can dismiss batsmen and they want fielders close to the bat to take the catching chances when they eventually come.

Treading carefully: Knowing when to set defensive fields

Captaining a fielding team isn't all attack, attack, attack! Sometimes you need to go on the defensive and wait for the batsman to make a mistake or the bowler to produce a great piece of bowling to bowl the player or trap him leg before wicket (LBW): Refer to Chapter 2 for more on the various modes of dismissal.

Packing the slips and crowding the bat

Attacking fields differ depending on the type of bowler. A typical attacking field for a seam or swing bowler involves lots of fielders standing in the *slip cordon* – located to the right-hand side of the wicket-keeper, presuming the batsman is right-handed. Some captains will deploy three, four even five fielders to stand at slip, because slip is the best location in which to field in order to take catches coming off the edge of the bat. The tactic of having lots of slip fielders in place is called *packing the slips*. Generally, when the condition of the pitch and the ball favours seam and swing bowlers, batsmen are prone to edge the ball in the air in the direction of the slip fielders.

Attacking fields set for spin bowlers, though, are an entirely different kettle of fish. When the condition of the ball and wicket favours spinners, batsmen are prone to offering catches to fielders located in front of and square of the wicket on the off and leg side. You rarely see more than one slip in place to a spin bowler but you may see a whole gaggle of fielders standing at silly mid off, silly mid on, silly point or the bizarrely named short backward square leg. This tactic is called *crowding the bat* in cricket speak, and can put the willies up the batsman as he knows one miscalculation could lead to a catch being snaffled by a close fielder. Refer to Chapter 7 for more on these fielding positions.

The captain may set a defensive field, such as the one shown in Figure 8-2, in the following situations:

- ✔ **If the ball is old**: When the ball is old and not moving off the seam, swinging in the air or spinning once bouncing off the wicket, less chance exists of the batsman making a mistake.

- ✔ **If the batsmen are playing well**: When good players have been batting for a long time they are at their most dangerous, able to judge the bounce and pace of deliveries and execute devastating scoring shots. At this point the fielding captain may feel he should go on the defensive.

- ✔ **If the game is a limited overs match:** In one-day, limited overs cricket the object is as much to prevent the batting team from scoring runs as to dismiss batsmen – though if you can do both all the better. As a result captains set more defensive fields in limited overs cricket than in test match cricket and longer first class matches. Check out 'Looking at One-day Captaincy' later in this chapter for more on tactics in one-day cricket.

The wicket-keeper is not allowed to move out of a close catching position into a run saving one on the boundary. This law change occurred after former England captain Mike Brearley sent his wicket-keeper to stand on the boundary rope during a one-day match against the West Indies, when the West Indians only needed four runs to win.

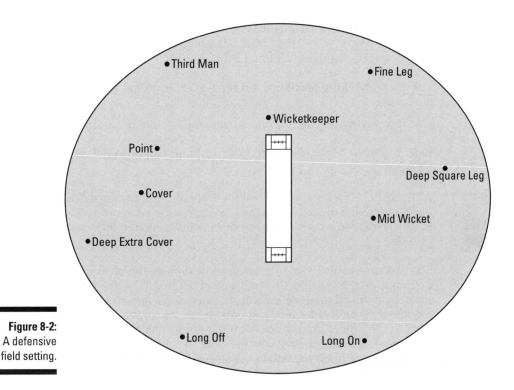

Figure 8-2:
A defensive
field setting.

Looking at fields that mix attack and defence

A lot of the time during a match captains don't set ultra-defensive or ultra-aggressive fields. Instead, captains like to keep their options open by placing some fielders in close catching positions and others in run saving ones.

Getting on with it

Fielding teams are expected to complete their overs at a decent pace. Umpires can be strict on captains and teams that bowl their overs too slowly. In some club cricket matches, the batting team has runs added to their total if the bowling side fails to bowl the set number of overs in a specified period of time. In professional cricket the captains of slowcoach bowling teams are often fined. As a general rule, the bowling side should look to complete a minimum of 15 overs during each hour's play.

In setting the field, the captain assesses where the batsmen are likely to hit the ball. A typical mixed field would combine some of the following fielding positions (refer to Figures 8-1 and 8-2):

- **Close catching positions:** Wicket-keeper, two slips, gully, short extra cover.
- **Run saving positions:** Point, cover, mid off, mid on, mid wicket, long on.

Refer to Figure 7-1 for where all these positions can be found relative to the batsman.

A cricket field is a big expanse and there simply aren't enough fielders to cover every inch of turf. The captain has to decide on a trade-off between having fielders to stop runs and being in pole position to take catching chances.

The captain usually looks to have some fielders on the off side of the wicket and some on the leg side. Generally, most field settings involve more players located on the off than the leg side, because seam and swing bowlers usually aim their deliveries at or just outside the line of the off stump. Refer to Chapter 6 for more on this line of attack. Occasionally, though, a captain will put more fielders on the leg side than the off, when perhaps the batsman has shown a desire to hit the ball in the air on the leg side. Refer to Chapter 2 for an explanation of the off side and the leg side.

Commonplace amongst cricket captains is to ask their slip fielders to spread out far and wide. For example, a captain may ask one fielder to stand in the first slip position while another stands at third slip. A substantial gap exists between the two fielders and the danger is that the ball could hit the edge of the player's bat and fly in the air between these fielders. The skipper, though, is backing the athleticism of his slip fielders, hoping they will be able to dive to catch the ball regardless.

Enforcing the follow-on

In a test or first class match, if the team has performed brilliantly in the field and dismissed the opposition – in their first innings – for not many runs, a funny thing can happen.

Provided the fielding side has already batted and scored a certain number of runs more than the team whose innings has just ended, the fielding captain has the right to enforce something called the *follow-on*. The number of runs is 200 in test cricket, and 150 in most first class cricket played around the globe. If the follow-on is enforced, the team whose innings has just ended has to come straight back out and bat again. The second time they bat is counted as their second innings and if on its completion their aggregate run total still isn't as high as the fielding side's, then they have *lost by an innings*!

The fielding captain makes the choice whether to enforce the follow-on. The captain has to assess lots of tactical factors before enforcing the follow-on, including:

- ✔ **The amount of time left in the match:** The less time left in the match, the more likely the captain is to enforce the follow-on. After all, less time means less chance of the opposition staging a winning fight back.

- ✔ **The tiredness of the bowlers:** The captain should try and gauge the fatigue suffered by the bowlers. If they have had to make a huge effort to bowl out the opposition then perhaps giving the bowlers a rest may be best, by choosing to bat and not enforcing the follow-on, so that they can be fresh for the second innings.

A danger always exists in making a team follow-on. On a few occasions in the past, teams that have been made to follow-on have scored lots of runs in their second innings, taking their aggregate score way past that of the first innings score of the fielding side. Then when the fielding team has batted they have been dismissed cheaply, giving the win and the glory to the team that had been made to follow-on. See Chapter 15 for my list of greatest ever test matches for some examples of these back-from-the-dead performances.

On average, nine times out of ten a captain who has the chance to enforce the follow-on does so.

Batting Tactics

A cricket captain's time is divided between marshalling the troops in the field, batting himself, or sitting in the pavilion watching the team bat. The tactical options open to the captain whose team is batting are fewer than occur in the field – after all, the batsmen facing the bowling are the ones who decide whether to play aggressive or defensive shots.

But, nevertheless, the tactics adopted by the captain can have a huge impact on how successfully the team bats.

When the team is in the field the captain can make constant adjustment to tactics such as moving a fielder or changing the bowling. When the team is batting tactical choices tend to be more sporadic but no less important.

Drawing up the batting order

All 11 players in a team have a chance to bat in an innings. The captain decides which players get to bat first, second, third . . . all the way down to eleven. The captain draws up a *batting order* before the team's innings begins and tells each player which number he will bat at. The players batting at numbers one and two go out first to face the bowlers: They are said to be *opening the innings*. When one of these players has been dismissed they are replaced by player number three in the order and this procession of players continues until only one player is left in the side who has not been dismissed. At that point the team is deemed *all out*. A team will be all out unless the captain declares the innings – see 'Declaring the innings' later in this chapter – or the bowling team runs out of overs in a limited-overs match.

Good captains don't just decide a batting order willy-nilly. They assess the abilities of each player and assign them a place in the batting order according to those abilities. The most capable batsmen are placed at or near the top of the batting order while the least capable go at the bottom. Two good reasons exist for this 'best batsmen go first' tactic:

- **The bowlers are at their freshest and the ball is at its newest:** The captain wants his most capable players at the top of the batting order to negate these twin dangers.

- **The captain likes good batsmen to bat together:** Good batsmen can build big partnerships; wearing down the bowlers and scoring lots of runs.

The best teams have a mixture of talents running through them. In the bowling department, they have seam, swing, and spin to make the most of the condition of the wicket. When it comes to batting, the best teams have some batsmen who have tremendous defensive skills and others who are best at playing attacking shots. Refer to Chapter 5 for more on defensive and aggressive batting shots.

Often a captain gives the job of opening the innings to players who are the top drawer at playing defensive shots; although they should be capable of playing aggressive shots too.

Sometimes though a captain will break with this tried and tested 'best goes first' rule and re-jig the batting order. This can happen when:

- **Quick runs are needed:** The captain may promote a player in the batting order because he is particularly adept at playing aggressive shots. Perhaps the side has to score a certain number of runs to win the game and they don't have much time, or they have a limited number of overs in which to score the runs.

✔ **Better batsmen need protecting:** In test and first class cricket when the batting side loses a wicket near the end of a day's play the captain will sometimes promote a less able player in the order. The captain would rather put the promoted batsman at risk of being dismissed than a more capable batsman who usually bats near the top of the batting order. A batsman promoted in this situation is called a *nightwatchman*. The nightwatchman is expected to play defensive shots with the aim of not being dismissed before the end of the day; refer to Chapter 5 for more on this tactic.

Conditions for the batsmen are often difficult at the end of a day's play. The light may be fading and late evening dew may even be on the pitch, helping the ball move off the seam. What's more, batsmen are at their most vulnerable to being dismissed early in their innings. Having to bat say for 20 minutes at the end of one day and start again bright and early the next day is a difficult task. By doing this, in effect, the batsman starts his innings twice – once late in the evening and again the next day. In the process, he has to get used to the bounce of the ball off the wicket, deviation of the ball in the air and concentrate fully twice over; all good reasons for deciding on the nightwatchman tactic.

In test and first class matches, *close of play* refers to the end of a day's play.

If all goes to plan, a nightwatchman is meant to avoid being dismissed until close of play. The next day, the nightwatchman is meant to defend for the first few overs, tiring the bowlers in the process. Once the nightwatchman is dismissed then normal service resumes with the more capable batsman (who moved down a number in the batting order to make way for the nightwatchman) taking over the batting and hopefully taking full advantage of the fatigued bowlers.

Promoting a player in the order brings risks. If you promote someone because they are good at playing aggressive shots then they're not likely to be that hot at playing defensive shots and could be easily dismissed by the bowlers. As for the nightwatchman scenario the risk is that he may be dismissed before the close of play, once again throwing the captain's tactics into turmoil.

Declaring the innings

Sometimes the batting team are well on top. The bowlers' deliveries are being flogged to all parts of the ground and runs are flowing freely. Happy days!

But the good times can't go on forever; a match has to be won. In test and first class cricket matches time is of the essence. The batting team has to finish their innings leaving enough time to dismiss the opposition and win the match.

The batting captain has the option of declaring the innings. This means that the captain says to the opposition captain 'We have made enough runs: now it's your turn to go out and bat'.

Declaring an innings is a tactic used in test and first class matches but not in professional one-day matches. Refer to Chapter 3 for more on the different match formats.

Sometimes in test and first class cricket – in which each side has two innings – when the batting side is set to declare their innings, the fielding side will go ultra defensive. The captain sets a field whose sole objective is to stop runs being scored. By doing this the fielding captain hopes to delay the batting side's declaration giving his own side less time to survive to draw the match.

In one-day matches each side has a set number of overs for their innings. No tactical advantage can be gained from declaring an innings in a one-day match.

Looking at declaration scenarios

Here are some typical scenarios when the captain of the batting side may decide to declare the innings:

- ✔ The batting side has made a huge first innings total but wants enough time left in the match to be able to bowl the opposition out twice.

- ✔ The batting side has built up a big lead in their second innings, so much so that there probably isn't enough time for the opposition to chase down the victory target.

- ✔ The captain is trying to force a result, by offering the opposition a tempting total. The idea is that the opposition batsmen will be tempted to play aggressive shots in order to reach the victory total, thereby increasing the chances of being dismissed.

No hard-and-fast rules exist dictating of and when a captain should declare an innings. The captain has to make an assessment of the match situation and decide on a run target he wants to set the opposition. He also needs to consider how much time is left in the match for his bowlers to dismiss the opposition team.

Sometimes in cricket games you see the twelfth man bring the batsman a drink, or a new pair of batting gloves. Sometimes the batsman has asked for this to happen but often the twelfth man has been sent onto the field by the captain to relay a message. The message will contain some useful tactical tidbit such as the batsman being urged to attack the bowling more, so that the innings can be declared as soon as possible.

Egg on the captain's face: Declarations that have gone badly wrong!

Sometimes a captain gets a touch overconfident about his team's ability to dismiss the opposition and cocks-up the declaration. This normally involves being too gung-ho; here are some examples:

✔ Back in 2001, at Headingley, Australia's skipper Adam Gilchrist declared his team's second innings on 176 for 3 wickets leaving England 315 to score to win the match during the final day. The subtext was that Australia were already 3-0 up in the series and going for a 5-0 series 'whitewash'. Now Australia had been beating England soundly for the previous decade or more and most expected the Aussies to dismiss all the England batsmen and win the match. However, one England batsman, Mark Butcher, had a different idea. He hit his highest score in test cricket of 173 to guide England to the victory total for the loss of only 4 wickets and the cricket world was stunned. However, the hoopla around Butcher's great innings didn't stop the Aussies winning the next test at the Oval cricket ground and taking the five match series 4-1!

✔ England were on the receiving of a duff declaration decision in 1984. England captain David Gower declared the team's second innings on 300 for 9 wickets on the morning of the final day of the test match against the West Indies. This left the West Indies needing 342 to win the game. Well on a bright sunny day, West Indian opening batsman Gordon Greenidge went berserk hitting boundary after boundary. West Indies made the victory target for the loss of only 1 wicket, thereby winning the match on the way to a 5-0 series whitewash of a sorry England.

✔ Another famous (or should that be infamous?) example – again involving England – occurred in 1968 in the West Indies. Home captain Garfield Sobers – see Chapter 14 on the greatest ever players for more – declared his side's second innings on 92 for 2 wickets; this left England 215 to win in less than four hours. The England batsmen went on the attack and reached the victory target with a few minutes of the match remaining. England had won the test match and the series 1-0 and the great Garfield Sobers was jeered and heckled by the local supporters.

✔ England yet again. In the second test match of the 2006-07 Ashes series at Adelaide, trailing 1-0 in the series, captain Andrew Flintoff declared the England first innings on a mammoth 551, only to eventually lose the match by six wickets on the final afternoon after a genius display by Aussie leg spinning great Shane Warne had seen the Poms bowled out for just 129 in their second innings. After this crushing reverse in fortunes, England lost all hope, it seemed, and were trounced 5-0 in the series.

Forfeiting an innings

Sometimes you may hear about a first class cricket match in which both teams choose to *forfeit* an innings. What happens is that the two captains agree to declare an innings each; thereby, in effect, reducing the match to one rather than the standard two innings. Forfeiture doesn't take place because both teams are bone idle. Instead, rain or bad light has usually taken time out of the game, but both captains still want the chance to win the match.

Looking At One-Day Captaincy

In one-day cricket, a match can be won without dismissing any of the opposition's batsmen – all you have to do is score more runs in the allotted number of overs. This emphasis on run-scoring and preventing the opposition from scoring runs is crucial to understanding one-day captaincy.

Some of the special tactics that are used in one-day cricket include:

- **Employing pinch hitters:** Some captains promote a player who is good at playing aggressive shots in order to exploit the fact that under one-day cricket law fielding captains have to have most of their fielders within 30 yards of the batsmen during the 10 overs of the innings; followed by another 10 overs later in the innings in two batches of five each selected by the batting and bowling captains. See Chapter 3 for more on one-day matches and these 10 'powerplay overs'.

- **Using more defensive field placing:** Because the emphasis on the fielding captain is to prevent the batsmen from scoring runs, captains often deploy more defensive run saving fields. In short, this means most of the players are located near the boundary but this is all subject to the one-day fielding restrictions laws. See the section 'Understanding one-day fielding restrictions' later in this chapter for more.

- **Rotating the bowlers:** In one-day matches a limit is put on the number of overs any single bowler can bowl in the innings. For example, in a 50 over match each bowler is limited to bowling 10 overs. This means the captain has to be canny, getting his best bowlers bowling at the right time in the opposition innings. In cricket speak this is called *rotating the bowlers*.

Organising the bowling

Usually, the best swing or seam bowler in the team bowls some of his allotted overs at the start of an innings when the ball is newest and most likely to move off the seam. The ace bowler then returns in the final few overs of the innings when the opposition batsmen are going for their shots. The idea is that the bowler has the skill to counter the batsmen's attack by ensuring deliveries are directed at the stumps and are difficult to score runs off.

For years, one of the best bowlers in one-day cricket has been Pakistan's Umar Gul. He was particularly adept at bowling at the end of the innings, often referred to as the *death*, and very skilled in varying the pace of his deliveries to bamboozle the batsmen and bowling directly at the stumps. The idea, as with all bowling, is to restrict runs and take wickets.

In one-day cricket umpires tend to interpret the wide rule very strictly. Refer to Chapter 2 for more on this rule. If the bowler delivers the ball outside the leg stump and the batsman fails to hit it then the umpire calls the ball wide. This means that the batting side gets a run added to their total and the ball has to be re-bowled. Understandably, fielding captains urge their bowlers not to deliver the ball down the batsman's leg side in one-day cricket.

Although getting batsmen out is not as crucial in one-day cricket as in other forms of cricket, dismissing the opposition can have a profound effect on the result of a one-day match. Dismissing a batsman means that a new player comes out to bat. This player may not find it easy to play aggressive shots straight away: Therefore, the rate of run-scoring slows. All in all, dismissing batsmen is a pretty sure fire way to slow the scoring rate of the batting side.

In professional one-day cricket the cricket ball used is white rather than red so that it can be more easily seen by players and spectators when floodlighting is used. For some strange reason – no-one quite knows why – a white coloured cricket ball tends to swing more in the air than a red one! In addition, a recent law change means in one-day international 50-over matches two new balls per innings are used.

Understanding one-day fielding restrictions

In order to stop fielding captains from putting all their fielders on the boundary from the start of the batting side's innings, one-day fielding restrictions were introduced.

These rules restrict the fielding captains to keeping nine fielders – including the bowler and wicket-keeper – within a 30 yard circle of the batsmen for a specified number of overs. The number of overs for which the restriction applies depends on the competition, but generally varies between 6 and 20 overs. The circle is marked by white markers or a whitewashed line on the pitch.

Often you find that batting sides go on the attack during the first 10 overs, looking to hit the ball over the fielders' heads to the boundary.

The first 10 overs of an innings in international one-day cricket use this *powerplay* system.. Basically, after the first 15 overs have elapsed, both the fielding and batting sides have the option to call an additional powerplay, which in essence reimposes the fielding restrictions which were in place in the first 10 over of the innings. Each separate powerplay lasts for 5 overs. But it's up to the captain's discretion when, after the fifteenth over, to call a powerplay, just as long as he does once before the start of the 41st over of the innings. A powerplay called by the fielding team is called a *fielding powerplay* and by the batting team – yes, you guessed it – a *batting powerplay*.

For example, after 15 overs of team A's innings have elapsed, the fielding captain of team B has to decide whether or not to call a powerplay. If he chooses to do so the fielding restrictions remain in place for another 5 overs. If he chooses to wait to call a powerplay, he has the advantage of spreading the field for while but is potentially storing up trouble for himself because he must opt for a powerplay by the start of the 40th over of the innings. Meanwhile, the captain of team A, which is batting, has his or her own powerplay to call, The captains of the batting and bowling teams cannot call powerplays at the same time: They have to be called separately. In a 50 over innings, therefore, the number of mandatory powerplay overs is actually 20. The idea of all these powerplays is to increase the number of tactical decisions the captain's have to make during a game, adding some excitement to proceedings for spectators.

In a game format in which the way to win is to score the highest number of runs, a powerplay, when it was originally designed was seen as disadvantageous to the fielding side. After all, a powerplay means that fewer fielders are allowed to be located on the boundary stopping the ball. But the experience has been different, with the need to have more fielders close to the bat often actually leading to more catches being taken and the batting team being brought under pressure.

Fielding captains look to call a powerplay when they feel they are on top of the batting side; for example, after they have dismissed a batsman. On the flip side, batting captains tend to call their powerplay when there are two batsman who have been at the wicket for a while or when a very aggressive batsman has just come into bat – the idea being to capitalise on the large open spaces in the field to score more runs.

Fielding restrictions apply in twenty20 one-day matches but the restrictions are in place for fewer overs – just 6. Refer to Chapter 3 for more on the ins and outs of twenty20 cricket.

If there is rain or bad light the number of overs in a one-day match are likely to be cut in order that the game can be finished in reasonable time. No one wants to play through the night, after all, unless the match is scheduled to be played under floodlights. If the overs are cut then the umpires will also reduce the number of powerplay overs by a pro rata amount. So, for example, if a 50 over match is cut to 30 overs each because of rain, equivalent to a reduction of 40 per cent, then the number of total powerplay overs – the initial field-restricted overs plus the batting and bowling powerplays – will also be cut by 40 per cent, from 20 to 12.

Deploying winning psychology

Mike Brearley was probably England's greatest ever test cricket captain. He had huge success in the late 1970s, winning two successive Ashes series against Australia. He wasn't a great player but as the former Australian captain Ian Chappell said, Brearley had 'a degree in people'. Good cricket captaincy is a bit like taking a crash course in psychology. Here are some tips on handling a team should you be lucky enough to get the chance:

✔ **Keep a little distance from the team:** Team captains have to make tough calls, such as dropping a player from the team. If they are all pally-pally with the rest of the team this can be harder to do. However, a captain shouldn't be so stand-offish that he's unapproachable and isolated.

✔ **Build confidence when necessary:** Sports people suffer doubts and occasionally they need to be told how good they are. On the flip-side, over confidence and complacency can lead to team underperformance; a few well-chosen words from the captain to the troops can build confidence and put complacency to sleep.

✔ **Offer constructive criticism:** Players and the team should have feedback on their performance. This feedback should be balanced and have positive and negative elements as well as an indication of areas of performance improvement. Launching into a critique of a team's performance in the dressing-room after a defeat is not always a bright idea. Emotions run high following a match – just let your feelings be known to the team in the days following the game.

✔ **Harness the power of team-mates:** No man is an island – no matter what his waist size! Good captains ask for tactical advice from their players – particularly those with lots of experience. But bear in mind, ultimately a decision has to be the captain's call.

Chapter 9

Talented Training and Cricket Coaching

. . . .

. . . .

*W*hen the famous South African golfer Gary Player was accused of being lucky on one occasion, he replied 'You know, the more I practise the luckier I get.'

I know that Mr Player was a golfer but his knowing maxim that high performance follows dedicated practice applies just as well to cricket.

In this chapter, I look at some of the basic drills to follow in order to hone your cricketing skills and boost your fitness levels.

Improving Your Fitness and Cricket Skills

People sometimes scoff when they are told that playing cricket requires physical fitness. No doubt they think that the most physically demanding thing a cricketer does is lift a cucumber sandwich on to their plate at the tea interval. True, being fit enough to deal with the demands of a good cricket tea can be a tough task – all those sandwiches, sausage rolls and pieces of cake. But turn on the telly and watch any game of cricket and you soon see that the modern cricketer is an athlete. The only six-pack they come into contact with is in their abdomen, not nicely chilled in the dressing room fridge!

Being physically fit can improve your cricket game in many ways:

- ✔ **Increased mobility:** The fitter you are, the quicker your reactions are. Quicker reactions improve your ability to move your body into the right position to execute a scoring shot or, when you're fielding, stop the ball.

- ✔ **Sharper mental approach:** The fact is well-known that the more tired you are, the less able you are to concentrate. Above all else, whether you're batting, bowling or fielding, cricket requires concentration. Every delivery is a match unto itself and you have a chance to influence its course. Ever heard the phrase healthy body, healthy mind?

- ✔ **Brute force:** If you're physically stronger, you can hit the cricket ball harder and farther, and deliver it faster when you're bowling.

As for developing your cricketing skills, you could just trust to raw talent. But unless you're exceptionally gifted, trusting to raw talent isn't going to get you very far. The history of cricket is chock-full of good players who became great players through dedicated practice.

Getting Match Fit

For the amateur, cricket is an incredibly time-consuming game – playing a match takes up most of a day and if you're working that's a big chunk out of your leisure time. And yet many club cricketers don't practise their game. If they're willing to invest so much of their free time playing the game why not invest just a little more to hone their skills? After all a match situation can be an unforgiving environment – even at club level – and not a good time for a spin bowler to perfect a new type of delivery or a batsman to play a shot he's never practised before.

 Give yourself the best possible chance of being good at cricket by becoming physically fit and practising your cricketing skills. Focus your cricket exercise regime on the four areas highlighted in Table 9-1.

Table 9-1	Cricket Fitness	
Type of Training	*What it Helps With*	*Possible Exercise*
Building upper-body strength.	Helps you hit the ball farther, bowl it quicker, and throw at the stumps with greater venom.	Free-weight training and resistance. Rowing.
Endurance training.	Stops you getting tired and aids concentration.	Long runs, cycle rides and gym step exercises.

Type of Training	What it Helps With	Possible Exercise
Explosive pace.	Allows you to run quickly between the stumps and chase down a cricket ball at pace. Bowlers can benefit as high levels of endurance help them to bowl more overs without tiring.	Short intense sprinting and spin cycle classes.
Flexibility.	Helps you get your body into position to play the right scoring shots, bowl, or stop the cricket ball when fielding. Also helps to prevent injury.	Yoga, Pilates (a variant of Yoga) and stretches.

Tiredness is one of the chief reasons why a bowler loses crucial accuracy. In addition, unfit batsmen tire more easily which in turn makes them more prone to making mistakes. Such mistakes can lead to dismissal.

A cricket pitch is 22 yards in length, so if you run down it a hundred times when batting, you cover the equivalent of 2,200 yards or 2 kilometres – all wearing padding, helmet and carrying a bat!

The faster and harder you run between the stumps, the more you can pressure the fielders into making mistakes, such as fumbling the ball, allowing greater opportunity to score more runs.

When batting to a spin bowler, advance to where the ball pitches so you can play your shot before the ball has the chance to spin off the wicket. You need to be pretty fleet of foot to move even such a short distance in the second it takes the ball to leave the bowler's hand and pitch on the wicket.

The exercises I outline in Table 9-1 are for guidance only. You should talk to your doctor before undertaking any rigorous exercise regime.

Before leaving the pavilion at the start of the match, and again before batting, spend a minute or two doing some stretching exercises. Stretching can stop you pulling a muscle. See the section 'Explaining Stretching' later in this chapter for more on stretching exercises.

In recent years, personal trainers have started appearing in gyms the length and breadth of the country. These super-fit and rather sickeningly well-toned individuals can design special training programmes which build strength, aid endurance and quicken the pace at which you move. They often also help you with diet advice. A personal trainer can set you back anything from £35–60 an hour but can be money well spent if you want to get fit for cricket.

The wicket-keeper is probably the most physically demanding of all fielding positions. A keeper crouches before every delivery bowled and has to be alert and fit enough to collect balls thrown to him by the fielders. The watchwords with keeping wicket are endurance and flexibility. Because of all the crouching they do, wicket-keepers are prone to bad backs. Stretching exercises, as outlined in the section 'Explaining Stretching' later in this chapter, can help.

Honing Your Technique in the Nets

In this section I introduce you to the concept of *net* practice. The nets are either fenced-off areas indoors or a specially prepared wicket outdoors where bowlers try to hone their bowling skills – and batsmen look to improve their defensive and attacking shots. They are called 'nets' simply because they are usually fenced in by netting.

Most players like nets because they:

- ✔ Provide practice sessions, in which players are free to make mistakes.
- ✔ Give an opportunity for coaches to see players' techniques and correct problems before they lead to potentially costly technical faults.
- ✔ Give batsmen an opportunity to get used to different types of bowling.
- ✔ Give bowlers an opportunity to bowl to both right-hand and left-handed batsmen.
- ✔ Can help develop something called *muscle memory* (in short, training the muscles to perform certain actions automatically without having to think about it). Batting involves co-ordinating the hand, eye and feet movements – nets can help make playing shots almost second nature. Likewise, bowlers can get used to bowling the ball on a particular spot on the wicket.
- ✔ Can be a good social occasion: In club cricket, most net sessions are followed up by a night in the bar!

Most professional cricketers have a net practice every day during the cricket season – which runs from April to September in the UK. Club cricketers, though, have day jobs – although of course most would rather be playing cricket – so you find most clubs run nets after work one or two days a week. When you first join a cricket club you're likely to be invited to a net where senior players will look at your ability before offering you a place in their team.

Some players treat nets very seriously: In the same way as some golfers need to spend time hitting drives before a big tournament, batsmen like to hit deliveries. On the other hand some players hate nets: They see the whole scenario as artificial, preferring to hone their skills in a match situation, when the adrenaline is pumping. In my experience of 20 years of club cricket, the former attitude to nets is usually the more successful.

Giving your batting a boost

A batsman only needs to make one mistake to find himself dismissed. This tightrope walker existence makes it crucial for a batsman to practise. The best way to practise is in the nets. Here are some tips for effective net practice:

✔ **Practise regularly:** Go to the nets at least once a week during the season. Regular practice helps build up muscle memory and aids footwork; it can also make you more confident.

✔ **Take practice seriously:** One of the keys to good batting is having sound judgement – when to play and when not to play a delivery. Use nets to hone your judgement. When a ball is delivered in the nets try to play that delivery in the same way that you would in a match situation. In addition, make sure that you take the same guard at the wicket as you would in a match. Refer to Chapter 5 for all you need to know about taking guard.

✔ **Work on your weaknesses:** If you are unhappy with a particular aspect of your batting, use nets as an opportunity to confront problems head-on. For example, you may not be happy playing spin bowling. If that's the case, make sure that you practise against spin bowling in the nets.

In the UK the cricket season is relatively short – only running from April to September – the rest of the time is called the *off season*. Many cricket clubs run off season net practice. Because of bad weather, these off-season net sessions are usually held indoors.

All players need to have some basic batting techniques off-pat if they want to succeed, including:

✔ **Taking a comfortable stance while facing the bowling.** Check out Chapter 5 for more on your batting stance.

• Stand at the crease with your feet a shoulder-width apart. In other words your feet should be parallel to your shoulders.

• Stand side-on, with your left shoulder pointing down the wicket at the bowler. (Reverse the stance if you are left-handed.)

- Ensure the eyes are level and facing the place from which the bowler is delivering the ball.

- Keep the knees a little bent, to aid flexibility.

✔ **Maintaining good balance at the crease.** Cricket is a game of fast reactions and being well-balanced means that you can turn these reactions into a shot in the blink of an eye!

- Have your weight evenly distributed between your front and back feet.

- Be on the balls of your feet. This allows you to move more quickly to the delivery to play a shot.

✔ **Being able to execute a backlift.** The backlift is the movement the batsman makes with the hands to propel the bat towards the ball.

- In order to get power and timing into the shot, lift the bat high behind your back so as to bring it back down in a pendulum action to meet the ball when it reaches you.

- Keep your head still throughout the backlift: Doing so helps you retain your balance. Failing to keep your head still can result in losing your balance which makes it harder for you to hit the ball.

- Keep the hands holding the bat close to the body during the backlift, to help ensure that the backlift is straight.

- At the top of the backlift the bat should be pointing around off stump. If the bat is pointed well away from off stump then the backlift isn't straight and your chances of connecting with the ball are reduced.

Taking Giant Steps Forward with Your Bowling

Bowlers are a little more fortunate than batsmen. If a bowler makes a mistake in a match and delivers a ball that is easy to hit, he gets another chance with the next delivery to dismiss the batsman and therefore redeem himself and snatch the glory. But this comfort zone doesn't last for long. If a bowler bowls poorly then, sooner rather than later, the team captain will replace the bowler with another one.

In truth, bowlers have to work at their game as hard – if not harder – than batsmen. The hard work is necessary because good bowling is all about rhythm – nothing Latin-American, but instead the ability to repeat the same action of delivering the ball out of the hands, time after time.

Key areas for bowlers to work on in net practice include:

- **Developing a run-up to the wicket:** A good way to practise is to start the run-up from the crease, heading away from the wicket. When it feels right, leap as if you're going to deliver the ball. Start your run-up in future at the point at which you leaped – this time towards the batsman. Don't forget to mark where your run-up should start.

- **Remembering to keep your head still:** Keeping your head steady and eyes still from the start of the run-up to delivery helps you direct the ball where you want it to go.

- **Concentrating on keeping the arms in close:** Keeping your arms close to your body as you run-up to the wicket to bowl helps you go through your bowling action smoothly, aiming the ball accurately. See Chapter 6 for more on the run-up.

- **Deciding how you are going to grip the ball:** Where you grip the ball across its seam has a crucial influence on how the ball behaves once it leaves your hand, whether in the air or once it bounces off the wicket. Refer to Chapter 6 for the different grips and their effects.

By all means use net practice as an opportunity to build greater variety into your bowling. Experiment with different ways of gripping the ball and angles of delivery. After you get something right in practice, you can try it out in a match. However, using the nets to master a stock ball (that you can use as a standard delivery) is also important in order to develop consistency.

Bowlers don't aim at the batsman. Instead, they usually try to make the ball bounce off an area of the wicket which makes it hard for the batsman to play an aggressive shot and heightens the chances of hitting the edge of the batsman's bat. Check out Chapter 6 for more on the areas of the wicket you should be aiming at to put the batsman in trouble.

One great way of building bowling accuracy is to put a marker, such as a handkerchief, on the area of the wicket you're aiming at. You're not allowed to use markers in match situations but you can use them in net practice.

You can break down the process of delivering a cricket ball into three phases:

- Running up to the wicket
- Jumping into a delivery stride and delivering the ball
- Following through

Refer to Chapter 6 for more on how to bowl.

Cricket is a game that requires good hand–eye co-ordination. Of course, good hand–eye co-ordination can be a natural talent but it can also be improved. Try playing a range of sports that develop hand–eye co-ordination such as golf, squash and tennis. The fact that top international cricketers are quite often excellent golfers is no coincidence!

Here are some basic drills that you can coach others to use, or use yourself, to help develop and refresh bowling skills.

- **One pace and bowl:** Perform this drill while stationary: no need for a run-up. If you're right-handed the ball should be in your right hand. Stand side-on – which means your left shoulder and head are pointed down the wicket at where the batsman is standing. Spread your feet about 50 to 60 centimetres apart – like a soldier at stand easy. Younger, smaller players should have their feet slightly closer together. The hand holding the ball goes down towards the knees – this action automatically brings the left arm upwards as a counterweight – then starts to rise in a windmill-like fashion until the right arm brushes past the ear when the ball is released towards the batsman. All the time the weight of the body is transferring from the right to the left foot. This drill perfects the basic technique of bowling a cricket ball.

- **The gather and explode drill:** Again you have no run-up to worry about in this drill. Instead you are trying to inject more momentum than with the 'one pace and bowl' drill. Stand with your feet together and your hands close to your chest. Now raise your left knee up close to your body (if you're holding the ball with your right hand) and step forwards. As you do this, the hand holding the ball should go straight out back and away from your chest, while your other arm, acting as a counterweight, should fly out in the opposite direction. This position is called the *gather* but you don't have time to think about that. The final stage is to bring the hand holding the ball over, past your ear and release – called *the explode* in coaching circles.

- **Run-up and bowl drill:** Stand about five paces from where you plan to release the ball. Step forward with your left leg, then with the right and again with the left. The next step is when your right leg plants itself in position and your left leg swings slightly across your body, so that the left foot lands in line with the right foot. The right hand holding the ball should go straight out back and away from your chest, while the left as a counterweight is high in the air. From here on in you simply bring the hand holding the ball past your ear as straight as possible and release. Automatically you will go into a *follow through*. Your right hand and arm, after the ball is released, swings across your body towards your left side and your left arm flies up above your head.

All these drills presume a right-handed bowler. If you're a leftie, simply reverse the drill.

Looking at Fielding Drills

The basics of fielding – how to catch, collect and throw the ball – are covered extensively in Chapter 7. But here are some drills you can practise on your own or coach others to help hone those fielding skills:

- **Improving your throwing arm:** Two players stand about 20 metres apart and throw the ball to each other. The players aim for the ball to bounce a few metres in front of each other.

- **Perfecting underarm throwing:** A group of players, ideally no fewer than four, form up in the outfield about 15 metres away from a set of stumps. Behind the stumps a player stands acting as wicket-keeper. Another player – standing near the stumps but not between the stumps and the players in the outfield – hits a ball with a bat into the outfield. Each player takes his turn to chase down the ball, collect it and throw it in underarm at the stumps; the wicket-keeper is there to stop the ball should the fielder miss. The wicket-keeper then chucks the ball to the player holding the bat, and that player then propels the ball back into the outfield for the next fielder to chase.

- **Practising slip catching:** One player throws the ball to a player holding a bat. The player with the bat, by turning the wrist at impact, then guides the ball to three or four fielders standing a couple of metres apart in the position of slip fielders. The idea is to replicate a slip catch in a match situation.

Try to attack the ball when fielding. Run as hard as you can to the ball, keeping your eye on it to ensure you collect it safely, and then throw the ball to the wicket-keeper. However, a smart play is sometimes to aim at the end of the wicket where the bowler is standing; doing so may give you a better chance of a run-out.

Wicket-keeping is a very specialist skill and takes years of practice. Wicket-keeping is looked at in greater depth in Chapter 7. Wicket-keepers benefit enormously from taking part in fielding drills. In many respects, wicket-keepers have to be the most flexible players in the team. That's why, if you watch a successful proponent of the art like England's Matt Prior, he is always bending and stretching between deliveries. The idea is to stay warm and loose, so that when he needs to spring for a catch or to stop a ball he can with ease and without fear of injury.

One way of sharpening your wicket-keeping skills is to practise in the nets. When the bowler is bowling to the batsman in the nets, go and keep wicket as you would in a match situation. However, don't do this to fast bowling because practice nets aren't long enough to give you a chance to react to the ball after it passes the batsman's bat. Ensure that you wear a helmet and protective padding – including leg pads, chest protector and a box – before wicket-keeping in the nets. Refer to Chapter 4 for more on cricket equipment.

Explaining Stretching

The game of cricket could almost be designed to cause muscle tears and hamstring pulls. Think about it: Cricket involves long periods of inactivity – such as sitting in the pavilion waiting to bat – followed by sudden bursts of physical exertion.

Therefore, warming up and stretching exercises are very important.

Warming up

Warming-up can be any moderately taxing physical activity such as jogging for 5–10 minutes. Professionals, though, will warm up for longer as the demands on their body are likely to be higher during the match.

You should stretch:

- Before play starts
- Before leaving the pavilion to bat
- A few minutes before starting to bowl
- Intermittently while in the field

The captain should tell you a few minutes in advance that he expects you to bowl. The message may come with a shout from the captain – typically 'Loosening-up' – or, alternatively, the captain may catch your eye and roll his arms about, mimicking a bowling action. Whatever method of communication is used, the captain wants you to stretch as he's likely to ask you to bowl soon.

Cricketers call warming-up and stretching exercises *loosening up*.

Cross training is becoming increasingly popular in professional cricket. In short, this means doing sports such as touch rugby or five-a-side football, which although not directly related to cricket, engage the interest of the player while exercising key muscle groups.

Looking at stretching exercises

Here are some basic stretches to get you flexible and fighting fit to do battle on the cricket pitch.

- ✔ **Flexing your back:** Lie on your back. Pull both knees to your chest. Now rock backwards and forwards with your chin tucked into your chest. Repeat a few times but hold the position for no longer than 10 seconds each time.

- ✔ **Stretching your hamstrings:** Lie on your back. Raise your left leg as straight as you can. Cup your hands behind your leg around the knee area, all the time keeping your right foot on the ground with your right knee bent. Hold this pose for 10 seconds and then switch legs and repeat.

- ✔ **Stretching your shoulders and triceps:** Place your left hand over your left shoulder and onto your back, with your elbow raised to meet your left ear. Now place your right hand on top of your left elbow and pull down the back. Hold this stretch for 10 seconds and switch to opposite arm and repeat.

- ✔ **Stretching your pectoral muscles:** Link your hands behind your back, ensuring your palms are facing upwards. Then push your hands down and back away from your body. You should feel a stretch in your pectoral muscles, which are located in your upper chest.

- ✔ **Stretching your upper arms:** Place your left arm across your body and over your right shoulder. Hold your left elbow with your right hand and pull the arm towards your chest. You should feel a stretch in your upper arm and across the shoulder. Hold this stretch for 10 seconds, then switch, placing your right arm across your body and repeat.

Executing stretching exercises incorrectly can be worse than not doing any stretches. Common errors that can lead to injury include hurrying through the stretch and making jerky, bouncing movements while undergoing a stretch.

Post-match warming-down exercises are very popular nowadays. In bygone days many cricketers' idea of post-match exercise was a pint of beer after the match. But the modern warm-down exercise involves stretches and gentle jogging. The idea is to prevent blood pooling in the limbs after intense periods of exercise. Blood pooling – as well as sounding gross – can lead to dizziness and a very melodramatic fainting fit.

Don't perform stretches while the bowler is delivering to the batsman. If the ball is hit to where you're fielding and you're busy stretching you're not going to be able to stop it; you can look a right charley in front of your team-mates!

How coaching transformed team England

From being an absolute shambles a decade or so ago the English cricket team now has the most advanced and progressive national coaching structure in place anywhere in the world. In fact the English system is so good that after the 2005 Ashes series, even members of the great Australian side said they could learn a thing or two from how cricket was run in good old blighty!

The keys to England's new found success are:

✔ **Specialist coaches:** The England cricket team now employs coaches who specialise in bowling, batting, fielding and wicketkeeping. The big idea is that no matter what skills the players have they can always call on the advice and support of a coach. Specialist dieticians and fitness experts have also been brought on board.

✔ **The academy:** Up-and-coming England cricketers have been sent to an academy in the winter in Australia to perfect their skills and their tans! An English Cricket Board (ECB) national cricket academy also exists at Loughborough University and many counties also have their own academies.

✔ **Central contracts:** England players used to be employed by their county clubs. This meant that when the players weren't playing for England they were slaving away for their counties. However, in 2000 central contracts were introduced. Under this arrangement a select band of England players are contracted to the ECB rather than the counties. The players play for their counties only when the ECB allows them to. This has helped combat player fatigue and reduced the incidence of injury amongst England players.

✔ **The Fletcher factor:** If one man has done more than anyone to oversee the transformation of the England cricket team, that man is Zimbabwe-born coach Duncan Fletcher. Fletcher set about putting in place a top-notch backroom coaching staff, central contracts, and helped with setting up the cricket academy. Although Fletcher resigned in 2007 his focus on supporting the players and working on the technical aspects of the game have been carried on by current coach and fellow Zimbabwean Andy Flower with considerable success.

Coaching Kids to Play Cricket

In order to ensure the future of the game of cricket, new talent is needed. In most cases this talent doesn't just arrive, but needs to be developed through coaching. Literally thousands of cricket coaches around the globe from Manchester to Mumbai are helping to show kids first how to play the game, and then how to play it well.

Coaches are the unsung heroes of cricket. If you want to join their ranks here's what you have to do:

✔ **Have a good understanding of the game:** You don't have to have been a top-notch professional cricketer but you should have a thorough knowledge of the laws of the game and match tactics. Kids are smart: They can spot waffle a mile off!

✔ **Practise good organisational skills:** Set a regular practice date and time and make sure that everyone is at the practice facilities promptly. This means telling both the youngsters and their parents. Break each practice session down to allow each player to bat, bowl and field.

✔ **Have plenty of spare time:** Coaching can be very time-consuming. Aim to be at the practice facilities well before the kids arrive in order to prepare. Preparation entails putting up netting, hammering the stumps into the wicket and ensuring that enough cricket balls are available. In addition, as your coaching duties expand, you may well find yourself organising colts' matches. Many coaches I know have in fact retired from their day job: You'll soon find your time filled up.

✔ **Take a flexible and innovative approach:** Ideally, you should try to vary practice sessions, perhaps from time-to-time spending a large chunk of the session on fielding or having an impromptu single-wicket competition, where players bat as pairs against their team-mates. When one batsman is dismissed he swaps places with a player who has been fielding; see the side-bar 'Making cricket fun' for more on how to throw a bit of fun into the mix.

✔ **Have patience in abundance:** The kids' skills aren't going to progress every time you see them. Sometimes you may find that they practise poorly or can't quite grasp something you're trying to show them. Never mind! Just keep plugging away. Patience is a virtue, particularly when it comes to coaching kids.

✔ **Apply a firm but friendly manner:** Kids are full of energy and tend to be a touch on the noisy side; sometimes for the good of the group and for health and safety reasons, you have to curb their enthusiasm. Firm but polite instruction from time to time doesn't go amiss, but don't become a sergeant-major and start bossing the kids around. They won't respond well. Don't talk for too long: Keep it short and keep to the point.

The best coaches are those who look to spend some time with every player no matter what their ability. If a youngster is ignored by a coach they quickly lose confidence, and with that interest, in the game.

For more on how to get involved in coaching youngsters, check out the England and Wales Cricket Board Web site at www.ecb.co.uk.

Encouraging all-round ability

If you're coaching youngsters try to encourage all-round cricketing ability. The youngster may show a preference for batting or bowling and that's great, but they have a better chance of succeeding if they develop skills in all aspects of the game.

Eventually the youngsters may decide on an area that they really want to focus on, such as spin bowling, but by giving them a wide range of skills you give them more options to choose from.

Don't fence off a player's cricketing options. Let the youngster make the decisions. Of course if they're really lucky then they may become good at both batting and bowling. This means they are an all-rounder, perhaps in the mould of England's Andrew Flintoff, and worth their weight in gold to any captain.

Safety is paramount in youth cricket. Parents trust their little treasures to the coach and he better look after them. A few years back wearing a protective helmet when batting became compulsory for every player under the age of 16 – check out to Chapter 4 on equipment for more. The only circumstance in which a player under 16 doesn't have to wear a helmet is when the parents sign a waiver.

Most coaches reckon that the key to coaching youngsters is to allow them to express themselves. If they want to run in and bowl fast or play aggressive shots in practice, allow them to do so. Trying to put a youngster in a straitjacket of cricket theory can damage their progress. Instead, look to introduce concepts to them gradually; such as the importance of being accurate when bowling and of playing defensive shots when they're warranted.

Michael Vaughan, the former England captain, has a very good piece of advice for all aspiring cricketers: Identify the parts of the game you are weakest at, and work to improve those. He says that if you only work on the bits of the game that you are good at – having lots of batting lessons when you have weaknesses as a fielder, say – then ultimately you will reach a plateau as a cricketer. 'Work hard on what you are good at, but harder at what you're not' is his mantra, and you'd be wise to follow it.

When coaching youngsters try to identify their stronger hand for batting and bowling. Get them to practise using the stronger hand. By the way, the stronger hand for cricket isn't always the one they use to write or open doors with. You can find lots of cases of players batting left-handed but doing nearly everything else right-handed. The only way to tell is to observe which hand the youngster is favouring.

Understanding coaching qualifications

Nowadays, having a cricket coaching qualification is all the rage. Many clubs now pay for members who show an interest in coaching cricket to go on an England Cricket Board (ECB) coaches' course. At these courses, prospective coaches are taught practice drills to develop player skills as well as basic health and safety.

Making cricket fun

Kids usually don't concentrate well – apart from when Playstation is involved – and cricket coaches have come to realise that plunging them into long games of cricket, spanning the best part of a day, is a sure-fire way to turn them off the sport for good. So in lots of schools and clubs, single wicket games have sprung up. This means that no 'teams' as such are involved, just a batsman, a bowler and fielders. When the batsman is dismissed he is replaced by one of the fielders as is the bowler. Now before you cast your eyes heavenwards at the idea of there being no teams, single wicket competitions have nothing to do with political correctness. In fact, they can be very competitive because all the players are itching to do their best and impress their mates.

Another popular innovation has been kwik cricket. Using soft balls and brightly coloured bats and stumps, the idea of kwik cricket is that a game can be played on virtually any patch of green space – you don't need a proper cricket wicket – with no fear of the ball damaging the youngsters or nearby property. Yet kwik cricket is authentic enough to allow youngsters to develop their bowling and batting skills. If you go and watch a test match in England don't just head off to the bar at lunchtime – stay in your seat and you'll probably be treated to the spectacle of a game of kwik cricket played by the boys and girls from local schools. Watch one of these matches and you soon realise that plenty of talented youngsters are out there developing a love of cricket!

ECB coaching qualifications come in four different grades:

- **ECB Coaching Assistant:** The first step on the coaching ladder, this course qualifies candidates to assist more qualified coaches.

- **ECB Coach:** This individual is able to deliver comprehensive coaching sessions to people of all ages and abilities. Most coaches stop at this stage.

- **ECB Head Coach:** Candidates are trained to plan, implement and revise annual training programmes. This grade is near the top of the tree as far as coaching is concerned.

- **ECB Master Coach:** This grade is the crème de la crème of coaching. A master coach is able to design, implement, and evaluate the process and outcome of long-term coaching programmes.

People looking to umpire can also go on ECB-sponsored training courses and receive accreditation. For more on umpiring courses check out www.ecb.co.uk or call 0121 440 1748.

Getting your son or daughter involved

Many of us would love our kids to become sporting stars. Unfortunately, professional cricket isn't the best paid of sports – closer to international tiddlywinks than top golfer in the pay stakes, I'm afraid – but ask most pro cricketers whether they'd rather have played any other sport and they say no – the job satisfaction is enormous.

So how can you get your little 'uns interested in playing cricket seriously?

- ✔ **Encourage enthusiasm:** Cricket is on our television screens a lot during the summer and you have lots of live games you can take youngsters along to, often for free or for a nominal charge. See Chapter 13 for more on being a cricket fan.

- ✔ **Find out what the school has to offer:** If your child shows a desire to play, you could send them to a school that has cricket in the sporting curriculum. Many independent schools have good cricketing facilities, equipment, and teachers well-versed in the skills of the game. Unfortunately cricket is virtually dead in state schools. Many hard-pressed state schools have sold off their playing fields and if cricket needs one thing, it's lots of open space.

- ✔ **Seek out your local cricket clubs:** Cricket clubs have taken up a lot of the slack of showing youngsters how to play the game. Dotted up and down the country, many clubs have volunteers who dedicate their time to running practice sessions and organising matches for younger players. The club cricket conferences have details of your local cricket clubs; check out their Web site at www.club-cricket.com.

In recent years, clubs have come on leaps in bounds in the way they approach young players. However, some clubs are better than others at catering for young players. Scan the local newspaper to see which club's matches are reported. Doing so gives you an idea of which local clubs have the most members and so are more likely to have youth sections. Also, before sending your child along call the secretary of the club and ask about what the club offers young players. Do they have a practice night dedicated to young cricketers, for example, and do they have an ECB-qualified coach at the club?

Watching heroic cricketing deeds gets youngsters hooked on the game. My love for the game was ignited by watching great players like England's Ian Botham and David Gower and West Indian batsman Vivian Richards put bowling to the sword in the late seventies and early eighties.

Taking it to another level: Colt cricket

If your son or daughter takes to cricket like a duck to water, you may want to get them involved in club *colt* cricket.

In colt cricket youngsters are divided into teams according to their age, and play matches against youngsters from other clubs who fall into the same age ranges.

In England, officials from professional county clubs scout colt cricket. Usually, the head coach of a colt team alerts the county to the fact that a promising young player is in the ranks. All going well, the youngster is then invited to practise and receive coaching at the county club. These tentative steps may be the first on the road to a cricketing career.

How some top players discovered the skills of the game

Donald Bradman was indisputably the greatest batsman of all time (see Chapter 14 for my top ten cricketers) famed for his hand-eye co-ordination. Part of the reason for Bradman's genius was that he spent hour upon hour in his youth hitting a golf ball against a wall in his back yard using only a tiny piece of wood as a bat – well, he did live in an Australian country town just after the First World War and there wasn't much else to do!

The Chappell brothers – Ian, Greg and Trevor – endured a more painful practice regime. Their father regularly bowled a cricket ball at them in the back garden, but the young Chappells weren't allowed by their dad to wear pads on their legs; so if they missed the ball with their bats the ball would more than likely hit their unprotected legs – ouch! The bruises must have been worth it, though; Ian and Greg Chappell became two of the best Australian batsman of all time and Trevor also played test cricket for Australia.

Part III
Welcome to Planet Cricket

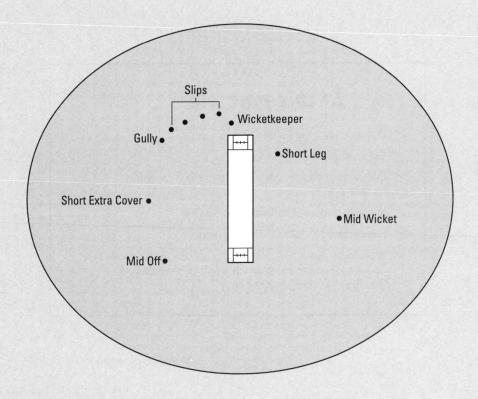

Go to www.dummies.com/extras/cricket for online bonus content.

In this part . . .

✔ Understanding the Ashes.

✔ Grasping global cricket rivalries.

✔ Coming to grips with the major international one-day tournaments.

✔ Immersing yourself in the domestic game.

✔ Knowing what it takes to become a fan.

✔ Go to www.dummies.com/extras/cricket for online bonus content, including an extra Part of Tens chapter: 'Ten Great Cricket Controversies'.

Chapter 10

Grasping the Global Rivalries

Cricket may not have the worldwide appeal of football, yet it can still lay a claim to be a major world sport. Not only is cricket the national summer sport of England and Australia, but it also has huge appeal throughout south Asia. Virtually every day of the year a test match takes place somewhere around the world, from Brisbane to Birmingham, and someone, somewhere is donning white clothing and strapping on the batting pads as you read this. With the advent of satellite television and YouTube you can sometimes even watch cricket 24/7. I know: I've done it!

In this chapter, I examine the history of cricket and some of the great players who spread the game's popularity far and wide.

In addition, I look at each of the ten test-playing nations in turn, explaining what makes them unique, and to top it all I take a peek at some of the great cricket stadia from around the world.

If you want the low-down on what makes test cricket special, this chapter is for you.

Exploring the History of Cricket

Cricket has more history than you can shake a stick at. Literally thousands of books have been written about every aspect of the game's history, all chock-full of stats. In this section I discuss some of cricket's landmarks.

From earliest times to test cricket

Pinpointing when cricket was first played is difficult. No cave drawings exist of prehistoric men playing an impromptu game of cricket to celebrate a particularly noble kill, nor cartouches of Egyptian pharaohs donning cricket whites and carrying bats. For the first mention of cricket – or 'creckett' as it was then called – you have to go way back to 1597, when records refer to boys in Guildford, Surrey, playing an early form of the game. Later on, in the seventeenth century, this time in Kent, one unfortunate bloke was recorded as having been killed after being hit over the head by a 'cricket staff' or 'cricket batt'.

However, it isn't until the eighteenth century that regular mentions of cricket start to crop up. In 1709 the first game between two English county sides, Kent and Surrey, took place, and in 1744 the first set of laws of the game were drawn up – surprise, surprise – in a pub!

For the next century or so cricket was mostly played by club sides and in public schools. The sport spread along with the British Empire to cover huge swathes of the globe and great stadia started to be built in England and Australia. Eventually, cricketers thought they may as well get a move on and bring global rivalries to the fore. The first test match was played in 1877 between England and Australia at the Melbourne Cricket Ground.

The 'Golden Age'

Cricket historians often talk about the 'golden age'. This was the period from around the end of the nineteenth century up to the outbreak of the First World War, when international and county matches were dominated by larger-than-life characters, members of the aristocracy and even the odd Indian prince. Back then there were more titles in a cricket team than on the shelves of a library. During this golden age, when the sun always seemed to shine, batsmen played with bravado and derring-do, hitting the bowling to all parts of the field. See the sidebar for more on two larger-than-life figures, WG Grace and CB Fry, from the golden age.

The good doctor and the would-be king of Albania

If two figures encapsulate the golden age of cricket, they are Dr WG Grace and CB Fry.

Dr William Gilbert Grace was the most famous cricketer of his time. He was instantly recognisable with a huge, bushy, black beard and in later years a hefty paunch. However, in his younger days he was a superb athlete. When just 18 years old he scored a huge 224 not out for All England against the county of Surrey and if that wasn't enough during the match he slipped off to win a 440 yard hurdles championship at Crystal Palace.

In a career spanning 43 years, Grace set cricketing records galore. He was the first player to score 100 centuries and to take 2,000 wickets in first class cricket. He scored the first test century by an Englishman.

Stories about Grace are legion. Probably the most legendary tale relates to a match at the Oval. In front of a packed crowd, Grace was bowled by a delivery. The crowd went silent and Grace simply picked up the bails, put them back on top of the stumps and told the bowler that the crowd 'have come here to watch me bat, not you bowl'. Such was the esteem that the good Doctor was held in, he apparently got away with it!

CB Fry was a true Boys Own hero. A first class honours graduate in something called Classical Moderations at Oxford, Charles Fry represented the university at cricket, soccer and athletics. As well as scoring over 30,000 runs in first class cricket and playing test cricket for England 22 times, Fry found time to equal the world long-jump record, play soccer for England, and edit a newspaper. All in a day's work, old chap!

He was deemed such a good egg that after the First World War, he was offered the throne of Albania, which he refused. But he did get to represent India at the League of Nations, the forerunner of the United Nations.

The golden age of cricket was associated with great batting feats. Back in those days, batting was considered a gentlemanly pursuit while bowling was seen as more, well, working-class. That's not to say, though, that there weren't star bowlers during this golden age, such as F. Spofforth and Wilfred Rhodes.

The Bradman years

The most fitting tribute to the genius of Australian batsman Don Bradman is that he gets a whole age of cricket named after him. But credit where credit is due, Bradman dominated test cricket from the late 1920s to the outbreak of the Second World War, scoring centuries galore. His effectiveness caused England to adopt the very controversial 'bodyline' tactics when touring Australia in 1932–33, see Chapter 17 for more on cricket's great controversies. What's more, after the war, Bradman carried on in the same way, putting bowling to the sword, until to the relief of bowlers around the globe he retired in 1948.

The Packer revolution

In the mid 1970s the staid world of cricket was rocked to its very foundations when an Australian TV mogul Kerry Packer signed up the world's best cricketers to play in a series of televised matches in Australia, dubbed super tests. Great players from the West Indies, England and Australia turned their backs on test cricket to play super tests in return for extra money. Previously test players had been paid a pittance, but Packer promised proper financial rewards for player talent.

These super tests and floodlight day-night matches were highly innovative – for one thing they brought us the West Indies team playing in shocking Salmon pink clothing – popular with the crowds and the cricket played was of a very high standard.

The fuddy-duddy administrators of test cricket, after having originally banned the Packer cricketers, eventually woke-up and smelled the coffee. In a few years the Packer players were back playing test cricket – on much improved pay – and Kerry Packer was sold the rights to broadcast test cricket in Australia.

But the 'Bradman years' weren't all about the master Australian batsman. England had some top notch players who would have shone even more brightly if they hadn't been eclipsed a little by Bradman. Great players such as Harold Larwood (a super fast bowler) and master strokemaker Wally Hammond would have starred in any era of cricket. What's more, these years saw a big expansion of cricket with West Indies, New Zealand and India all starting to play test match cricket.

Steady as she goes

The 1950s and 1960s were a strange time for cricket. England and Australia kept drawing matches ad nauseam and several of the nations that had recently joined test cricket – New Zealand, India and Pakistan – were yet to find their feet against the big two, Australia and England. The Australians were probably the best side in the world at the time – by a whisker. Through the inspired leadership of leg spin bowler Richie Benaud and fast bowling skills of Graham McKenzie and Alan Davidson Australia managed to keep ahead of the pack. But during this time successive West Indian teams were also making their mark as did teams from South Africa, particularly the side that whitewashed Australia in 1970, boasting great names such as Barry Richards, Graham Pollock, Eddie Barlow and Mike Proctor. Soon afterwards, though, South Africa was sent into sporting isolation due to apartheid. See Chapter 17 for more on the Basil D'Oliveira affair, which signalled the start of two decades in the wilderness for the Springboks (the former nickname of the South African cricket team).

Calypso cricket

West Indies carried all before them in the late 1970s, 1980s and into the early 1990s, thanks to the tactic of deploying four fast bowlers. Opposition teams just couldn't cope with the accuracy and pace of the bowling. They also had great batsmen like Clive Lloyd, Vivian Richards and Gordon Greenidge to turn the screw on the opposition bowlers.

However, not everyone welcomed the West Indies' tactics. Because bowling quickly requires long run-ups the West Indies took forever to complete their overs. Consequently the average number of runs scored in a day fell sharply and the crowds were turned off the game. See the section on the West Indies later in this chapter for more on the ups and recent downs of West Indian cricket.

The 'New Golden Age'

From the mid 1990s to the end of the first decade of the twenty-first century the Australians were firmly at the top of the cricketing tree again and they got there by playing wonderfully aggressive cricket. Australian batsmen consciously gone after the bowling, looking to score as fast as possible in order to leave themselves enough time in the game to bowl the opposition out twice and claim the win.

Other countries, particularly England and India, decided that if you can't beat them, join them, and started to play much more aggressively too. As a result, very few boring draws happen in test cricket any more, with most teams going for it hell for leather.

Some reckon that the past fifteen years have seen some of the best batting in the history of the game and the bowling wasn't bad either with great spinners like Australia's Shane Warne, India's Anil Kumble and Sri Lanka's Muttiah Muralitharan plying their trade.

Although the basics of cricket have not changed during its history, the laws of the game have evolved. The law-makers are not afraid to tinker with the game to improve it. For instance, umpires can now call for video replays of disputed catches, stumpings and run-outs. Cricket may have a stuffy, staid image but over the years the sport has proved surprisingly innovative and able to adapt to changing tastes and technology.

Jockeying for position: the 2010's

The relative decline of the great Australian cricket team from about 2005 onwards has given all the other test-playing nations the hope that they could, with a bit of hard work and skill, take the number one slot in international cricket. India, South Africa and England have all made it to the top of the test match rankings at some point in recent years, and such is the competitiveness in top-level cricket at the moment that surprise results and close fought series are the order of the day. There is at present no great team that has emerged to sweep all before it – like the West Indies in the 1970s and 1980s and Australians in the 1990s and 2000s – and this makes top level test and one day international cricket so fascinating to watch.

In many respects there has never been a better time to be a cricket fan!

Looking at the Test-Playing Nations

England gave the nations of the British Empire cricket, and these countries have been thanking them for it ever since by giving their old colonial masters some proper hidings at the game.

Ten nations have full test-playing status, which means that only matches between these ten countries are deemed to be test matches. These teams play each other home and away every few years.

Teams don't just meet to play one test match. Test nations compete in *series* of test matches. These series consist of between two and five test matches. The team winning the most test matches in the series is deemed to have won the series. See Chapter 3 for more on what constitutes a test match and makes them such red-letter occasions in the cricket calendar.

England and Australia

These countries are the two founding test nations and in terms of the number of test matches won they remain the most successful. They played their first test match in 1877. At different times in test cricket history one of these two nations has usually dominated the global game.

England had much the better of the first 25 years of test cricket, up to the First World War, thanks to a host of great players, such as WG Grace and Wilfred Rhodes.

Between the wars, Australia dominated thanks in large part to the emergence of the exceptionally talented batsman Don Bradman; see Chapter 14 for my all-time ten great cricketers.

After the war the balance of power swung to and fro with both sides having their heroes. Australia could boast great all rounders such as Richie Benaud and Keith Miller, while England could point to master batsmen such as Len Hutton, Peter May and Dennis Compton.

Just when it looked as if the England–Australia axis would dominate *ad infinitum* the great West Indies teams of the 1970s and 80s emerged.

The West Indies juggernaut put successive England and Australian teams to the sword.

But since the early 1990s normal service has been resumed with Australia in particular – buoyed up by the emergence of a great players such as Shane Warne, Glenn McGrath and Steve Waugh – beating all-comers. Of late, England too has been on the comeback trail – after a dreadful run of results in the 1980s and 1990s – culminating in the 2005, 2009 and 2011 test series victories over the old enemy, Australia.

Even today, with ten test-playing nations, Australian and English cricketers prefer nothing more than to square off against each other. This rivalry is explored in greater detail in Chapter 11.

South Africa

South Africa were invited into the test-playing club in 1889 when England and Australia realised that they needed somebody else to play apart from each other. The Springboks, as they were commonly called, proved to be a tough nut to crack, particularly on their own turf. Great South African players such as batsmen Trevor Goddard and Jackie McGlew proved more than a match for their Australian and English counterparts.

Away from home, though, they would regularly be beaten by both England and Australia.

But at the time, white South African society was racist and the cricket team chose to only play other white nations, ignoring the West Indies, Pakistan and India. This could not go on and in 1970 South Africa was excluded from international cricket.

Ironically, the exclusion occurred just when South African cricket was at an all-time high. The team was full of star players such as Barry Richards and the Pollock brothers, Graeme and Peter, and had just hammered a champion Australian team.

South Africa remained banned for more than 20 years before the political winds of change swept Nelson Mandela's African National Congress to power, and paved the way for South Africa's re-admission to international cricket.

The South Africans took part in the 1991 cricket World Cup, the premier international one-day cricket tournament, and reached the semifinal. This set down a marker that South Africa were back. Since their re-admission to test cricket South African sides, with batsman Jacque Kallis, Graeme Smith wicket-keeper Mark Boucher and fast bowler Shaun Pollock, son of Peter, in the ranks, have again proved to be of the highest class.

The new South Africa even managed to reach number one in the world test cricket rankings in 2010: See the sidebar later in this chapter for more on the test cricket world championship rankings system. The cricketing nation was shaken to the core though, when captain Hansie Cronje was embroiled in a match fixing scandal; see Chapter 17 for more on this.

India

Cricket is the number one sport in India. Yet for the first 25 years of their test-playing history India struggled.

England started playing test cricket against India in 1932 and although India were competitive at home they were soundly beaten when coming to England. In fact India did not manage to win a test match in England until 1972.

But gradually Indian performances improved. They triumphed in the World Cup of 1983, thanks in large part to the inspirational batting and bowling of Kapil Dev.

Indian teams have traditionally performed poorly in test matches away from home but have lorded it over opponents in their own back yard. The reason is that pitch conditions in India tend to favour spin, whereas in England, for example, pitch conditions strongly favour seam and swing bowlers. Great spin bowlers from India's past include the left-armer Bishen Bedi and more recently Anil Kumble.

In recent years India's performances have been the classic curate's egg. Sometimes, they have swept all opponents before them – reaching world number one for a brief period in 2011 and winning the 2011 cricket one-day World Cup. Crackerjack batting talents such as Sachin Tendulkar (see Chapter 14 for this little batting master), Rahul Dravid, Virender Sehwag, and MS Dhoni led the way in this golden period for India. However, following successive defeats to England and Australia in 2011 (in both cases India were whitewashed) the great Indian juggernaut had appeared to come off the road. However, the wealth of the Indian Premier League (see Chapters 3 and 11 for more on this) means that India is the new powerbroker in world cricket. What the Indian Cricket Board says normally goes in international cricket, replacing the English and Australian Cricket Boards at the top of the game.

Pakistan

In 1952, four years after partition from India, Pakistan started to play test cricket. Like India, Pakistan initially struggled to compete against the older, more established test nations, but gradually performances improved and they became very hard to beat, particularly at home.

Pakistan followed India's lead by winning the World Cup in Australia in 1991. Two Pakistani all rounders, Imran Khan and Wasim Akram, took the tournament by storm.

Pakistan teams have suffered down the years when playing away from home, rather like India, and for the same reasons – pitch conditions in Pakistan don't help players adjust to playing overseas.

Pakistan has had their share of great spin bowlers, such as Abdul Qadir and Saqlain Mushtaq. But in the 1980s and 1990s Pakistan also produced a crop of lightning-fast bowlers including Imran Khan, Wasim Akram, Waqar Younis and more recently Shoaib Akhtar, who terrified batsmen around the globe and made the country truly competitive in test matches away from home.

In 2010 it seemed that Pakistan cricket had reached a nadir, when several top players were found to have taken money in return for match fixing. At the same time, the performance of the Pakistan team was dreadful, as they lost heavily to both England and Australia. In addition, political instability at home meant that Pakistan was unable to play international cricket in their own country, instead basing themselves in Dubai and Abu Dhabi. But like a phoenix from the flames, Pakistan cricket seems to have undergone a bit of a renaissance under the inspired leadership of captain Misbah-Ul-Haq. The mercurial talents of this team appear to have been properly harnessed, and they managed to whitewash England 3-0 at the start of 2012 in a 'home' series played in Dubai and Abu Dhabi. Cricket fans around the world will be hoping that the Pakistan recovery continues.

To say that political relations between India and Pakistan have been a touch unfriendly over the years is something of an understatement. As recently as 2000 these two great nations came close to war over the disputed territory of Kashmir. However, the shared love of cricket has gone a considerable way to ease the troubles. In recent times, conflict between the two nations has been consigned to the cricket field; see Chapter 11 for more on this rivalry.

The West Indies

The West Indies, a collection of Caribbean nations from Jamaica in the north to Guyana in the south, first played test cricket in 1928 and from then on world cricket reverberated to the calypso beat. In the early years great players such as Learie Constantine and George Headley meant that the West Indies were instantly on a par with England, although Australia continued to beat them easily.

But Caribbean cricket really came of age in the 1950s. Under the captaincy of John Goddard, a side brimful of talent – including a trio of great batsmen known as the three Ws, Frank Worrell, Everton Weekes and Clyde Walcott, and spinners Alf Valentine and Sonny Ramadhin – beat England in England.

As the 1950s became the 1960s, the great all rounder Gary Sobers captained the side and produced outstanding performances to beat both England and Australia. See Chapter 14 on the ten greatest players for more on Gary Sobers.

Under the captaincy of first Clive Lloyd, and then Vivian Richards, the West Indies became dominant in the 1970s and 1980s. Their success was based on the policy of having four fast bowlers. Bowlers such as Michael Holding, Joel Garner, Malcolm Marshall and more recently Curtley Ambrose and Courtney Walsh terrified batsmen with their speed and accuracy of delivery. Thanks to this tactic, for the best part of two decades the West Indies were virtually unbeatable.

If this book had been written a decade ago then the story of West Indian test cricket would have been almost totally upbeat. However, such has been the decline in cricket standards in the Caribbean over the past ten years that many people fear for the future of the game in the West Indies.

The test side has gone from champions to chumps in a decade, losing heavily at both home and away to most test-playing nations, apart from Zimbabwe and Bangladesh. This slide culminated in a humiliating test series *whitewash* – defeat in every test – against England in 2004. And few silver linings can be found; no great players have emerged since Brian Lara, over a decade ago, and West Indian youth seem keener on playing basketball than cricket.

Where once a deep love for the game existed, injured pride and indifference are largely what remain. The cricket authorities hoped that the World Cup to be played in the West Indies in 2007 will help reignite interest in the game. But the tournament was widely seen as a disaster, with poor cricket played, local people priced out of spectating by high admission prices, and even the normally reliably sunny Caribbean weather turning windy and wet.

Sadly, cricket fans around the globe and in the Caribbean are still waiting on a re-emergence of the once all-powerful West Indies. Fingers crossed it won't be too long.

New Zealand

The New Zealand cricket team – or Kiwis as they're known – started playing test cricket in 1929 but only began to make their mark in the 1970s and 1980s. In fact, Australia didn't play New Zealand in test matches for a quarter of a century on the grounds that they were so awful. However, England carried on playing New Zealand, if only because it meant a succession of easy wins, something they never got from the other test-playing nations at the time.

The emergence of a crop of great players such as Glenn Turner, Martin Crowe, and in particular all rounder Richard Hadlee, turned New Zealand's fortunes around. In fact during the 1980s the Kiwis had a strong case to be considered the second best team in the world, behind the West Indies.

Although, not yet quite reaching such heights again, more recent Kiwi sides have remained good, competitive teams but without enjoying much success. The Kiwi's are rarely easy to beat, but likewise rarely excel.

Sri Lanka

Sri Lanka played their first test match in 1982 and like India and Pakistan have relied on high quality batsmen and spin bowling for success. After initially finding the cut and thrust of international cricket difficult, slowly but surely Sri Lanka became a force to be reckoned with.

The country's greatest triumph was winning the 1995 World Cup, helped by the exhilarating batting of Sanath Jayasuriya. More recently, the team's series victories in test cricket have been mostly at home, thanks in the main to the off-spin bowling of Muttiah Muralitharan. But the retirement of the great Muralitharan has left Sri Lanka sadly bereft of top-class performers, and despite a drawn home series against England in 2012, this once proud cricketing nation has fallen somewhat on hard times.

Zimbabwe

Hopes were high when Zimbabwe was granted full test-playing status in 1992. Previous Zimbabwe teams had competed well in one-day international cricket tournaments. However, after a run of good early results, including a test victory over India and a drawn series against England, Zimbabwean cricket has been dogged by infighting and player strikes. In addition, the International Cricket Council, which administers the game of cricket globally, has been angered by what it sees as interference in Zimbabwe cricket by some of the country's politicians. As a result, over the past decade, there have been short periods when Zimbabwe has been suspended from test and even one-day international cricket. However, they did play during the last World Cup, although sadly with very little success, being eliminated in the group stage of the competition. See 'Understanding the Zimbabwe controversy' later in this chapter for more on the troubles in Zimbabwe.

Bangladesh

Bangladesh, the newest test nation, were granted test status on the back of good performances in the 1999 World Cup and on the insistence of the powerful Indian lobby (which aimed to increase the number of Asian test-playing nations) at the International Cricket Council (ICC); see the section 'Who Runs World Cricket?' later in this chapter for more on India's growing stature in cricket's corridors of power.

Bangladesh's performances have been in the main woeful with a single test victory over Zimbabwe and a stunning one-day international triumph over Australia the only bright spots. See 'Struggling Bangladesh' later in this chapter for more on Bangladesh woes.

England has traditionally scheduled a series of five-match tests against Australia, South Africa, and the West Indies. When it comes to Pakistan, India, New Zealand, and Sri Lanka, three- or occasionally four-match tests in a series have been the order of the day. Zimbabwe and Bangladesh, world cricket's minnows, only get to play in series of two-match test matches against England. Why the discrepancies? Pure economics: England try to play more test matches against countries that pull in the crowds.

Recently the ICC went back and looked at all the test cricket played around the globe since 1953 and ranked retrospectively which test playing nations would be ranked number one. Over the 60 year period Australia have far and away been the most successful test nation – being number one ranked for the longest time – followed by the West Indies and then England.

The test cricket world championship

Under International Cricket Council (ICC) rules, test teams are supposed to play each other home and away in a series consisting of at least two test matches within a three-year period. This schedule of matches allows the ICC to draw up an ongoing test championship league table. How points are scored is fiendishly complex. More points can be won for winning a test series against teams higher in the table. Some teams play more tests than others so the ICC averages the points scored per test and that constitutes the ranking and dictates where the team stands in the championship.

In the summer of 2012 the championship was shaping up like this:

Country	Tests	Points	ICC rating
1 England	44	5,124	116
2 South Africa	32	3,709	116
3 Australia	46	5,153	112
4 India	46	5,103	111
5 Pakistan	35	3,781	108
6 Sri Lanka	38	3,780	99
7 West Indies	34	2,898	85
8 New Zealand	28	2,366	85
9 Bangladesh	18	135	8

Zimbabwe is currently unranked, since it has played insufficient matches. It has 167 points and a rating of 22.

There has been a lot of speculation that in the future there will be a sort of World Cup final of test cricket where at the end of a specified five-year period the two or four highest ranked test teams will play each other for the right to hold a test world championship trophy. However, the TV companies – particularly the big-paying Indian ones – have shown little appetite to broadcast such an event. As a result, the ICC has put the idea on ice, for the time being at least.

Cricket's second division

Cricket isn't just played in the ten test-playing nations: A host of countries field national teams.

These countries don't get to play test cricket – it wouldn't be fair as they aren't up to the standard of the other test-playing nations – but they do get to compete with each other for the chance to field a team in the one-day World Cup.

This second division of cricket countries includes:

- Afghanistan
- Canada
- Kenya
- Ireland

- ✔ Namibia
- ✔ The Netherlands
- ✔ Scotland
- ✔ United Arab Emirates
- ✔ United States of America

Very occasionally, when one of the second division sides gets to play a test-playing country in a one-day match, they pull off a shock. Back in 1995 Kenya beat the West Indies and in the 2003 World Cup Kenya actually made the semifinals after beating Bangladesh (by then a test-playing nation). However, the minnows are almost always rolled over by the test-playing nations.

The most successful minnows of recent world cups has been Ireland. In 2007 they beat Pakistan in the cricket one day world cup and actually progressed from the group to the knockout stages of the competition. Four years later they were at it again, this time triumphing in a one day group game over England, chasing down more than 300 runs in an innings to bring about a historic victory against their traditional rivals from the other side of the Irish sea.

The ICC calls the smaller second division nations Associate Members, whereas test-playing countries are referred to as Full Members.

Stop press . . . cricket more popular than baseball in the USA!

Americans, generally, don't get cricket. How is it, they ask, that two teams can play a game for five days and at the end it can be a draw? However, this wasn't always the case.

For a big chunk of the nineteenth century cricket was a big sport Stateside. In fact, some even argue cricket was more popular than baseball! Lots of clubs existed and even a national team, which played the world's first international match with Canada in 1844. In fact, the first test match could just possibly have been played between England and America instead of England and Australia. But as the nineteenth century progressed, baseball captured the hearts of Americans and cricket became a minority sport. A United States cricket team still exists, and has competed in major one-day tournaments. But most of the players in team USA are drawn from ex-pat West Indian cricketers living in Florida.

Taking in the Cathedrals of Cricket

Cricket fans are a lucky lot. They get to watch their sport in some of the most historic stadia in the world. Historic isn't merely code for 'dilapidated'; many test grounds have been redeveloped in recent years and now offer modern spectator comforts, while managing to retain their own unique sense of tradition. This section features some of the great cricket stadia. Go to one of these and you're set fair for a unique experience.

Lords, England

Lords is the world's most famous cricket ground, often referred to as 'The Home of Cricket', or 'Headquarters'. Laid out by Thomas Lord – hence the name – in 1813, Lords cricket ground is in a prime St Johns Wood location within strolling distance of central London. Lords is owned by the Marylebone Cricket Club (MCC). See the later sidebar 'Who Runs World Cricket' for more on the MCC. The ground was originally used by the MCC for its matches and for set piece occasions such as the annual game between Eton and Harrow schools. Lords has hosted test matches since 1884 and traditionally every test-playing team to tour England gets to play the host country at Lords.

The appeal of Lords is aesthetic as well as historic. The ground's architecture manages the rare feat of marrying up the old with the new. At one end of the ground is the nineteenth century pavilion with its famous Long Room, while opposite is the media centre which looks like something out of Star Trek. But somehow it all works.

The Oval, England

The Oval is London's second cricket ground but in many respects it can claim to have more history than even Lords. Australia triumphed over England in a test match at the Oval in 1882 and the Ashes conflict was born: See Chapter 11 for all you need to know about the Ashes. Don Bradman also made his last ever test appearance at the Oval in 1948. For once the great Bradman failed, bowled without scoring, and thereby missing out on a career test batting average of 100.

Traditionally, the last test match of the English summer is played at the Oval and over the years this has lent a sense of drama to the tests played there. England reclaimed the Ashes at the Oval in 1953 after nearly two decades of Australian dominance, and repeated the feat, again at the Oval, in 2005. The Oval also hosted the climax of the 2009 Ashes series, with England triumphing again to grab an unlikely 2-1 series win and take back the precious Ashes urn.

Melbourne Cricket Ground, Melbourne, Australia

The Melbourne Cricket Ground, or 'MCG' as it is affectionately known, is Australia's Lords. The first test match ever was played at the MCG in 1877, with Australia beating England by 45 runs. Whereas Lords has its architecture, the MCG has sheer size. The playing surface is the biggest in the world and the capacity dwarfs that of Lords or the Oval. The MCG is one of the great stadia in global sport.

One of the highlights of the global cricket calendar is the annual Boxing Day test match at the MCG, where the ground is usually packed to the rafters. In the Ashes series of 2006–2007, during Australia's whitewash of England, Melbourne saw the great Aussie leg spin bowler Shane warne claim a then world record 700th test wicket, dismissing England's future captain Andrew Strauss. The Melbourne cricket ground was also the venue for the Centenary test in 1977 between Australia and England. The game was remarkable for many reasons, not least the fact that the final result, a 45 run win for Australia, was the exact same result as had occurred in the first match 100 years earlier.

Sydney Cricket Ground, Sydney, Australia

The Sydney Cricket Ground (SCG) is another nineteenth century ground with oodles of history. Sydney has hosted test cricket since 1882, when Australia beat England – again!

Sydney has been the scene of many Australian triumphs over the years and is particularly noted for having a noisy crowd ready to barrack players from visiting teams at the drop of a can of Fosters.

The Hill at Sydney was traditionally where the most vocal locals liked to sit and dispense their wisdom, though that area of the ground has now been redeveloped. The modern Sydney cricket ground manages to incorporate both tradition, in the shape of the Victorian green fronted Lady's Stand, and up-to-the-minute modern stands and facilities. There are few places better to watch a game of cricket than the SCG.

Newlands, Cape Town, South Africa

Newlands has plenty of history; the first test match played there was way back in 1889.

But if awards were handed out for stunning backdrops then Newlands cricket ground would win top billing.

Newlands nestles in the shadow of Table Mountain in Cape Town. Nothing is quite like relaxing with a cold beer watching a game of cricket at Newlands. And the beer is guaranteed to be fresh because on one side of the ground is the famous Castle brewery, with cold refreshments pumped straight into the bars. The experience is especially fine if you're at a floodlit one-day match, when you can see the African sun setting behind Table Mountain.

Sabina Park, Kingston, Jamaica

Sabina Park first played host to test cricket in 1930. Jamaica is traditionally one of the strongest cricketing nations in the West Indies. The ground was a long time fortress for the West Indies. The wicket at Sabina Park is bouncy and aids fast seam bowling – just the type of bowling the West Indies excelled in during the 1970s and 1980s. Add to this the sunny weather and permanent party in the stands – helped no doubt by the local rum – and you can see why a Sabina Park test is on the must-do-at-least-once list for many cricket fans around the world.

India and Pakistan, partly because of their large populations and geographic spread, tend to use more grounds for test cricket than say England. Quite often grounds are used for a few years and then dispensed with. However, watching cricket in these countries is always a tremendous experience. The local fans are something to behold – both passionate and knowledgeable and welcoming to those fans from abroad in their midst.

Troubling Times for Test Cricket

Test cricket is well over a century old and has seen plenty of ups and downs. Check out Chapter 17 for some of the great controversies to affect the game. With ten test-playing nations spanning the globe, the odd bit of friction is bound to happen. At present, three major problems face administrators: The ongoing political problems in Zimbabwe, Bangladesh's struggles to cope with the demands of top-flight international cricket, and the drop in popularity of the game in Asia.

Understanding the Zimbabwe controversy

Zimbabwe, many independent observers suggest, is a country on the slide. Allegations abound against the ruling Zanu PF party, headed by president Robert Mugabe, concerning vote rigging and human rights abuses. If that wasn't bad enough, the economy is in freefall and the spectre of famine hangs over large parts of the country.

The chaos has also infected Zimbabwe's cricket establishment. The national team, elected to test-playing status in 1992, has suffered from a succession of controversies. First, some players have alleged that selection has been racist, with black players favoured over whites. Second, allegations of corruption continue against the country's cricket governing body. Both issues have led to player boycotts and a haemorrhaging of cricketing talent. In more recent times though, with the political situation quieting a little, there has been a bit of a comeback for cricket in the country. After periods of isolation where teams from overseas refused to travel to Zimbabwe, or the country was temporarily suspended from international completion, we are now seeing more games being played and playing standards beginning to rise again. The problems of Zimbabwe cricket are still a long way from being solved, but there is at least now some hope.

Struggling Bangladesh

Bangladesh have performed very poorly since they were granted test status in 2000. Many prominent ex-test players around the globe have suggested that Bangladesh are so bad that they're devaluing test match cricket. Bangladesh's record is truly horrible. Out of 73 test matches played they have lost all but 10, winning just three. They have managed only one series win, in 2009 against a West Indies team weakened by a player strike.. There is the odd bright moment though: For example in 2005 Bangladesh pulled off a huge shock by beating world champs Australia in a one-day match. In 2011 Bangladesh co-hosted the cricket world cup along with India but failed to progress from the group stage, becoming the first test nation to be bowled out twice in a world cup for under 100 runs in an innings.

 The one saving grace for Bangladesh is the unstinting support of the administrators of world cricket, and in particular India. See 'Who Runs World Cricket' later in this chapter for more on the importance of India in world cricket's corridors of power.

Falling popularity in Asia

Cricket is the national sport in India, Pakistan and Sri Lanka. Literally hundreds of millions of people in these countries follow cricket. Star players, such as India's Sachin Tendulkar, are treated like movie stars, with their image adorning billboards and television screens. But all is not well with the state of cricket in South Asia. One-day cricket, and in particular twenty20 cricket as embodied by the Indian Premier League is hugely popular, with stadia always packed to the rafters, but the same can't be said for test cricket. Attendances at test matches are at an all-time low. Administrators are scratching their heads wondering how to make test cricket appealing. Often, crowds are let in for free, yet still stadia are nowhere near full. Long term, the danger is that if test cricket in these hotbeds dies, its days will be numbered in the rest of the world too.

Who Runs World Cricket?

For a large part of cricket history the bigwigs at the Marylebone Cricket Club (MCC) ran the game. The MCC bigwigs were the self appointed 'guardians of the spirit and laws of cricket' – very pompous sounding!

The Imperial Cricket Conference was formed in 1909 with England, Australia, and South Africa running the show.

However, as more nations joined the test club these uppity newcomers started to demand a say on how things should be run in world cricket. You can imagine the monocles of MCC members falling into their gin and tonics at the thought of that!

By 1965, The Imperial Cricket Conference (ICC) had eventually morphed into the International Cricket Council. The ICC gave all the test-playing nations a say but England still ran things because they could rely on the support of Australia and New Zealand. But as Sri Lanka, and then lately Bangladesh, joined, England's hold on the game waned as the playing prowess, economic and political clout of other nations grew, in particular of India.

Today the balance of power has well and truly shifted away from Lords and England. The ICC has moved its HQ from Lords to Dubai, while in the corridors of power India, with its billion plus consumers, growing wealth and intense love of the game, is now the dominant power. India can marshal the support of Pakistan, Sri Lanka and Bangladesh to get its way. India, after all, is by far the richest cricketing nation. The financial clout of the Indian Premier League guaranteeing huge television audiences means that the Indian Cricket Board can command huge fees from broadcasters looking to screen games. As with most things in life, money and power go hand-in-hand.

Breaking the Hoodoo: England's Renaissance

One of the striking aspects of international cricket in recent years has been the return to prominence of the England cricket team.

In 1999, after a 2-1 home test series defeat to New Zealand, England were ranked the worst test-playing nation by the ICC (this was just prior to Bangladesh's admittance to the test-playing club). English cricket had become a global joke. But slowly at first, and then more rapidly, English cricket turned itself around.

The old approach of chopping and changing players was ditched. Instead, the concept of Team England was born. The big idea behind Team England was that the best players in the country would be identified and then developed as a team largely outside the cut-and-thrust of the domestic County Championship (see Chapter 12 for more on this competition). Top coaches specialising in batting, bowling, fitness and fielding were brought in to work with Team England. At the same time, the most promising youngsters received intense coaching at a new cricket academy.

In short, English cricket got its act together and for once made the most of the player talent available.

England can attribute a lot of this recent success to the appointment of two Zimbabwe-born coaches. First, Duncan Fletcher oversaw an uplift in playing standards from 2000 to 2006, including the 2005 Ashes triumph. Then from 2008 onwards – after a dip in performance – Andy Flower, a successful Zimbabwean test cricketer, was appointed coach. He has helped bring about two Ashes triumphs in 2009 and then again in Australia in 2010–2011. Both Fletcher and Flower had the same calm demeanour while emphasising the need for greater fitness and hard practice.

Chapter 11

Taking in Big International Tournaments

. . . .

In This Chapter

▶ Exploring the magic of the Ashes

▶ Looking at some past Ashes heroes

▶ Fighting it out around the globe

▶ Understanding what beating England means

▶ Putting on a big show: the 50-over and twenty20 World Cups

▶ Considering some of cricket's superstars

. . . .

Cricket fans are spoilt. Ten test-playing nations lock horns in test and one-day international cricket day-in-day-out around the globe. They do this for trophies as well as for pride.

In this chapter, I look at the main international cricket tournaments and some of the rivalries that have developed over the years. What's more, I take a look at some great players from the past as well as the superstars lighting-up today's cricket firmament.

If you want to familiarise yourself with the landscape of the cricket world, this chapter is for you!

Raking over the Ashes

The Ashes is cricket's longest running and most richly historic competition. The contest only involves two countries: England and Australia. Every couple of years these countries play five test matches to decide which team is better. Each country takes its turn to host an Ashes series and such is the aura surrounding the competition that full houses at most of the grounds can be guaranteed.

What are the Ashes?

The Ashes have their origin in a Victorian joke. The day after England were beaten by Australia in a test match at the Oval in 1882, *The Sporting Times* published the following mock obituary.

'In affectionate remembrance of English cricket which died at the Oval, 29th August 1882, deeply lamented by a large circle of sorrowing friends and acquaintances. RIP. N.B.: The body will be cremated and taken to Australia.'

The following winter England managed to beat Australia at Melbourne and some unnamed ladies burnt a cricket bail (one of two small pieces of wood which rest on top of the stumps), put the ashes into a little urn and presented it to the captain of the England cricket team, the wonderfully named the Honourable Ivo Bligh (In those days the poshest toff in the team was usually made captain. Even if he couldn't play, he knew how to pass the port correctly!)

Ever since, Australia and England have competed in test matches for the right to hold the Ashes. However, the original urn is very fragile and doesn't leave the cricket museum at Lords – where the curators charge people to see it! When Australia win the trophy the urn is simply moved from one trophy cabinet to the other.

But a run of easy victories for Australia over England in the 1990s and early 2000s prompted many Australians to ask for the urn to be handed over to them permanently.

The team that wins the most tests in the series claims the Ashes (see the sidebar, 'What are the Ashes?'). If the series is drawn, the team that won the previous series gets to keep the Ashes.

Understanding what makes the Ashes unique

For most of the first hundred years of test cricket, the Ashes were where 'it was at'. England and Australia were the two best cricket nations on the planet – not that difficult as up until the 1920s, only three countries played the sport to international standards (the other was South Africa). Therefore, games between these two countries were considered the pinnacle of the sport.

Several factors have helped fan the flames of Ashes competition:

✔ **The colonial issue:** Australians love beating the English, and vice versa. For a long time some Australians saw the English as stuck-up and condescending. On the flip side, some of the English played up to this stereotype by regarding the Australians as uncultured. However, despite occasional name-calling, deep down there has usually been great respect between the teams.

✔ **Infrequency of test cricket:** Fewer test matches were played before the Second World War and cricket fans on both sides would feast on the deeds of the great players in Ashes battles. When the matches were played at home, fans crammed into the stadia; when played away they would have to wait for newspaper reports and Pathé newsreels in the cinemas – no satellite sports coverage back then.

✔ **Always competitive:** For most of their history, Ashes test matches have been extremely hard-fought contests. No one side could ever relax as they knew the other was always up for the fight. This competitiveness made most Ashes series compulsive viewing for spectators.

Ashes contests have not been without their controversy. The grand-daddy of them all was the infamous bodyline tour of 1932–33 when England's fast bowlers aimed their deliveries at the bodies of the Australian batsmen with the aim that the batsmen would hit the ball in the air to fielders placed on the leg side of the wicket. The tactics of the England team caused a furore in Australia and damaged diplomatic relations between the countries; see Chapter 17 for more on this episode.

In recent years some commentators suggested that the Ashes were losing their appeal. The reason they gave was that Australia were so much better than England that it wasn't a proper contest anymore. These commentators had a point. However, England's triumphs in the 2005, 2009 and 2011 Ashes series and the way that cricket caught the popular imagination has shown that the clashes between these two great cricketing nations still have plenty of life in them.

In many respects a lot of the history of cricket is tied up in the Ashes; refer to Chapter 10 for more on cricket's development from a game played in the south-east of England to a major global sport.

Understanding the secrets of Australian success

Ask any England cricketer and they'll tell you that beating the Australian cricket team is a very tough task. The Australians have brilliant individual players and are usually well organised.

For most of the history of test cricket, Australia have ruled the roost. Theories abound as to why Australia are so good. Here are some of the most plausible:

- ✔ **Warm climate:** The Australian climate is warm and sunny and this has helped breed an outdoors culture. Most Australian youngsters enjoy getting outdoors and playing sport.

- ✔ **School system:** In many Australian schools, sport is an important part of the culture. After-school sports clubs are common and sporting achievements bring kudos.

- ✔ **Strong club teams:** Cricket clubs in Australia are a conveyor belt for talent. If a player is successful in club cricket, he has a chance of being selected for a state side – the Australian version of the English county teams – and from there good performances can bring selection for the national team.

- ✔ **Competitive culture:** In Australia finishing second is not an option. Teams from 'Down Under', regardless of the sport, always go for the win.

In Australia a player can progress from club cricket to the national team. On the other hand, if you fail for the national and the state side, you can soon find yourself playing in club cricket.

Australian cricket teams like to play aggressively. However, Australians pride themselves on their sportsmanship and showing respect for opponents who succeed against them.

Australia's Ashes heroes

Australia have had the better of the Ashes battles with England, and their cricketing heroes include some of the greatest names in the history of the world game.

Donald Bradman

The Don as he was nicknamed was unquestionably the greatest batsman of all time and helped Australia beat all-comers for most of the 1930s. His batting average – the number of runs he scored on average each time he batted – was about double that achieved by any other player with a claim to be considered great in the history of the game. The Don's achievements are looked at in greater detail in Chapter 14.

Dennis Lillee

Dennis Lillee was a thoroughbred amongst fast bowlers. He could bowl at lightning pace yet rarely lost accuracy, thanks in large part to his well-honed and rhythmic bowling action. He terrified batsmen around the globe throughout the 1970s and early 1980s, taking 355 test wickets in only 70 tests.

Allan Border, Mark Taylor, and Steve Waugh

These three players were successive captains of Australia, and they managed to win every Ashes series from 1989 to 2003. All three led by example, scoring lots of runs. Under the astute and ruthless leadership of Border, Taylor and Waugh, Australia became, and have stayed, the world's best team.

Shane Warne

In 1993, at Old Trafford cricket ground in Manchester, Aussie leg spin bowler Shane Warne became an instant legend with his first ball in an Ashes test match. He spun the ball a huge distance to bowl England's best batsman of the time, Mike Gatting. This was dubbed *the ball of the century* by the cricketing press. For more than a decade, Warne tormenting England batsmen. He went on to capture more than 700 test wickets, the highest proportion of which were English.

England's Ashes heroes

Although England have often been on the end of test series defeats by Australia, it hasn't been for the lack of great players.

Jack Hobbs

Before the arrival of Bradman, Jack Hobbs was the genius batsman whom everyone tried to emulate. In a long and glorious career he scored an incredible world record 197 centuries in first class cricket matches. In tests his run scoring prowess – particularly against Australia – was no less impressive and for this reason he is the only Englishman to make it into my list of the ten greatest ever cricketers: See Chapter 14 for the full run-down.

Len Hutton

The finest opening batsman of his generation, Hutton broke the record for the highest ever individual score in a test match at the age of just 23 – against Australia. His score of 364 helped England to a rare triumph over the Australians – although Bradman was injured. His career was interrupted by the Second World War, but after the war he became one of England's best ever captains – taking his team to Australia and beating the home team in a test series in 1955.

Ian Botham

Botham is one of the great all rounders in cricket history and was the scourge of Australia during three Ashes series in 1981, 1985, and 1987. He is best remembered for his role in the 1981 series. Sacked as captain after the second test of the series, Botham went berserk with bat and ball, scoring centuries and taking wickets galore. Almost single-handed the incredibly powerful Botham won the Ashes, capturing the imagination of the entire country. See Chapter 15 for more on the extraordinary events of the 1981 Headingley test.

Developing Rivalries around the Globe

England and Australia don't have a monopoly on cricket rivalry; with ten test-playing nations other major contests also draw in the crowds.

Pakistan v India: Asia's 'Ashes'

The Ashes maybe the oldest and most historic test rivalry but the contests between India and Pakistan can claim to be the most exciting and colourful in world cricket.

Whenever Pakistan and India meet – whether in a one-day international or in a test match – more than just the result of a cricket match is at stake. If one side beats the other, the loser's national pride takes a real hit. There have been instances of fans rioting following defeat.

The reason for such passion isn't difficult easy to work out. Pakistan was once part of India, but since the countries were divided in 1947, they have been political and military rivals. This rivalry has been fuelled by the fact that Pakistan is a Muslim country while India is mostly Hindu.

But don't go thinking that India versus Pakistan cricket matches are simply marked by out-and-out aggression: The cricket is usually of the very highest quality with great batsmen and bowlers on both sides.

In England and Australia cricket has to vie with other sports for popular attention. But in India and Pakistan cricket is the number one sport – particularly one-day internationals – a bit like soccer in Brazil.

The clash of the titans: West Indies v Australia

The West Indies were the best team in the world during the 1970s and 1980s, but eventually their crown was snatched by the Australian team. Throughout the 1990s a riveting battle existed for top spot between these two cricketing powers. The West Indies had two great fast bowlers – Curtly Ambrose and Courtney Walsh – while the Australians had Shane Warne, Glenn McGrath, and Steve Waugh. These contests took on epic proportions, with the advantage swinging to and fro. Eventually, though, Australia started to win the matches consistently and have dominated ever since. In fact, West Indian cricket has sunk quite low, making contests between the two nations very one-sided in Australia's favour.

The International Cricket Council continuously ranks the test playing nations, Since 1953 the ICC figures show that Australia have spent the longest period ranked at number one in the world, but it's the West Indies who have spent the second longest period in the number one spot. See Chapter 10 for more on the ICC rankings.

Southern hemisphere rivalry: South Africa v Australia

When South Africa was suspended from international cricket in 1970 – in reaction to the country's racist apartheid policy – the team had just become the best in the world by thrashing Australia. When, after 21 years in the wilderness, South Africa was re-admitted to international cricket in 1991, the country felt it had something to prove. Every time South Africa play Australia the South African players see a chance to prove that they are number one again. Although the matches between these two countries have always been hard fought, usually the Australians have continued to come out on top – much to the annoyance of the South Africans.

Crossing the final frontier: India v Australia

During the late 1990s and the turn of the millennium, the Australians were beating everyone all around the world; with one big exception. No matter how hard they tried, Australia couldn't beat India in India. Steve Waugh, the former Australian captain, described winning a test series in India as 'the final frontier' – very Star Trek. In 2001, the two teams played a three-match test series which Australia, under the captaincy of Steve Waugh, looked set to win until an amazing fight back by India snatched victory from the jaws of defeat; see Chapter 15 for this match's place in the list of greatest ever matches.

In 2004, Australia finally managed to cross the final frontier and beat India in a test series on India's home turf. Sadly for him, Steve Waugh had by then retired. Since then, though, the pattern has returned to the familiar one with Australia generally beating India at home but losing when travelling to the sub-continent.

Tuning into test cricket in England

Test matches in England often have a very special atmosphere. Britain in general is a very diverse country with huge numbers of people with Pakistani, Indian and West Indian roots. When test teams from these countries come over to play England, many fans turn out to cheer on the visitors. Back in the 1970s and 1980s, when the West Indies visited England, grounds reverberated to the calypso beat as West Indian fans blew horns and played the drums. More recently, Pakistani and Indian cricket fans have been turning up the volume at grounds. Sometimes this vociferous support has got the hackles up of some more fuddy-duddy cricket aficionados, but most fans welcome a bit of noise, thinking it adds to the sense of the occasion.

Cricket fans in England are almost unique in loving test matches as much as one-day international matches – if not more so. International grounds in England are often packed to the rafters for test matches and admission charges in recent times have skyrocketed. See Chapter 13 for more on being a cricket fan.

Fears have been raised that test match cricket could eventually die out because too few people are going to see it around the globe. Crowds in New Zealand, West Indies and the Indian sub-continent have been falling for years. And even more recently in Australia test matches and one day internationalshave been struggling to pull in the crowds. Refer to Chapter 10 for more on the dwindling crowds at test cricket in Asia's cricket heartlands.

If a team loses regularly, the captain and coach usually get it in the neck. Back in the 1980s and 1990s when England were being consistently beaten by the other test-playing nations, there was a lot of chopping and changing of the team coach and captain. During the summer of 1988, England had no fewer than five different captains over the course of five test matches against the West Indies. However, they still lost the series 4-0.

Australia and India compete for the Border–Gavaskar trophy. This trophy is named after two former great players, one from each side: Allan Border from Australia and Sunil Gavaskar from India.

Beating England is Everyone's Goal

Cricket is a game spread by the British Empire, and the former colonies like nothing better than to beat England at their own game. Previously, only Australia were able to beat England on a regular basis, but since the emergence of the great West Indian team of the 1970s, the other test-playing nations have been making up for lost time, winning lots of games. When England tour other test-playing nations they normally draw a big crowd because the home fans want to see their heroes triumph.

Competing for the World Cup

Every four years cricket teams from all the test-playing nations and other selected countries compete in the World Cup: Find out who can qualify in the section 'Examining how the World Cup works' later in this chapter.

During the World Cup, the teams play each other in one-day, limited-overs internationals. Eventually, after about a month of matches, two teams play in a final and the winners are crowned world champions.

In World Cup one-day international matches, each side has one innings limited to 50 overs. An *over* is made up of six deliveries, therefore during an innings lasting 50 overs, 300 deliveries are bowled, excluding illegal deliveries.

Another rule used in all international one-day matches requires the fielding captain to keep most fielders within 30 yards of the batsmen during the first 10 overs of the innings. This gives batsmen the incentive to play aggressive shots as fewer fielders are near the boundary to catch the ball. As a result many teams employ a *pinch hitter*. This is a batsman who is known for being able to play aggressive shots and therefore take advantage of the fielding restrictions. Refer to Chapter 8 for more on one-day tactics and Chapter 3 for more on how one-day cricket matches work.

In one-day, limited-overs cricket, each bowler is limited to bowling a maximum of one fifth of the total number of overs in an innings. As a result, at least five players have to bowl in an innings. The fielding captain decides which players bowl.

Growing out of humble beginnings

The first three World Cups, in 1975, 1979 and 1983 were all held in England. The one-day international cricket format had only just been invented in 1970 and many teams still hadn't cottoned on to the fact that special tactics were needed to win. Teams tended to play the same players as they did in test cricket and hope for the best. West Indies won the first two tournaments – which was just as well as they were the best team at the time. In 1983, India caused an upset by beating the West Indies in the final.

The 1987 tournament in India was the first to be held outside England. By 1987, the competing countries had started to select players who were adept at playing the one-day format rather than test cricket – though the best players could excel at both forms of the game. Australia won this tournament after beating England in a tense final.

Taking off in Australia

The 1991 World Cup in Australia is regarded as the most exciting to-date. All the then eight test-playing nations took part, plus Zimbabwe. All nine sides played each other once, in a round-robin league. Ultimately the four teams that won the most matches made it through to the semifinals. Pakistan won the cup after beating England in yet another close final.

The 1995 tournament, staged jointly by India and Sri Lanka, was noted for its tactical innovation. Captains and coaches had at last worked out different tactics for one-day cricket. Eventually Sri Lanka beat Australia in the final, due in large part to their use of a pinch hitter at the top of the batting order.

Stumbling in England and South Africa

The World Cups held in England and South Africa in 1999 and 2003 respectively, were disappointing affairs. Both times the home side was knocked out early on and the format of the tournaments has drawn criticism.

What's more, the decision to include teams from countries that don't play test cricket, such as The Netherlands and Namibia, has drawn fire. Critics suggest that these teams can't compete with the big boys and this makes many games in the group stages of the tournament a real turn-off for spectators.

Shaming of the world cup: West Indies 2007

The world cup held in the West Indies in 2007 will be remembered for many things, none of them good. Early in the tournament there was the tragic death of Pakistan coach Bob Woolmer from a heart attack – although a murder enquiry ran for several months. Local people were priced out of the tournament by high ticket prices, so was attendances were low, generating a poor atmosphere in the grounds. The cricket was often of a low quality, with many one sided matches between test playing nations and the minnows. And to cap it all the final, which was won by Australia, was thrown into chaos by an umpiring blunder over delays for rain and bad light. Even the normally reliable West Indian weather let down proceedings with several matches being curtailed by downpours.

Fighting back: India 2011

After the tragi-comedy of the 2007 event in the West Indies, the 2011 tournament in India had to be better, and thankfully it was. The cricket was of a higher standard, with some fine matches played. Ticket prices were kept under control so the locals could attend and add to the atmosphere. Matches were played in three subcontinental countries – India, Bangladesh and Sri Lanka – guaranteeing lots of interest from fans and TV audiences. The tournament even brought a home triumph, with India beating Sri Lanka in the final.

Examining how the World Cup works

In the most recent format under which the World Cup has been played, fourteen teams start the competition: The ten test-playing countries and four associate members of the ICC. These fourteen teams play in round-robin groups of seven, made up of five full test playing countries and two associates. The top four teams from each group then progress to the knockout phase of the competition. Quarter finals, semi finals and a final are then played. The last team standing is crowned world champions of one-day international cricket.

In order to win the cricket World Cup a team needs to negotiate two barriers. They must:

✔ Qualify from the round-robin pool.

✔ Win the quarter-final, semi-final and final matches.

The ICC is made up of full members and associate members; refer to Chapter 10 for more information on who the associate members are. Full members are test-playing nations, ten in total, and associate members are countries that aren't quite up to playing test cricket. These associate members play each other in a separate competition for the right to take on the big boys in the World Cup.

Qualifying from the pool

The fourteen teams taking part in the World Cup are broken down into two groups of seven. The teams in these groups play each other and the teams finishing in the top four places go through to the quarter finals.

Under starter's orders for the 2015 World Cup

The next World Cup will be upon us quicker than you think; it will be staged jointly in Australia and New Zealand in 2015.

The competition promises to be intense but here are the prospects for the main runners and riders:

- **Australia:** The team from down-under will be favourites in their own backyard to lift the trophy. They have fantastic batsmen and bowlers and their fielding is second to none. However, the Australian team isn't as good as it once was and at the last World Cup they were eliminated at the quarter-final stage.

- **England:** England have gone through a marked revival in test cricket over the past few years, but this upsurge has not been mirrored in one-day international cricket. England seem incapable of stringing together more than a couple of wins.

- **India:** The beaten finalists in the 2003 World Cup won it on home territory on 2011 On their day the Indians can be a match for anyone, particularly with an array of batting talent to call on.

- **New Zealand:** Always difficult to beat in one-day cricket and with a host of good all rounders, the Kiwis are usually a good outside bet to make the semi-finals. However, they lack the genuine world-class performers to take the title, and have never made a World Cup final.

- **Pakistan:** Real dark horses, Pakistan have improved enormously in recent times under the leadership of ace batsman Misbah-ul-Haq. They have good batsmen and bowlers, and their fielding has improved.

- **South Africa:** The Proteas have a very good recent record in one-day international cricket, thanks to the talented batting of captain Graeme Smith and Jacques Kallis. The South Africans also have fine fast bowlers in particular Dale Steyn. But they tend to underperform in the World Cup.

- **Sri Lanka:** Famous for winning games at home but losing them away. They made the 2011 world cup finals but without the likes of retired ace spin bowler Muttiah Muralitharan and left arm seam bowler Chaminda Vaas they lack world-class performers.

- **West Indies:** Years of cricketing decline will be difficult to reverse and their best hope may be a semi-final berth. The West indies, once the kings of one-day cricket, have had a poor record in the past few World Cups.

- **Bangladesh, Zimbabwe:** These two countries are way behind the other test-playing nations in terms of quality of personnel and leadership. They may pull off a shock and beat one of the other test-playing nations but in reality they are headed for an early exit.

Four associate countries will take part in the 2015 world cup but they haven't had their play-off tournament to decide which ones will take part. Ireland, though, with their success in the 2007 and 2011 world cups will be hot favourites to make it to the 2015 tournament.

Setting up the quarter finals

Once the top four teams in each round robin group have been decided, the knockout phase of the competition begins. Teams are ranked according to where they finished in their group, and this determines which team from the other group they play in the next round. For example, the team that qualified first in group A plays the team which qualified fourth in Group B. The team that qualified second in Group A plays the team that qualified third in Group B. The idea is that winning more matches in the round robin is rewarded with an supposedly easier quarter-final draw, while teams that played each other in the round robin will avoid each other at the quarter-final stage. Going for the trophy

Once the quarter finals are done with, there are four teams left, and these play each other in the semi–finals. The winners of these two games go to – yes, you guessed it – the World Cup final. This is a single match played between the final two teams in the competition. A World Cup final only happens once every four years, so for many players it is a rare chance to take away what is arguably cricket's biggest prize – game on!

The format of the 2011 World Cup, with fourteen teams in two groups and then knockout stages, was deemed a success. The previous three tournaments had a 'Super Eight' stage between the groups and semi finals which was fiendishly complex to understand and was cited as a major reason why those tournaments flopped.

Looking at Other One-Day International Tournaments

One-day cricket goes down a storm with the crowds. Therefore lots of tournaments have sprung up around the globe looking to cash in on this popularity.

The Asia Cup

Every couple of years teams from India, Sri Lanka, Pakistan and Bangladesh compete in a one-day international tournament. The teams compete in a round robin group and the top tow teams progress to the finalal. The winner of the Asia cup is usually one of the big three – India, Pakistan or Sri Lanka – and gets the continent's bragging rights. Pakistan is the current holder of the Asia cup beating Bangladesh in 2012 final. The next tournament will be held in 2014, with the venue to be decided.

The Australian Tri-series

Marketing people in Australia cottoned onto the money-making potential of one-day international cricket long before their English counterparts. Since the late 1970s Australia has played two other test-playing nations each winter in a round-robin tournament. Teams play each other eight times and after this round-robin the top two sides go through to a three match final series of games.

The NatWest series

The NatWest series is the English equivalent of the Australian Tri-series. Each summer, since 2000, two test-playing nations have come over to England to compete with the hosts. Each team plays each other and at the end of this round-robin the top two teams make it through to the final, which is played at Lords. Sadly, England weren't that good at one-day cricket and often fail to make the final of the NatWest series. In recent summers the format has changed slightly, with the NatWest series becoming a straight shoot out over five matches between England and another test playing nation.

Virtually all one-day and international cricket is now televised, at least on digital pay channels. Interestingly, the administrators running cricket gain far more cash from selling the rights to broadcast cricket than they get from charging spectators at the ground.

The Champions trophy: a competition too far?

A few years back the International Cricket Council (ICC), the body that runs world cricket, decided that another major one-day trophy was needed for teams to compete in. As a result, the Champions Trophy was born. Teams from the test-playing nations join two associate members of the ICC – refer to Chapter 10 for the lowdown on which countries these are – to play in round-robin group matches. The top team in each of the four groups qualify for the semifinals and the winners of these go through to the final. The Champions Trophy suffers from the same problems as the World Cup in that the associate countries such as the United States and The Netherlands are no match for the likes of Australia and India. This means that a lot of the group matches are very one-sided. In addition, in the past, some countries have been reluctant to take part because they are already busy playing one-day international and test cricket. But long term there may be a role for the Trophy. 2013 the champions trophy will be held in England, the ICC has said that this will be the last edition of the trophy.

Putting bums on seats: the ICC Twenty twenty world cup

Whereas the likes of the ICC World Cup and the Champions Trophy have had more downs than ups in recent times, one international tournament which has gone from strength to strength is the ICC twenty20 World Cup. It attracts big crowds and the TV companies love the excitement of the shorter twenty over game, with matches being completed in around three hours.

Such has been the success of the tournament that three finals have taken place since 2007. The winners have been:

- **2007**: India (hosts South Africa)
- **2009**: Pakistan (hosts England)
- **2010**: England (hosts West Indies)

There are three more ICC twenty twenty world cups already in the international calendar for 2012 (in Sri Lanka), 2014 (in Bangladesh) and 2016 (In India).

Twelve teams take part in the twenty20 World Cup – they are divided into four groups of three. Matches in these groups are in a round robin format, and the top two teams in the groups go through to the next round. The eight remaining sides are then split into two groups of four who play each other – the Super Eights stage – and the top teams inform each of these two groups progress to the knockout semi-finals.

England's triumph in the 2010 world cup was the country's first in a major international one day tournament.

In the 2007 tournament Indian batting ace Yuvraj singh hit six sixes in one over bowled by England's Stuart Broad. He scored a world record 36 runs in the six-ball over, an amazing feat which may never be repeated in top-class international cricket.

Checking Out the World's Leading Cricketers

The world's great tournaments – from the Ashes to the World Cup – are a showcase for the leading cricketers.

So that you can easily familiarise yourself with the movers and shakers in world cricket, here's the low-down on some of the game's current superstars.

The great batsmen

The world of cricket is blessed with a plethora of fantastic batsmen. In this section I introduce some of the true world greats gracing the cricket fields of the world.

Virender Sehwag (India)

When he first came into test cricket, Sehwag was dubbed 'little Tendulkar' because his stature and the way he stands at the crease is the spitting image of the great Indian batsman, see Chapter 14 for more on the great Sachin Tendulkar. However, Sehwag soon moved out of Tendulkar's shadow, scoring century after exhilarating century. He is the first Indian batsman to score more than 300 runs in one innings and averages more than 50 runs each time he bats.

Kevin Pietersen (England)

The South-African born Pietersen has made a huge impact since his England debut in 2005. His 158 at the Oval in the final test of the 2005 Ashes series was one of most remarkable innings of modern times. Pietersen is an incredibly brave batsman, willing to back his own ability and attack the bowling. He is a natural gambler: Sometimes it pays off, sometimes not. Whatever the outcome, though, Pietersen is always exciting to watch.

Michael Clarke (Australia)

The Australian captain and middle order batting maestro is nicknamed 'Pup' for his boyish good looks. But as he enters his early thirties there is nothing inexperienced about his batting or his leadership. Since taking on the captaincy in 2011, Clarke's already excellent batting has gone up a level, and he now has a test batting average of around 50. He is a match winning performer and recognised by observers in the know as one of the most elegant performers out there.

Mahela Jayawardene

The Sri Lankan captain is one of the most consistent performers in modern test cricket. His batting average is around 50 and he has played in over 130 tests, scoring a remarkable 31 hundreds. He is also regarded as a fine captain and cricketing superstar in his homeland.

Shivnarine Chanderpaul (West Indies)

The diminutive West Indian cricketer has been in the top echelons of the international game for well over a decade. While playing in a substandard West Indian team, Chanderpaul has produced some performances of the highest quality. In 140 test matches to date, Chanderpaul has become one of only a handful of cricketers to score more than 10,000 runs. His performances in the 2012 series in England were again out of the top drawer.

Graeme Smith (South Africa)

Smith took on the South captaincy in his early twenties but took to it and the job of opening the batting for South Africa like a duck to water. He has played in over 100 matches for his country, captaining in most of them, and has scored more than 8,000 runs. He is not the most elegant of players to watch, but his determination and ability to concentrate are rated amongst the finest in the test arena. If you wanted someone to bat for your life, Smith would be a very good choice.

You calculate a player's batting average by dividing the number of runs he scores by the number of times he is out. For example, if a batsman scores 1,000 runs in his career and is out 20 times his batting average will be 1,000 divided by 20, which works out as 50.

A batting average of 50 or above is considered to be the hallmark of a top class batsman.

The great all rounders

A player who is an excellent batsman and bowler is called an all rounder. Players who can bat and also bowl or keep wicket are worth their weight in gold to a captain.

Kumar Sangakkara (Sri Lanka)

The Sri Lankan wicket-keeper is a genuine all rounder. He is the team's best batsman. He averages a score of around 50 each time he bats and has made many big innings scores of over 100. Sangakkara is also a fine wicket-keeper although in recent years he has only done this job in the one-day international arena, preferring to concentrate on his batting in test cricket. It seems that he has discovered how to control his temper. He had to because early on in his career he had several run-ins with the cricketing authorities. In 2011, he was named by the *Wisden Cricketers' Almanack* as the world's top cricketer – some accolade.

Stuart Broad (England)

Stuart Broad is an electrifying cricketer. A hard-hitting batsman and aggressive fast bowler, he has taken the cricketing world by storm over the past few years. In 2009 he helped secure the Ashes for England with a remarkable bowling performance at the Oval. His emergence as a top class all-rounder has been a key component in England surging to the top of the world rankings. The one cloud on the horizon, though, is that the large framed Broad is prone to injury, and missed much of the 2011 Ashes in Australia with a side strain.

Shahid Afridi (Pakistan)

On his day Shahid Afridi is one of the most exciting players in world cricket. As a batsman he plays aggressive powerful shots, exciting the crowd and putting fear into his opponents. He is particularly effective as a one-day international batsman due to his panache as a batsman. Overlooking Afridi's leg spin bowling is all too easy, but he is an exceptional one-day international bowler. For a leg spin bowler he delivers the ball at an unusually high speed – often around 70 mph – catching batsmen unaware. The irresistible mix of attacking strokeplay and leg spin bowler mark Afridi out as a real crowd pleaser and has earned the nickname 'boom boom' for his hard hitting batting antics.

Jacques Kallis (South Africa)

Kallis is good enough to be selected for his team as both a batsman and as a bowler. In fact as a batsman he is one of the very best in the world, scoring nearly 13,000 runs at a remarkable average of 56. As a bowler he has taken nearly 300 wickets at an average of little over 30 – itself a very good performance. Add superb fielding skills to the stellar batting and high-quality bowling and you have the most complete cricketer in the world.

The great bowlers

Dale Steyn (South Africa)

Probably the fastest bowler in the world today, Steyn is a fantastic performer at test level. Still under the age of 30, the South African speedster has taken nearly 300 wickets in a little over 50 test matches. He is not only quick, but he has the ability to move the ball off the seam with great control. See Chapter 6 for more on the art of bowling fast. In short, Steyn has all the weapons that a bowler needs to dismiss the very best batsmen.

Saeed Ajmal (Pakistan)

Ajmal made his test debut at the relatively advanced age of 31, but he has more than made up for lost time. He is a high-class spin bowler, able to deceive the batsman with the way he flights the ball and the bounce it gets off the wicket. See Chapter 6 for more on what makes a top class spin bowler. Perhaps Ajmal's finest hour to date was against England in a test series played in the United Arab emirates in early 2012. His bowling during the series bamboozled the England batsmen and ensured a whitewash 3-0 win for resurgent Pakistan. In 20 matches to date he has rushed to over 100 wickets, and if he can stay fit he will claim the scalps of many more batsmen before his career comes to an end.

James Anderson (England)

Anderson is widely recognised as the finest swing bowler playing today. He bowls the ball fast, at nearly 90 miles per hour, and is able to swing the ball through the air to deceive the batsman and force an error almost at will. See Chapter 6 for more on the intricacies of swing bowling. He was once seen as a bowler who did well in England, with its swing friendly conditions, but less well overseas. The 2011 Ashes series in Australia changed all that, as he stepped up to the mark in fine style and produced several outstanding bowling performances.

Graeme Swann (England)

The England spin bowler has a bit of a reputation as a joker, always laughing on the field and teasing colleagues and opponents with his quick wit. But this should not detract from the fact that Swann is probably the finest spin bowler playing today. He is aggressive and accurate, and able to turn the ball off the wicket consistency. He can also bat as well, and is a fine fielder. He has already taken nearly 200 test wickets in a relatively short test career, and opposition batsman know he is certainly no joke.

Peter Siddle (Australia)

Siddle's nickname is 'Vicious' possibly because he has a slightly punkish look about him but it could be just as appropriate for some of the deliveries he bowls. He bowls at up to 90 miles per hour regularly, and can move the ball off the wicket both towards and away from the batsman – a good skill. Siddle is a wholehearted cricketer, who on his day can be a match winner and strike fear into the hearts of even top-class international batsmen.

Chapter 12

The Domestic Cricket Scene

Cricket isn't all about test matches and one-day internationals. Cricket has a thriving domestic scene as well. For around 150 years, each April to September, professional cricket teams the length and breadth of the county have been doing battle.

In this chapter, I explain how professional cricket is run in England, what competitions you can follow, and which teams are top performers and which are also-rans. I also take a look at how cricket is trying to ditch the stuffy image, by introducing some much needed razzmatazz. Finally, I look at the emergence of the women's game.

Laying Bare the English County Cricket Scene

Professional cricket in England and Wales revolves around 18 county sides. Seventeen of these county sides are from England and one, Glamorgan, hails from Wales. These county sides compete in several competitions ranging from four-day, two-innings matches to quickfire games of twenty overs a side that last just a few hours.

All these competitions together are known as *county cricket*, the chief importance of which is that people who perform well put themselves in line for being picked to play for the England cricket team.

Scotland, although not a county side, field a team in the Pro40 competition. Flip forward to the section 'The Pro40 league' later in this chapter for more on this competition.

All the test-playing nations have their own domestic competitions. The major islands of the West Indies enter teams into the President's Trophy – which sounds like quite a posh sponsor to me. In South Africa state teams compete in the Super Sport series. Teams from the different states in New Zealand play in the Plunket Shield! Indian club sides compete for the Ranji Trophy, and the Pakistan equivalent is Quaid-e-Azam Trophy. Both competitions are highly skilled and very competitive. But probably the highest quality domestic competition in the world is Australian. This competition is called the Sheffield Shield and is fought over by six state teams.

Understanding different county cricket formats

Counties play each other in several competitions divided into two main formats.

- ✔ Four-day first class matches.
- ✔ One-day limited over matches.

First class cricket matches are of a standard just below test match level. The England and Wales Cricket Board (ECB) decides if a fixture played is worthy of being given first class status. In other countries, such as Australia, it's the domestic cricket board which decides if a fixture deserves the title of first class.

In England first class matches are played over four days with each side having two innings. Limited overs matches, even when played between county or even international teams, are not granted first class status. Refer to Chapter 3 for more on how games of cricket are divided between first class and non-first class.

When county teams play each other in four-day first class matches they are competing in the County Championship.

When county teams play each other in limited overs matches they can be competing in any of the following competitions:

- ✔ The Pro40 League
- ✔ The Twenty20 Cup

I look at all of these competitions in detail later in this chapter.

Explaining the County Championship

This championship is the most prestigious cricketing competition in the country. Eighteen county sides take part in the County Championship. The sides are divided into two divisions, intuitively enough called Division One and – wait for it! – Division Two. The best teams compete in Division One, the rest in Division Two.

Nine sides compete in each division. Teams in the separate divisions play each other twice, home and away, during the season. Therefore, teams in Division One only play teams in their same division; like the Premiership in soccer.

Teams play a total of 16 four-day first class matches. At the end of the season the top two teams in Division Two are promoted to Division One for the beginning of the following season. The bottom two teams in Division One are relegated to Division Two. The team that finishes top of Division One is called the County Champions: Cue popping of champagne corks and lots of high fives.

With each team playing 16 games, lasting up to four days a time, the County Championship is a marathon rather than a sprint. The team that comes out on top normally needs to have a good squad of players in order to cover for injuries – and for when England selects players from their ranks.

In 2000, the ECB introduced central contracts for England players. In essence, this means that centrally contracted players are employed by the ECB and not the counties. As a result, the ECB can tell county sides to give centrally contracted players a rest and can pull them out of games at anytime.

Declining attendances at County Championship matches

The County Championship started way back in 1864. Early in the twentieth century the championship was a big spectator sport: Not quite a rival for soccer but not that far behind. Back then it was not unusual to see county grounds packed to the rafters with thousands of cricket lovers – all seemingly wearing hats! And at the time games between successful county sides such as Surrey and Yorkshire were big news, and newspapers dedicated lots of column inches to reporting on them.

Boy, how times have changed! Today, the County Championship matches are watched at best by a few hundred spectators. Because games are played in the week, people are working, and have far more ways to spend leisure time than at a county cricket match.

So with so few spectators turning up, why bother with the championship at all? The answer is that the true purpose of the championship is to develop cricketing talent for test matches.

However, county cricket club members still get delighted when their side does well in the championship and winning the whole kit and caboodle brings great prestige.

Attendances at County Championships are so low that gate receipts wouldn't cover the wages of the players. Counties rely in large part on hand-outs from the ECB to survive. The ECB gets its cash from ticket sales at test matches and charging TV companies broadcast rights.

Looking at the first class counties

Eighteen county sides compete in the two divisions of the County Championship. Here is the low-down on each one.

Derbyshire

Only one championship to Derbyshire's name, back in 1936, says just about all that needs to be said. Oh yes, the home ground of Derby is famed for being cold, even in August, and Derbyshire teams have had few star players over the years.

Durham

They have only been playing county cricket since 1992. The Durham side spent most of this time languishing at the bottom of the league. However, thanks to a smattering of experienced high quality campaigners and some good young players Durham won back to back Division One titles in 2008 and 2009 – some achievement. What's more the county's Riverside stadium is now allowed to stage test matches by the ECB.

Essex

The most successful county side of the 1980s thanks to star player Graham Gooch and captain Keith Fletcher. The side has gone through a poor patch since, never threatening to take the big prize. However, in recent seasons, although their performance in the County Championship has been rather ordinary, they have proved a very effective side in one-day cricket.

Glamorgan

The only Welsh county to play in the County Championship has a chequered history. Brought into the championship in 1921, Glamorgan spent most of the time since near the bottom of the pile. However, ever so often a good team comes together in the valleys and they scoop the top prize. The last time Glamorgan won the championship was in 1997.

Gloucestershire

This West Country county can claim more success than Somerset, having won the championship last time around the small matter of 135 years ago. Difficult to say if Gloucestershire have ever enjoyed a 'golden age' but the past decade and a half has seen some success in one-day competitions.

Hampshire

Very infrequent winners of the championship but have become a force in recent years. In 2005, under the inspired leadership of great Australian leg spin bowler Shane Warne, the county were just pipped at the post in the championship. The county's new Rose Bowl ground is considered a model for cricket stadia and now hosts one-day international matches regularly and occasionally a test match too.

Kent

Undoubtedly, the best county side in the country – 30 years ago! Kent have shown signs in recent times of getting back to the top. They have finished as bridesmaid in 2005 and 2006. They then claimed the twenty20 Cup in 2007. All seemed on the up. Then came a dramatic collapse in form, and the county was relegated from Division One in 2008. They have remained in the lower tier ever since.

Lancashire

Play their home games at the impressive test venue Old Trafford – not the Old Trafford of Manchester United fame but its namesake, only a stone's throw away from the home ground of the red devils. Lancashire has a reputation for being good at one-day competitions but not so good in the County Championship. But this was slightly disproven by the county claiming its first Division One County Championship crown in 2011.

Leicestershire

Leicestershire have managed occasionally to throw off the reputation as also-rans to take three County Championships, most recently in 1998. The Leicestershire's Grace Road ground vies with Derbyshire's for the title of least impressive county ground in the country.

Middlesex

Middlesex players have the good luck to play most of their cricket at Lords. Refer to Chapter 10 for more on the special surroundings of Lords. After a decade of mediocrity, the Middlesex team seems to be on the up again, gaining promotion to Division One in 2011 and now the question is will they be able to stay there?

Northamptonshire

Northamptonshire have never managed to claim the top prize but have come close on a couple of occasions. For most of its history Northamptonshire have largely made up the numbers in the County Championship – cannon fodder for the likes of Surrey, Middlesex and Yorkshire. Recent performances suggest that this state of affairs isn't going to change soon.

Nottinghamshire

Play their home games at Trent Bridge, one of the finest grounds in the country. Nottinghamshire dominated the County Championship during the first quarter century of its history. Since then, championship titles have been few and far between but in 2005, after nearly 20 years in the doldrums, Nottinghamshire claimed their nineteenth title, followed in 2010 by their twentieth.

Somerset

One of only three counties never to have won the championship, the wicket at Somerset's home ground of Taunton is famed as being very good for batting. The county enjoyed its heyday in the 1980s when the great West Indian cricketers Joel Garner and Vivian Richards played there along with England legend Ian Botham. However, since those heady days not much has happened on the cricketing front down in Somerset.

Surrey

Surrey is one of the two most successful county sides in history. They play their cricket at the Oval ground in London, England's oldest test venue; See Chapter 10 for more. Achieving huge success at the turn of the millennium under the leadership of crackerjack captain Adam Holyoake, Surrey were dubbed the Manchester United of cricket. Therefore, relegation from Division One in 2005 was a crushing, humiliating blow. They bounced back in 2006, winning the second division championship at a canter, only to be relegated again in 2008. They made it back into the top flight thanks to winning their final four games of the 2011 season.

Sussex

The south coast county team have been described as unfashionable – in cricket speak this means that the team and ground facilities have never been up to much. However, that all changed in 2003 when, for the first time in its long history, Sussex won the championship, a trick they repeated in 2006 and 2007.

Warwickshire

In the past decade or so, Warwickshire have often challenged for top spot. Finally, after a nine-year wait, they claimed the championship in 2004. However that was a high watermark for the county and the have rarely challenged since.The team play their home matches at the Edgbaston ground in Birmingham, a regular test match venue.

Worcestershire

The wonder of Worcestershire cricket is the county's stunning New Road ground. It sits nestled between the river and the beautiful spire of Worcester cathedral. When the sun shines Worcester is a cricket ground made in heaven. Oh and yes, Worcestershire have won five championships and can boast some great names such as England's Tom Graveney, Graeme Hick and for a couple of happy years, Ian Botham.

Yorkshire

Yorkshiremen and women love their cricket and the county's huge success in the 1950s and 1960s were a great source of pride to them. Since the glory days, however, intermittent infighting in the dressing room and in the boardroom has seen the county only play a bit-part role in the championship. After winning the title for the first time in 32 years in 2001, the county was promptly relegated the next season. In 2011 after a brief return to the top flight they were once again relegated.Who knows what will happen next in the Yorkshire melodrama?

The English cricket season is very short – due to the notorious weather – only running from mid April to late September. Playing cricket in April is no joke. On occasion the first day of the cricket season in England has been interrupted by snow!

At the start of the English cricket season, some county teams warm-up by playing fixtures against teams drawn from the nation's universities. As you'd imagine these matches are often one-sided affairs with the students taking a real hiding. Occasionally, though, a student impresses so much that a county side takes him on. What's more, some of the students who play in these games have already signed a contract to play for a county side once their studies are complete.

Four-day two-innings matches between county teams and the two 'great' universities Oxford and Cambridge are given first class status. First class status is a big deal because it means that runs and wickets scored in the match count towards the players' *first class career records*. At the end of the player's career he will be judged on how many runs and wickets he took (see Chapter 13 for more on cricket statistics). So why are Oxford and Cambridge afforded first class status? Well, it's simply a preserve of the good old British class system.

Taking on board overseas players

Each county side is allowed to field two players who do not qualify by birth to play for England. These players are referred to as *overseas players*. The idea of limiting the number of overseas players that a county side can field is to ensure that enough young England qualified players get a chance to play and develop their skills. After all, potentially, they could one day be playing for the national team.

Overseas players started to be introduced in the 1960s and ever since opinion has been divided over their merits. Supporters and opponents of overseas players have been arguing since they first appeared in the English game.

Opponents of overseas players say:

- **Overseas players are just in it for the money:** They are often signed for a single season or even on some occasions just a few weeks. How can they, therefore, be fully committed to the team?

- **Overseas players block young England-qualified players:** Fewer English-born players are able to play professional cricket if their places are taken by overseas players.

- **Overseas players gain inside knowledge by playing county cricket:** This knowledge prepares the overseas players for when they play England at test or one-day international cricket.

Supporters of overseas players say:

- **Overseas players are often the crème de la crème of world cricket:** As the best players in the world they bring experience and know-how to a dressing-room. Young England-qualified players benefit from playing alongside overseas stars.

- **Overseas players bring in the crowds:** Paying fans are attracted to the glamour of seeing the best players in the world compete.

The overseas player argument has been going for 40 years and is likely to keep going for just as long again.

Passport get-out clause

The European Free Movement of People law, which Britain as an EU member is signed-up to, guarantees the free movement of people to work anywhere in the EU, and it's having a strange impact on, of all things, county cricket. The law means that if a player has the right to a passport in any EU member country they can come and play for a county side, without being deemed an overseas player. Therefore, an Australian cricketer with Greek parentage could come and play in England and not be counted as overseas. Some counties have been taking advantage of this quirk in the law to sign up good quality cricketers from around the globe, without using up their overseas quota.

The trend of people from outside the EU exploiting their right to an EU passport started when Maros Kolpak, a handball player, went to the European Court in a bid to play in Germany without being classed as a foreigner, claiming restraint of trade. Maros Kolpak won his case.

The reality is that counties are going to keep signing overseas players because all the other counties are doing it. The first county to break ranks and go without an overseas player is on a hiding to nothing, because they will be at a big disadvantage when they play the other counties, which have quality overseas players in their ranks. Until the 1990s, diehard Yorkshire wouldn't even pick players who were born outside the county's borders. They have now gone with the flow and employ players from other parts of the UK and overseas.

Sometimes a county's overseas players can change several times during a cricket season. This is because the top international players may have to leave part way through the season to play for their national side. What tends to happen is that when an overseas player is away on international duty the county will bring in another overseas player as cover until the original overseas player returns.

A person can play cricket for England if he meets one of the following criteria:

- ✔ Born in the UK
- ✔ Parents or grandparents born in the UK
- ✔ UK resident and playing for an English county side for at least four years

Anyone meeting these criteria is referred to as *England-qualified*.

Scoring points in the County Championship

As if cricket wasn't complex enough – what with all the crazy jargon – the ECB has designed an almost impenetrable points system for the County Championship. Even top boffins find understanding how teams score points in the County Championship a bit of a stretch but here's how it works in plain English.

- ✔ For winning a game, a team gets 16 points, the losing team gets nothing.

- ✔ If the two teams draw the match they both get 3 points. In a tied match – where both teams have completed their two innings and the scores are level – each teams scores 8 points.

- ✔ If the match is abandoned without a ball being bowled, each side earns three points.

Easy so far, I hear you say, but now we come to the *bonus points system*.

Under the bonus points system, teams earn bonus points on top of the ones they gather for the result of the match. Bonus points are earned for scoring runs and taking opposition wickets in each team's first innings. Teams are only awarded bonus points for the first innings of a match. Performances in the second innings do not count towards bonus points. Furthermore, all bonus point calculations are made on the first inning score after 110 overs, or when the innings ends, whichever comes first. The points are awarded as shown in Table 12-1.

Table 12-1	English County Championship Bonus Points
First innings score after 110 overs	*Batting Points Awarded*
200–49 runs	1
250–99	2
300–49	3
350–99	4
Over 400	5
Opposition wickets taken after 130 overs	*Bowling Points Awarded*
3–5	1
6–8	2
9–10	3

Teams in the County Championship have points deducted if they bowl their overs too slowly. Teams are required to bowl an average of 16 overs an hour, and the two teams undertake to complete 104 overs in a full day's play.

Counties are supposed to produce wickets that allow an even contest between batsmen and bowlers. This mean that the condition of the wicket is such that it provides some assistance to the bowlers but not so much that playing shots is incredibly hard for batsmen. Occasionally, a county fails to prepare a wicket that conforms to this rule and the ECB docks points.

As if the County Championship wasn't excitement enough, all the county teams also compete in the Second Eleven Championship. Second eleven teams are made up of the county playing staff that aren't quite good enough to play in the main county side at any given time. Second eleven matches are mainly an opportunity to test younger cricketers and gently ease older cricketers back from injury. The Second Eleven Championship trophy doesn't carry anywhere near as much prestige as the main County Championship gong.

Gauging how counties are run

Unlike soccer clubs – which tend to be run by a board elected by shareholders, a rich local businessman or the occasional Russian billionaire – county cricket clubs are run by the membership.

Members get to vote on who they want to sit on the board. The board run the whole show; appointing the team captain, coaching staff and making sure that the inevitable financial losses are minimised. Any member is free to stand for election to the board. See Chapter 13 for more on how to become a county member.

The Minor Counties

England and Wales have dozens of counties yet only eighteen play in the County Championship. What happens to the rest?

Well, these counties still have representative teams but they get to compete in the Minor Counties Championship rather than the full County Championship. Much less attention is paid to the Minor Counties Championship because the games aren't deemed to be first class. Minor county sides tend to be made up of good club cricketers and ex-county professionals.

One of the key differences between County Championship sides and minor counties is that the former have a paid professional staff of players who are signed to play for a season. Minor counties don't have much money so they can't afford to keep full-time playing staff.

The reasons for a county only being allowed to play in the minor counties competition is normally a combination of history, home ground facilities and simple economics. Minor counties are like non-league clubs in soccer.

Sometimes the minor counties get to play the big boys, normally in one-day limited overs competitions. Regular as clockwork, every couple of years, one of these minor counties teams plays out of its skin and beats the big boys in a game. Usually, though, the matches are very one-sided in favour of the County Championship side.

No automatic promotion or relegation exists between the County Championship and minor counties championship. But a minor county showing lots of ambition can gain first class status. The last minor county to be allowed to join the County Championship was Durham in 1992. But the transition isn't easy; Durham spent most of their first decade in the County Championship getting beaten.

Losing Cricket's Stuffy Image: Introducing One-Day Cricket

Take a survey of people's perception of county cricket and the following are bound to crop-up; men in whites (some with what look suspiciously like beer bellies) who stomp off the field at the mere presence of a black cloud on the horizon and a smattering of elderly spectators slumped asleep in their chairs.

But English cricket has been making a big effort to throw off this old stuffy image. The main weapon in this battle has been one-day limited overs cricket matches.

Limited overs – or one-day – cricket began in the 1960s with the 60 overs Gillette knock-out cup competition and the 40 overs a side Sunday League.

The one-day concept caught on fast. In fact, the money it generated probably rescued several counties from going to the wall.

Fans loved the idea that they could see a complete game of cricket in one day and were thrilled that the batsmen may have to get a move on and try and actually score runs fast. County Championship matches were slow, tactical affairs. One-day cricket offered some welcome crash, bang and wallop.

Since the 1960s, the one-day competitions have changed but the basic idea hasn't: Provide the crowds with some excitement and they'll come back.

Today counties compete in the following one-day competitions:

- ✔ The Pro40 League
- ✔ The Twenty20 Cup

Here's a look at each competition in turn.

The Pro40 League

In the Pro40 League, teams are divided into two divisions, just like the County Championship. Each team plays every other team home and away. Again, just like the County Championship, three teams are promoted from Division Two at the end of the season, while three are relegated from Division One. The Pro-40 has gone through many incarnations. Back in the 1960s it was called the John Player League (JPL), with 40 over-a-side matches played on a Sunday. More recently, the JPL became the Norwich Union League in which matches were played any day of the week, with each side given 50 overs to bat. Pro 40 is like an amalgam of the two. Team innings are limited to 40 overs a side (like the JPL) but games take place throughout the week (like the Norwich Union League). Some games start in the mid afternoon and end under floodlights: They can be a real spectacle.

The Twenty20 Cup

The Twenty20 Cup is the new kid on the block and has taken English cricket by storm since it was introduced in 2003. Each side has twenty overs to score as many runs as possible. Frantic, exciting cricket is the object and judging by the large crowds the format has been attracting, it seems to be hitting the spot. Teams are divided into tworegional zonal groups – north and south. Teams play each other on a round-robin basis home and away, so that means 16 matches per side, normally played over a period of a few weeks. As a result, neighbouring counties get to play each other. Four teams emerge from the regional zonal groups to compete in the quarter-finals. The winners of these quarter-finals go through to Twenty20 finals day. On this day – held at a major venue – both semi finals are played and the winners of each then play off under the floodlights in a final game. Twenty20 finals day is a massive set piece occasion, normally played in front of a capacity crowd with lots more watching at home on television. The viewers really get their money's worth as it involves 120 overs being bowled, fast action, big hits and spectacular fielding exploits – just as long as the rain holds off!

A word from our sponsors

The current sponsor of the Twenty20 cup is Friends provident. The Pro 40 is backed by Clydesdale Bank, and Liverpool Victoria (or LV= for short) has sponsored the County Championship for around a decade. The money brought in by these sponsorship arrangements is key to the economics of cricket in England and Wales.

Putting on a party: One-day razzmatazz

One-day limited overs matches are all about bums on seats. In effect, the money made in the limited overs games, when combined with cash made through test cricket, keeps the first class counties afloat.

In order to keep the turnstiles turning, the counties have tried to inject some colour and fun into one-day games.

Some attempts at jazzing the game up have been more successful and longer lasting than others but here are the main ways that a little pizzazz has been brought into cricket.

- ✔ **Coloured kits:** In one-day matches boring old cricket whites are passé. Instead teams have their own coloured strips. These kits are sometimes referred to as *pyjamas*.

- ✔ **Floodlighting:** This allows games to take place in the evening. Combined with coloured kits it helps create a unique atmosphere. Most major grounds in England, Australia and India now have permanent floodlights, and they are even being used in test cricket.

- ✔ **White ball:** Instead of using a traditional red ball, a white coloured cricket ball is used. The big idea is that the batsmen, fielders and spectators can see it more easily under the floodlights. More recently some one-day games have seen the use of a bright pink ball. The idea is that the colour is easier to pick out in the night sky when many games are played under lights.

- ✔ **Squad numbers and names on shirts:** This helps the crowd identify who is who on the cricket field more easily.

Games that start in the afternoon and end in the evening under floodlights are called *day night matches*. Floodlighting at English grounds doesn't tend to be as powerful as at grounds overseas, in particular South Africa and Australia. Most English grounds are old and a little tatty and don't have built in floodlights. Therefore, counties have to hire floodlights and cranes to hoist them high in the air. This cobbled-together floodlighting does the job – just. But this floodlighting is nothing compared to the lighting at grounds like Melbourne, Sydney or Newlands in Cape Town.

Injecting some excitement: Twenty20 cricket

Twenty20 cricket has been a phenomenal success. When it started in 2003, no-one was sure how it would go. But county clubs were shocked that suddenly they had thousands of people *wanting* to come and watch cricket.

For once cricket seems to have found a winning formula, one that adapts to changing tastes and patterns of work.

The main objections to traditional cricket from potential paying customers are:

- ✔ Matches take too long. Even 50 overs an innings matches can take a whole day to complete.
- ✔ Matches are often played in the week and in the daytime when most people are at work.
- ✔ Matches have too many hold-ups in play.
- ✔ Matches stop for bad light and rain, and the weather is often bad.

Twenty20 is cricket's latest and most successful answer to these objections. Here's why it appeals:

- ✔ Matches are often played in the evening, after spectators have left work.
- ✔ Some matches are floodlit: These allow the later starts and stop the practice of going off for bad light.
- ✔ Games are held in high summer, when the weather should be at its best and the nights warm for spectators.
- ✔ Teams are under strict instructions to bowl their 20 overs quickly which means fewer hold-ups and games are normally done and dusted in a little over three hours.

Some critics have warned that counties could be in danger of killing the golden goose. At present, the Twenty20 Cup competition is played at the height of summer when the notoriously dodgy English weather should be at its best. However, the number of fixtures is expanding and the danger is that, in time, games could be held early or late in the season; when the weather isn't so good. What's more, the risk is always there that the public could get bored with the format. As the saying goes 'familiarity breeds contempt'.

Outlaws, Sabres and your dad getting on down

County cricket clubs have been desperate to jazz up their image to appeal to young people. They reckon that unless they can attract younger fans then they may as well shut up shop. But this is not an easy task with the typical member of a county club being between 60 and 70 years of age.

Counties have tried re-branding. In short this involves sticking a snazzy, exciting word on the end of the county name.

Therefore, Nottinghamshire has morphed into the Nottinghamshire Outlaws, Somerset into the Somerset Sabres and Kent into Kent Spitfires.

The whole re-branding exercise may have helped shift a few shirts from the county shops but for many cricket fans the whole exercise is a bit embarrassing: Akin to watching your dad bop away to a hardcore house music track!

And its not just the English who are into the renaming thing. In Australia the historic Victoria cricket club now call themselves the Bushrangers. While the new Indian premier league is full of snazzy names the Deccan Chargers for instance and the very regal Chennai Super kings, see chapter three for the low down on the Indian Premier League and its growing importance in the global game of cricket.

If the umpires deem that the light conditions are so bad that the batsmen can't see the ball properly, and are therefore in physical danger of being struck, then they can take the players off the field.. When the players are off the field, play is said to have *stopped for bad light*. Refer to Chapter 2 for more on how this law works in practice.

In giving twenty20 cricket the thumbs up, a note of caution must be struck. Some cricket fans aren't keen on the format, suggesting that games are too short and are all about batsmen hitting the ball as hard as possible, and bowlers seeking only to restrict them. They argue that this takes some of the finesse out of batting and bowling and ultimately could lead to a decline in skill levels.

Picking up the pace of scoring

A funny thing has been happening in one-day limited overs cricket in recent years. Teams have been scoring far more runs and this has led to more exciting matches.

When one-day limited overs matches started in the 1960s many teams used similar tactics as they did in County Championship cricket. The opening batsmen looked to defend against the new ball and the innings would wind-up gradually into a crescendo of run scoring at the end of the innings. Typically, innings scores of 200 runs plus were considered good.

However, when fielding restrictions were introduced batting tactics started to change. Under the new restrictions, the fielding captain was forced to keep most of his fielders within 30 yards of the batsmen for the first 10 overs of the batting side's innings, in an area called the *infield*. This meant that the batsmen had less chance of being caught if they hit the ball in the air, just as long as they cleared the infield. See Chapter 8 for more on one-day batting tactics.

Batsmen were thus encouraged to play more aggressively at the start of the innings and they haven't looked back since. In fact, some teams go for their shots from the off and a total of between 280 and 300 runs in a 50 over innings is now considered par for the course.

Run scoring tends to be fastest in twenty20 cricket because teams know that with eleven batsmen the bowling side is unlikely to dismiss them all in just twenty overs. Normally batsmen in twenty20 games take a couple of balls to get themselves accustomed to how the ball is bouncing off the pitch and the pace of the bowler's deliveries and then go for their shots.

In one-day cricket matches, the umpires tend to be very strict in calling deliveries wide. A wide is called when the umpire believes that the batsman didn't have a fair chance to hit the ball because it was directed outside his reach. But in one-day cricket almost any delivery that is directed past the player's leg stump, which the player fails to hit, is called as a wide. If a wide is called then the batting team is awarded a run and the bowler has to deliver the ball again.

Coming Up Trumps: English Women's Cricket

English women's cricket goes back almost as far the men's game. But, in truth, throughout its long history, the women's game has been overshadowed by the men's. The women's game, although skilful, lacks the physical strength associated with matches between teams of men. But of late, English women's cricket has been coming out of the shadows and showing the world what it has to offer.

Looking at competitions for women

All the first class counties, along with a host of minor counties, field teams in the Women's County Championship. Players are selected from the counties' own coaching academy and local clubs.

Bringing home the Ashes

In 2005 under the captaincy of the bright Sussex cricketer Clare Connor, the England women's team triumphed over their Australian rivals for the first time since 1963. Since then these good results have continued, with England retaining the Ashes in 2009 and 2011. Winning the women's one day World Cup in Australia in 2009 was particularly sweet for the English, and add to that triumph in inaugural women's twenty20 World Cup in 2011 and these are golden days for women's cricket.

The structure of the Women's County Championship is different to the men's. Teams are split into four divisions of six, each meeting twice. There is no divide between county teams and minor county teams. So for example division four currently contains Derbyshire and Northamptonshire – both county sides with men's teams who play first-class cricket – and Cornwall, a 'minor county' side. To help spread the game further afield the women's county championship contains a team from the Netherlands. A season consists of ten matches, but these games are all 50 overs a side one-day affairs. There is promotion and relegation between the four divisions. In addition, there is a twenty20 cup for women with the top two teams in the two divisions – northern and southern – playing semi-finals and the winners of these progressing to a grand final.

Women's cricket is an amateur game. Therefore, players have to juggle the demands of work and family with pursuing their sport. Nevertheless, top women cricketers are fine athletes, taking their sport deadly seriously.

Getting involved in women's cricket

If you're a male club cricketer you may not want to read the following lines: I'm afraid the chances of a club cricketer being picked for England are zilch. The gap in skills between club and test players is absolutely huge. However, if you're a female club cricketer, the situation is very different.

The skill gap isn't quite as great in the women's game. In fact, many of the English women's team play club cricket. Good performances at club level can bring county then national recognition. Therefore, if you're keen on playing women's club cricket and, crucially, show plenty of talent, it could, fingers crossed, provide a route to playing for your country!

Women's cricket teams are normally run under the umbrella of a large men's cricket club. To find your local women's cricket check out the English Cricket Board Web site at www.ecb.org.uk.

Chapter 13

Becoming a Cricket Fan

. . . .

. . . .

*1*n this chapter, you find out everything you need to know to become an A1 cricket fan.

You discover how you can get your hands on tickets for the really big games and what to take with you on your big day out at the cricket. You also find out the benefits of joining a county club – or the famous Marylebone Cricket Club – as well as how to enjoy cricket for free in the local park. Armchair fans are also catered for with the low-down on cricket on the box, radio, online and inside the pages of national newspapers.

A peek at the complex world of cricket statistics completes the joys of being a cricket fan.

Watching International Cricket Live

For many cricket fans a day at a test or one-day international match is the bees knees. They get to watch the best players in the world going head-to-head, soak up the crowd atmosphere and partake of the odd beer or ten and perhaps the occasional glass of something chilled and sparkling. Cricket crowds are almost always good-natured, applauding the efforts of opponents. Also, cricket is a family-friendly sport, with reduced prices for children.

Poring over the rain ticketing rules

Cricket is the only major spectator sport that can be derailed by a few spots of rain or even dark clouds overhead.

The two umpires get to decide whether the players should play through rain or bad light or trudge off the field back to the pavilion, waiting for the sky to brighten and wet weather to subside. Umpires usually stop play in a professional cricket match when

✔ The condition of the pitch is being altered by rain.

✔ The batsmen are unable to sight the ball properly because of poor light.

At one time umpires would take players off and stop the match at the drop of a hat, all to the general dismay of the spectators. However, these days, it seems, umpires are a little more considerate of the paying public. Often umpires allow play to continue through short, light showers of rain: They get weather forecasts during the day and can better judge whether

any rain is set to hang around or pass over the ground in a jiffy.

What is more, the umpires often extend the hours of play if, at some point during the day, they have had to take the players off the field due to rain or poor light.

In addition, refunds to spectators when rain or bad light stops play are more generous than ever.

If your day at the test match is spoilt by rain or bad light you can expect a partial or full refund. The refunds policy for test matches works like this:

✔ Fewer then 10 overs played in a day's play: full refund

✔ Fewer than 10–25 overs played: 50 per cent refund.

However, if rain or poor light stops play, you receive no refund of transport or any other costs you may have incurred.

Even people who aren't completely clear about the rules of the game can still enjoy their day at the cricket.

Each summer England play six or seven test matches, with two teams from the test-playing nations touring England every summer. Tests in England usually start on a Thursday and end on a Monday.

Each test match is scheduled to last five days but sometimes one side runs away with the game and the match finishes a day or two early. Therefore, in order to be guaranteed a full day's cricket, you should try to get tickets for one of the first three days.

The cricket rule makers, the International Cricket Council (ICC), have been getting tough on captains whose teams do not bowl their overs in quick time. In recent years, there have been several instances of captains being fined part or all of the pay they receive for playing in a match because of a slow over rate. Some captains have even suffered short suspensions from playing when their teams have failed to get through their overs in time. Does this tough stance make a difference? Not really, it seems, as over rates in one-day and test match cricket are still below what they ought to be and innings take too long to complete as a result.

Grabbing yourself a ticket

Test and one-day international cricket in England is riding a wave of popularity. Improved performances by the England test team are the key to this popularity. Ever since the 2005 Ashes triumph the English and Wales Cricket Board (ECB), which runs test and county cricket in England, reported unprecedented spectator interest. No doubt about it, test cricket is the hot sport of the moment!

But this good news story presents cricket fans with a problem – how to get hold of a test or one-day international match ticket?

Tickets for test matches go on general sale over the winter, a few months before the start of the cricket season, which starts in April. The sale of tickets is managed by the individual venues. You can order these over the phone or through the venue's Web site. See the sidebar 'English test match grounds' later in this chapter for full details on all the venues.

But in recent years some matches have already been sold out before the general sale starts, because members of the England Supporters' Club, county cricket clubs, and Marylebone Cricket Club (MCC) get first bite of the cherry. They are able to enter a ballot for tickets before the remainder go on general sale.

If you want the best chance of getting your hands on test and one-day international match tickets, you should join a county club, MCC, or the England's Supporters Club. Joining the MCC is not easily done; see 'Hob-Nobbing with Cricket's Elite: Joining the MCC' later in this chapter for more. Check out www. ecb.co.uk for more on joining the England Supporters' Club.

English cricket grounds are not big, particularly when compared to Australian venues. The largest, Lords, holds just 28,000 spectators.

Try to get a seat that gives you a good view of the giant video replay screen in the ground. The video replay screen can really add to your enjoyment of your day at the cricket. Usually, giant video replay screens are only operational when a television company is broadcasting the match.

English test match grounds

The ECB decides which grounds get to host one-day international and test matches. As far as the county cricket clubs, who run the venues, are concerned getting international cricket is a financial bonanza. These matches mean big crowds all paying top whack for tickets as well as a fortune to be made from catering.

The ECB chooses which venues get their hands on the golden goose of international cricket based on a number of factors including ground facilities and transportation links.

Some of the main venues for international cricket in England are:

- **Lords:** The most famous ground in the world; read more about this cathedral of cricket in Chapter 10. Address: Lords Cricket Ground, London NW8 8QN. Ticket line: 0207 432 1000, www.mcctickets.com or www.lords.org.

- **The Oval:** The oldest test venue in England which traditionally holds the last test of the summer. Address: The Brit Oval Kennington, London SE11 5SS. Ticket line: 0207 582 6660 or try http://www.surreycricket.com/.

- **Edgbaston:** Famed for its raucous atmosphere. Address: Warwickshire County Cricket Club, County Ground, Edgbaston Birmingham, B5 7QU. Ticket line: 0870 062 1902 or http://www.eticketing.co.uk/edgbaston.

- **Trent Bridge:** One of the most picturesque cricket grounds in the country. Address: Nottinghamshire County Cricket Club, Trent Bridge, Nottingham, NG2 6AG. Ticket line: 0115 982 3000 or www.nottsccc.co.uk/ticket.cfm.

- **Headingley:** This ground has seen many of England's greatest cricket triumphs over the years. Address: Yorkshire County Cricket Club, Headingley Cricket Ground, Leeds LS6 3BU. Ticket line: 0871 222 0994 or try www.yorkshireccc.com.

- **Old Trafford:** Lancashire's headquarters has held test matches for more than 100 years and has a spectacular pavilion – also England's wettest major ground. Address: Ticket office, Lancashire County Cricket Club, Old Trafford, Manchester, M16 0PX. Ticket line: 0870 062 5050 or try www.lccc.co.uk.

- **Riverside:** A relatively new test venue, Riverside's far north location can mean inclement weather. Address: Riverside, Chester-le-Street, Durham, DH3 3QR. Ticket line: 0870 389 1991 or try www.durhamccc.co.uk.

- **Cardiff:** Hosted its first test match in 2009 and what a match as it was a crunch Ashes encounter Address: SWALEC Stadium, Cardiff, CF11 9XR, (ticket line 0871 2823401).

- **Rosebowl:** The latest ground to be added to the test circuit, with the first test played there in 2011. A lovely place to watch cricket, and the home of Hampshire county cricket club. Address: Rosebowl, Botley Road, West End, Southampton, Hampshire SO30 3XH; ticket line 023 8047 2002.

Tickets are far easier to acquire if you don't live in England. In Australia, apart from games against England, it is unusual for a test or one-day international match to be sold out, and you can turn up on the day and pay at the turnstile. The same is true in the other test playing countries, but to an even greater extent.

Counting the cost of rising ticket prices

The England and Wales Cricket Board (ECB) was quick to wake up to the growing demand for test and one-day match tickets. And guess what? They've been putting up the price of tickets. In fact, ticket prices at many English test venues have more than doubled in the pastdecade . Expect to pay between £50 and £80 for a ticket for a day at a test or one-day international match. The most expensive venues are the two London grounds, the Oval and Lords.

Ticket touts are becoming an ever-present feature at test and one-day match venues throughout the country. They have been known to charge fans up to ten times face value and cases exist of fraudulent tickets being sold. Ticket touts are vultures – best walk away!

Under 16s and OAPs enjoy discounted ticket prices.

Going on an overseas tour

Following the England cricket team on its travels to play cricket abroad can be a lot of fun. When the England cricket team plays abroad it is said to be *on tour*.

The other test-playing nations such as Australia, India, West Indies and South Africa are top holiday destinations and great places to watch cricket. What's more, England tour in the winter, so if you travel to watch the team play you can escape cold and wet Blighty and get some welcome sunshine.

England's one-day and test record isn't very good away from home. If you follow the England team on tour, be prepared for the possibility that you may end up watching the side lose.

Travelling with a supporters' tour

Holiday companies specialising in sports tourism have been offering package holidays for England cricket fans to follow the exploits of their heroes abroad for about two decades. These packages are called supporters' tours.

Some of the advantages of going on a supporter's tour are:

- ✔ Flights, accommodation and transfers are arranged by the tour company.
- ✔ Some companies offer meals and nights of entertainment hosted by ex-test cricketers. These can be good occasions for autograph hunting.
- ✔ Tickets to the cricket are included in the price.

The most famous supporters' tours are run by an organisation called the Barmy Army. Hundreds and sometimes thousands travel with the army and they often get good deals with local hoteliers and, yes, pubs! The Barmy army like to sing and dance and have added a lot to the atmosphere of test and one-day cricket around the world. To find out more about their tours check out www.barmyarmy.com.

Travelling independently

Of course, you don't have to travel in a group, you can do things – pardon the pun – off your own bat.

Things to bear in mind if you're thinking of travelling independently include:

- ✔ **You can draw up your own itinerary:** This allows you to go where you want, when you want, rather than joining the herd.

- ✔ **You can travel within a budget:** Travelling independently is generally a lot cheaper than going on a supporter's tour.

- ✔ **You are not guaranteed tickets:** This is potentially a big downside. You have to source and buy tickets yourself.

The price of supporters' tours has increased markedly in recent years. Holiday companies take a big mark up on hotels, flights and tickets. If you want to support on a budget then the most cost effective way is travel independently, booking your own flight, hotel and sourcing tickets locally.

If you go on a supporters' tour, try to go with a friend. The holiday companies offering supporters' tours tend to charge whopping big single occupancy supplement fees.

Before going to the airport to catch your flight double check that your passport and other documents are in order. Some countries such as South Africa and Australia won't accept your passport if it has less than six months left before expiring. Many non-EU nations require you to have a valid visa, so check before travelling.

Becoming a County Member

For an annual membership fee normally of around £150– £250 a year anyone can become a county member (see Table 13-1).

Being a member brings you some real advantages:

✔ Free entry to home County Championship matches; some counties also throw in free entry into the club's home limited overs matches.

✔ Free entry to away county matches.

✔ Early entry into ballots for test match tickets.

✔ Seats in the pavilion on match days and drinks in the members' bar.

✔ A vote on which individuals get to sit on the management board of the county cricket club.

Some counties also offer heavily discounted membership rates for people over 65, the under 16s, and those who live more than 50 miles from the ground.

If you have plenty of time to spare to watch live cricket then county membership can make financial sense. The average county plays something like 50–60 days of cricket at home each year.

Table 13-1	County Cricket Club Membership Details	
County	*Telephone Number*	*Website*
Derbyshire	01322 383 211	www.derbyshireccc.com
Durham	0191 387 1717	www.durhamccc.org.uk
Essex	01245 252 420	www.essexcricket.org.uk
Glamorgan	0871 282 3401	www.glamorgancricket.com
Gloucestershire	0117 910 8000	www.gloscricket.co.uk
Hampshire	02380 472 002	www.hampshirecricket.com
Kent	01227 456 886	www.kentccc.com
Lancashire	0870 062 5000	www.lccc.co.uk
Leicestershire	0871 282 1879	www.leicestershireccc.co.uk
Middlesex	0207 289 1300	www.middlesexccc.co.uk
Northamptonshire	01604 514 455	www.nccc.co.uk
Nottinghamshire	0870 168 8888	www.nottsccc.co.uk
Somerset	0845 337 1875	www.somersetcountycc.co.uk
Surrey	0207 820 5715	www.surreycricket.com
Sussex	0871 282 2003	www.sussexcricket.co.uk
Warwickshire	0870 062 1902	www.thebears.co.uk
Worcestershire	01905 337 921	www.wccc.co.uk

Hob-Nobbing with Cricket's Elite: Joining the MCC

The Marylebone Cricket Club (MCC) is known the world over, and is the most exclusive cricket club on the planet. The MCC owns the wonderful Lords cricket ground – refer to Chapter 10 for more on this cathedral of cricket – and members get to watch games at the ground, in the historic pavilion.

A real snob factor goes along with being a part of the MCC. Members get to sport the famous 'egg and bacon' tie – orange and red in colour – and hob-nob in the famous MCC members' bar at Lords.

Many of the top people in Britain are members of the MCC, ranging from rock stars to cabinet ministers. But the MCC has a reputation of being stuck in the past and only started to admit women members a few years back.

Joining the MCC isn't as straightforward as becoming a county member. Existing members have to propose candidates, who then go on a long, long waiting list. Apparently a candidate can expect to wait around 20 years before getting through the door. Why such a long wait? Existing members have to die off or leave before new ones can join!

As you'd expect, joining the MCC isn't cheap or easy. You have to be proposed, seconded and sponsored by a full member of the MCC. You have to pay an upfront £215 registration fee plus a unspecified joining fee when, hopefully, you get invited to join.

You can beat the queue in one way, by becoming a playing member of the MCC. This entails being picked for the MCC's own cricket team. The MCC plays big prestigious club teams. To be picked you have to be recommended by an MCC playing member.

MCC teams usually consist of a handful of existing playing members and trial-lists – people who are trying to prove their worth and gain admission through the playing membership route.

Once picked you have to play well for at least half dozen matches – maybe more – over two years. The captain of the MCC team has to write a glowing report about you, saying what a great player you are and a smashing bloke. Just the sort of chap we should have at the club!

At this point the club may grant you playing membership or it may not. Becoming a playing member isn't easy, or else everyone would do it. Even some very good club cricketers fail to make the grade.

Having the MCC team visit is a big deal in club cricket. The MCC teams turn up in their orange and red club blazers and even fly their flag from the club's flagpole, if one exists, during the match.

I have played against MCC teams on a few occasions and you can tell which players are the triallists. They are on their best behaviour, and desperate to impress the captain, so there's no swearing and they have their shirts always tucked firmly into their trousers. Check out www.lords.org/mcc or telephone 0207 616 8660 for more on joining this very exclusive club.

Enjoying Your Day at the Cricket

Nothing is quite like being a spectator at a big cricket match, particularly if the weather is nice and sunny. You not only get to enjoy the action on the pitch but the crowd itself are quite a spectacle – from knowledgeable types who know the ins and outs of the game to groups of friends there purely to soak up the atmosphere and partake of a drink or two, cricket matches can be great fun. Here's a guide to all you need to know to enjoy your day at the cricket.

Understanding the times of play in test matches

A day's play in a test match in England is split into three *sessions of play*. The morning session of play runs from 10.30 a.m. or 11.00 a.m. for 2 hours. The players then troop off for lunch which lasts 40 minutes. The middle session of play also lasts two hours, when again players leave the field and take tea. After a 20 minute tea break teams emerge for the final session of play which lasts two hours. Ideally the day's play should finish between 5.30 p.m. and 6.00 p.m.

Often, however, a day's play is extended for any one of three reasons:

- **Not enough overs have been bowled:** In test matches the fielding side is supposed to bowl 90 overs in a day's play. If they fail to do this the day's play can be extended for up to an hour until the full allocation of overs is bowled.

- **Bad light or rain stoppages have reduced play:** If the players have left the field for any time during the day for bad light or rain, the umpires can extend the day's play by up to an hour. Sometimes, when a substantial amount of time has been lost to rain or bad light early in the match, the umpires may decree that play will finish later on each of the remaining days of the match.

✔ **The chance exists of a result:** If the captain of the fielding team reckons that he has a chance of dismissing all the opposition's batsmen in their second innings, and thereby win the match, he can ask for extra time at the end of the day to finish the job. The umpires decide whether play should be extended. The right to request extra time to finish the match doesn't apply on the final day of the test.

When 10 out of 11 of a team's batsmen are dismissed the innings comes to an end, the players leave the field – yet again – this time for 10 minutes. This stoppage in play is called the *change in innings*. The umpires subtract two overs from the amount allocated to be bowled during the day.

If the umpires take the players off the field due to rain or bad light and feel that play has no chance of resuming, they will call off play for the day. The crowd then leaves the ground and may be able to claim a refund on tickets. Flick back to the sidebar 'Poring over the rain ticketing rules' for more information on refund rules.

If rain and bad light stops play for a large part of the day then the umpire will extend the playing time but this may not be enough to compensate for the time lost out of the match.

Understanding the times of play in a one-day international

Fortunately, the rules governing hours of play in a one-day international match are far more straightforward.

Players do not take a lunch or tea-break. Instead play stops at change of innings – for anything up to an hour. If the weather and light is good teams play on until all the overs in the match have been bowled and a result achieved.

But if rain or bad light persists, the umpires may start to cut the number of overs. Therefore, games can be reduced from 50 to say 40, 20 or even 10 overs a side.

If the match is seriously disrupted by the weather then you may find the Duckworth-Lewis system may come into play.

The idea of Duckworth-Lewis is that a result can be achieved even if the number of overs each side has to bat is different. Refer to Chapter 3 for more on this fiendishly complex system.

Observing proper etiquette

Cricket is a lot less stuffy than it once was but nevertheless there is still etiquette to observe. Mostly this etiquette is about being considerate to your fellow spectators.

Try to avoid the following cricket faux pas and you'll enjoy your day at the cricket and hopefully so will those around you – even if your team is beaten!

- ✔ **Keep chanting to a minimum:** Nothing is more distracting than having someone bawl out a player's name or sing a repetitive song for hours on end, although this doesn't stop some members of the Barmy Army after a few ales have been consumed!

- ✔ **Avoid standing during play:** Only leave your seat at the end of an over, or you could be obscuring the view for fellow spectators. This big no-no will have your fellow spectators tut-tutting and shaking their heads.

- ✔ **Never walk in front of the sight screens:** Sight screens are the white-washed large wooden boards at both ends of the ground. The sight screens exist so that the batsmen can more easily spot the ball leaving the bowler's hand. If you wander in front of these sight screens at any time during play, the batsman is allowed to ask the umpire to stop play until you have moved. Stopping play like this is a sure-fire-way to make yourself public enemy number one.

- ✔ **Follow the instructions of stewards:** Grounds employ stewards to manage the crowd. Their job is to ensure that everyone has a good time but stays safe, and doesn't interfere with play. If they ask you to do something, such as move seat or wait in a stairway before returning to your seat while an over is completed, just do it. If you don't follow their instructions, or are rude to them, you can be ejected from the ground. You can tell who the stewards are at cricket grounds because they wear fluorescent bibs.

Some test match spectators like to listen to the radio coverage of the cricket while they are watching the game. See the section 'Following cricket on the radio' later in this chapter for more on what's on offer over the airwaves. If you choose to listen to the radio commentary while spectating, be considerate to your fellow spectators and use headphones.

Don't feel tempted to run onto the field of play during or after the match. It will lead to you being thrown out of the ground and you're likely to get arrested!

Not just test and one-day international matches attract big crowds. Twenty20 matches also pull in the punters.

Deciding what to take with you to the cricket

You're free to go as you are to the cricket but you may want to consider packing a small bag with some useful items:

- ✓ **Binoculars:** At most grounds you are a long way from the action. A pair of binoculars can help you view the action close up as well as spot the best fancy-dress outfit in the crowd.

- ✓ **Liquid refreshment:** Why not take your favourite tipple to enjoy? Don't overdo it so that you fall asleep and miss the action, though.

- ✓ **Packed lunch:** Catering facilities at many cricket grounds tend to be limited to burgers, chips and chicken. If fast food isn't your thing then you'll have to bring your own packed lunch.

- ✓ **Reading material:** A good book or a newspaper can help you pass time during the lunch and tea intervals or gaps between innings.

- ✓ **Sun cream:** If you're stuck outside for hours at a time the sun's UV rays may well damage your skin. Be safe, slap on the sun cream to protect yourself, even when the sky is cloudy overhead.

- ✓ **Umbrella:** The rain is a sad fact of life for the cricket fan. Some experienced cricket watchers turn up to matches with umbrella and sou'wester packed.

Lots of test match venues limit the amount of alcohol fans can take into a ground on match days, some even bar it – pardon the pun – altogether. They claim these limits are for 'health and safety' reasons and, oh, by the way, completely coincidentally, venues make a big pile of cash from selling booze to fans in the ground.

Bags are searched on entry and you won't be able to bring a metal knife into the ground, even one for cutting up bread or dealing with a particularly hefty piece of Stilton.

Partying on the terraces

The atmosphere generated by a big cricket crowd can be something to savour. You find scores of spectators in fancy dress: Two fans actually travel the globe following England dressed as Sylvester the Cat and The Pink Panther! Every so often the crowd breaks into a Mexican wave and during lunch and tea intervals you're often entertained by live music and games of kwik cricket. A nice sunny day at the cricket is heard to beat.

Being an Armchair Fan

Only a fraction of cricket fans actually go to games; most sit at home and watch from the comfort of their armchair. Who can blame them? They don't have to fork out a king's ransom for tickets or travel to a venue and they have a ready supply of refreshments in the fridge. What's more, they don't have stewards telling them what to do, and television coverage can offer the cricket fan a uniquely close-up view of the action.

A major shift in cricket broadcasting has taken place in recent years. For decades the BBC had the rights to screen England's home test matches, but then in 2000 Channel 4 came along and bought up the rights. Auntie Beeb wasn't very pleased but the majority of cricket fans were, as Channel 4's coverage of cricket was top-notch. They explained the intricacies of the game in layman's language – a bit like this book – helping to broaden its appeal. At the same time, cricket anoraks were catered for with oodles of serious analysis and a cracking commentary team.

But this was a brief burst of glory for Channel 4, as Sky Sports then bought the broadcast rights for English cricket. The coverage on Sky is normally of a high standard – they have broadcast England's overseas test matches for over 15 years – but anyone wanting to watch has to pay a subscription fee. The size of this fee depends on which channels the user buys; check out www.sky.com for more details.

Cricket fans who don't want to subscribe to Sky have a crumb of comfort; the terrestrial channel Five has bought the rights to televise highlights of the test cricket.

Following cricket on the radio

As far as many England cricket fans are concerned, radio, not TV, is king. The BBC started broadcasting ball-by-ball coverage of test cricket on the radio way back in 1957.

Over the years, the BBC's Test Match Special radio programme has become part of the social landscape of the country. For many people the programme is the soundtrack of summer. The programme is free to listen to and can be found on BBC Radio Four long wave (LW 198) and the digital radio Five Live Extra station.

Currently, the BBC has the rights to broadcast radio commentary of England's test and one-day international matches both at home and abroad.

Keeping up with cricket through the newspapers

Some national newspapers give more prominence to cricket than others. Generally, the upmarket newspapers – *The Times*, *The Daily Telegraph*, *The Independent* and *The Guardian* – dedicate plenty of column inches to the game. On the other hand, the tabloids, such as *The Sun* and the *Daily Mirror*, tend to be soccer obsessed, relegating cricket to only a cursory mention.

If you want more in-depth written coverage of cricket matches and the issues in the game, you may want to check out *The Wisden Cricketer*, the country's bestselling cricket magazine. You can find a copy at most newsagents or you can subscribe on 0870 220 6538.

Each April the *Wisden Cricketers' Almanack* is published. This vast work contains, among other things, details of all the test and one-day international matches played around the world in the previous twelve months. The *Almanack* is often referred to as cricket's 'bible', and with editions running to nearly 1200 pages you have plenty to take in.

Stump Microphone, Snickometer and Hawkeye

In recent years, TV coverage of cricket has been transformed through the introduction of new technology.

The whiz-bang toys deployed by the broadcasters to boost the viewing experience include:

✔ **Stump microphones and cameras:** These allow viewers to get down and dirty with the action. They see the ball hurtling towards the stumps and can hear every word exchanged between batsmen and bowlers – sometimes a bleeping device is needed to drown out the more colourful language.

✔ **Snickometer:** The stump microphone is also used to detect if the batsman makes thin contact with the ball. This thin contact is called a snick and TV companies have developed technology to tell whether a sound is due to the ball making contact with the bat or just, say, a part of the batsman's anatomy such as the forearm.

✔ **Hawkeye:** Hawkeye is an impressive technological toy. The Hawkeye computer tracks the ball once it leaves the bowler's hand until it reaches the batsman. The computer then calculates the direction the ball is headed. Even if the ball strikes the batsman's pads, Hawkeye will be able to say with almost 100 per cent accuracy whether it would have hit the stumps or not. At present, umpires don't get to see Hawkeye but the lucky viewer at home does.

✔ **Hotspot:** This nifty piece of kit allows viewers and the off-field third umpire to see whether the batsman has hit the ball or not.

It does this by detecting heat emitted from the surface of the bat resulting from friction from contact with the ball. The technology is super-sensitive and can detect the slightest touch of ball on bat.

Hawkeye and Hotspot are key components of the decision review system (DRS). This allows fielding captains and batsmen to have an LBW or caught decision on the field reviewed by the off-field third umpire. The umpire looks at a TV screen and at the information from Hotspot and Hawkeye to determine whether or not the original on-field decision was correct or not. See Chapter 3 for more on the intricacies of the DRS.

Experiencing Grass Roots Cricket

You don't have to pay to see a game of cricket: Literally thousands of cricket clubs around the country welcome spectators. Check out the Club Cricket Conference www.club-cricket.com or call 0208 973 1612 for a list of your local cricket clubs. Club matches may be a million miles away from the glitz and razzmatazz of international games but they can still offer the spectator plenty of tension and, on occasions, good quality cricket.

Many cricket clubs have their own Web sites with lists of fixtures and even player profiles. In addition, you may want to check your local newspaper for the inside track on how local clubs are performing.

Getting to Grips with the Statistics

Cricket is chock-full of statistics. Nearly every action in a cricket match creates a statistic which is noted down by the *scorers*, people whose job is to keep track of runs scored and wickets taken. Refer to Chapter 3 for more on the role of the scorer.

You can use some of these statistics to gauge how good an individual player is, compared to his peers and players from the past. These statistics are called batting and bowling averages.

Reading a scorecard

Figure 13-1 shows a typical cricket scorecard. At first glance it may look like a plethora of names, numbers and letters, but discover how to read and decipher it and the events of a match unfold before your eyes. To keep things as simple as possible the following scorecard is from a one-day international match, which means each side only had one innings and the team that scored the most runs – in this case England – won the match.

West Indies Innings			
Chris Gayle	run out		23
Shivnarine Chanderpaul	c Jones	b Harmison	3
Devon Smith	c Jones	b Harmison	2
Ramnaresh Sarwan	c Collingwood	b Trescothick	46
Brian Lara*		b Anderson	6
Dwayne Bravo	c Jones	b Anderson	5
Ridley Jacobs+		b Anderson	2
Ricardo Powell		b Harmison	36
Ian Bradshaw	c Jones	b McGrath	12
Ravi Rampaul	c Anderson	b Gough	10
Jermaine Lawson	not out		0
Extras: (LB 4, W 9, NB 1)			14
Total: (40.1 overs)		(all out) 159	

England bowling: Gough 8.1-2-23-1; Harmison 10-2-31-3; Anderson 8-1-37-3, McGrath 10-1-36-1; Trescothick 4-0-28-1.

England Innings			
Marcus Trescothick		run out	55
Michael Vaughan*	c Gayle	b Bravo	14
Robert Key		b Bravo	6
Andrew Strauss	not out		44
Andrew Flintoff	not out		21
Extras: (LB 8, W 4, NB 8)			20
Total: (22 overs)		(for 3 wickets) 160	

Did not bat: Paul Collingwood, Anthony McGrath, Geraint Jones +, Darren Gough, Steve Harmison, and James Anderson.

West Indies bowling: Bradshaw 6-0-29-0; Lawson 7-0-50-0; Bravo 4-0-29-2; Rampaul 3-0-28-0; Smith 2-0-16-0.

Match result England won by 7 wickets

Figure 13-1:
A cricket scorecard.

Now here's how to decipher the scorecard line by line.

- **Chris Gayle run out 23:** Gayle scored 23 runs and was then dismissed run-out. This means that a fielder has managed to hit the stumps and dislodge the bails with the ball before the Gayle has completed a run. Refer to Chapter 2 for more on being dismissed run-out.

- **Shivnarine Chanderpaul c Jones b Harmison 3:** Chanderpaul scored 3 runs and was then caught out by Jones off a delivery from Harmison. The 'c' in the scorecard stands for caught and the 'b' for bowled. Looking at the England innings scorecard, you see a '+' next to Jones's name. This denotes that Jones is the wicket-keeper. Refer to Chapter 7 for more on this specialist fielding position.

- **Devon Smith c Jones b Harmison 2:** Like Chanderpaul, Smith – after scoring 2 runs – hit the ball in the air off a delivery bowled by Harmison and was caught out by the England wicket-keeper Jones.

- **Ramresh Sarwan c Collingwood b Trescothick 46:** Sarwan made 46 runs and then hit the ball in the air off a delivery bowled by Anderson and was caught out by Collingwood.

- **Brian Lara b Anderson 6:** After scoring 6 runs Lara had his stumps hit – and bails that rest upon them dislodged – by the ball delivered by Anderson. The '*' after Lara's name denotes that he is the captain of the West Indies.

- **Dwain Bravo c Jones b Anderson 5:** After scoring 5 runs Bravo hit the ball, delivered by Anderson, in the air, and was caught by the wicket-keeper Jones.

- **Ridley Jacobs b Anderson 2:** Jacobs had scored only 2 runs when he had his stumps hit – and the bails that rest upon them dislodged – by the ball delivered by Anderson.

- **Ricardo Powell b Harmison 36:** Powell had done quite well, scoring 36 runs when he had his bails dislodged by a ball delivered by Harmison.

- **Ian Bradshaw c Jones b McGrath 12:** After scoring 12 runs Bradshaw hit a ball delivered by McGrath in the air and was caught by the wicket-keeper Jones.

- **Ravi Rampaul c Anderson b Gough 10:** Rampaul had scored 10 runs and then hit the ball in the air off a delivery bowled by Gough and was caught out by Anderson.

- **Jermaine Lawson not out 0:** Lawson did not score a run but he was not dismissed. The other ten batsmen in the team had been dismissed. Under the laws of the game, an individual batsman is not allowed to continue batting after all his team-mates have been dismissed. As a result, at least one batsman is always not out in a cricket innings.

- **Total 159 all out (40.1 overs):** This means that the West Indies as a team scored 159 runs. *All out* means the West Indies had ten of their eleven batsmen dismissed; the innings is over. It took England's bowlers 40.1 overs – that is 40 completed overs plus 1 delivery – to dismiss the ten West Indian batsmen.

- **Extras: 14 (LB 4, W 9, NBs 1):** West Indies scored 14 runs which were classified as *extras*. These are awarded by the umpire (refer to Chapter 2 for when the batting side earns extras). These extras were broken down into leg byes (LB), wides (W) and no-balls (NBs).

Now look at the England bowling figures.

- **Gough 8.1-2-23-1:** Gough bowled 8 overs and 1 delivery. 2 of the overs were *maidens* – that is, had no runs scored off them. Gough conceded 23 runs to the batting side and dismissed 1 batsman.

- **Harmison 10-2-31-3:** Harmison bowled 10 overs, 2 maidens, conceded 31 runs to the batting side and dismissed 3 batsmen.

- **Anderson 8-1-37-3:** Anderson bowled 8 overs, 2 maidens, conceded 37 runs to the batting side and dismissed 3 batsmen.

- **McGrath 10-1-36-1:** McGrath bowled 10 overs, 1 maiden, conceded 36 runs to the batting side and dismissed 1 batsman.

- **Trescothick 4-0-28-1:** Trescothick bowled 4 overs, did not bowl any maidens, conceded 28 runs to the batting side and dismissed 1 batsman.

Now turn to England's innings; remember they need 160 runs to win.

- **Marcus Trescothick run out 55:** Trescothick did well and scored 55 runs but was then dismissed run-out. This means the fielder managed to throw the ball at the stumps, hit them and dislodge the bails before Trescothick had completed a run. See Chapter 2 for more on being dismissed run-out.

- **Michael Vaughan c Gayle b Bravo 14:** Vaughan had scored 14 runs and then hit the ball in the air off a delivery bowled by Bravo and was caught out by Gayle. The '*' after Vaughan's name denotes that he is the captain of the England team.

- **Robert Key b Bravo 6:** Key had scored just 6 runs when he had his stumps hit – and bails that rest upon them dislodged – by the ball delivered by Bravo.

- **Andrew Strauss not out 44:** Strauss scored 44 runs and was not dismissed by the West Indies.

> ✓ **Andrew Flintoff not out 21:** Like Strauss, Flintoff was not dismissed by the West Indies. When an innings ends early because a result has been achieved, two batsmen are always *not out*. In this case England had reached their victory target of 160 runs while Strauss and Flintoff were batting together.

> ✓ **Did not bat: Paul Collingwood, Anthony McGrath, Geraint Jones, Darren Gough, Steve Harmison and James Anderson:** This is fairly obvious; these players didn't get to bat because England had already reached their victory target and the innings was over.

> ✓ **Total; 160 for 3 wickets (22 overs):** This means England scored 160 runs in their innings but only had three batsmen dismissed. The England team took only 22 overs to reach the victory target.

Now look at the West Indies bowling figures.

> ✓ **Bradshaw 6-0-29-0:** Bradshaw bowled 6 overs, 0 maidens, conceded 29 runs to the batting side and dismissed 0 batsmen.

> ✓ **Lawson 7-0-50-0:** Lawson bowled 7 overs, 0 maidens, conceded 50 runs to the batting side and dismissed 0 batsmen.

> ✓ **Bravo 4-0-29-2:** Bravo bowled 4 overs, 0 maidens, conceded 29 runs to the batting side and dismissed 2 batsmen.

> ✓ **Rampaul 3-0-28-0:** Rampaul bowled 3 overs, 0 maidens, conceded 28 runs to the batting side and dismissed 0 batsmen.

> ✓ **Smith 2-0-16-0:** Smith bowled 2 overs, 0 maidens, conceded 16 runs and dismissed 0 batsmen.

> ✓ **Match result:** England win by seven wickets. England made their victory target while losing just three of their 10 innings wickets.

When a side triumphs, the result is recorded in one of two ways. If the team winning the match does so while batting, the victory margin is said to be the number of wickets they have spare. For example, team A scores 250 and team B scores 251 but only has one batsman dismissed: The margin of victory is nine wickets. On the other hand, if the team winning the match does so in the field then the victory margin is said to be the total number of runs that side had to spare. For example, team A scores 250 runs and team B scores 150: Team A is said to have won by 100 runs.

Working out a batting average

Put simply, the batting average is the number of career runs scored by a player divided by the number of times he is dismissed. For example, player A scores 1,000 runs in his career and is dismissed 20 times during this career, and so the batting average is 50.

Most averages aren't as clear cut as this example but the principle is always the same.

On occasions the batsman will be not out when the team's innings ends. The runs scored by the batsman count towards his career run total but no dismissal is recorded.

Test match and County Championship cricket has been going for well over a century. During that time hundreds of players have represented each county or country. Statistics are a way in which an individual player's performance can be put into historical context.

Working out a bowling average

The bowling average is the number of runs conceded by the bowler during his career divided by the total number of batsmen he dismisses. For example, bowler A has 6000 runs scored off his bowling during his career but manages to take 200 wickets; therefore, bowler A has an average of 30.

In one-day cricket matches, another key stat is the average number of runs conceded by the bowler off each over – called the *economy rate*. Again, this stat is easy to work out: A bowler's economy rate is the number of runs he concedes divided by the number of overs he bowls. Therefore, if a bowler delivers 10 overs in a match and concedes 40 runs the economy rate is 4. An economy rate around 4 or below is considered pretty good in one-day cricket matches.

Telling good from bad players using statistics

You can set a player's batting and bowling average against the following benchmarks to ascertain whether he is any good.

Batting benchmarks

The quality of a first class batsman is usually clear from his batting average: the higher, the better.

> ✔ **Less than 10:** The player is a poor batsman, and probably earns his corn primarily as a bowler: In cricket jargon these poor batsmen are often referred to as *rabbits*.

- ✔ **Between 10 and 20:** The player can bat competently but rarely makes big match-changing scores.

- ✔ **Between 20 and 30:** Every now and then the player makes a big match-changing score but doesn't do so consistently.

- ✔ **Between 30 and 40:** This average indicates a good player who makes big scores but fails badly on other occasions.

- ✔ **Between 40 and 50:** Now we're cooking with gas. This average is the benchmark for being a good batsman, consistently making high scores.

- ✔ **Over 50:** Players who average more than 50 in first class cricket can have a claim to the title of great. They are world-class performers, regularly winning matches through their batting prowess.

Look out for the batting and bowling averages quoted in newspapers and television coverage of cricket.

As a general rule, the higher the batsman's average the more likely he is to occupy a high position in the batting order. Refer to Chapter 5 for more on batting orders.

Bowling benchmarks

As a measure of a bowler's ability, things are the other way round. The lower a bowler's average, the better he is.

- ✔ **Over 50:** Unfortunately the bowler isn't doing well, dismissing too few batsmen.

- ✔ **Between 40 and 50:** Again, the bowler isn't much good. He occasionally joins the party, dismissing a few players, but must do better.

- ✔ **Between 30 and 40:** Getting better! The bowler is capable on occasions of producing a match-winning performance.

- ✔ **Between 20 and 30:** This average is the benchmark for being a good bowler. The bowler consistently dismisses batsmen. A first class bowler with an average in the low 20s is likely to be considered a great player.

- ✔ **Below 20:** The bowler is an absolute star and a terror to the batsmen. Very few bowlers in cricket history average below 20 over a long period of time.

As far as batsmen are concerned the higher the batting average the better. Bowlers, on the other hand, strive to secure as low a bowling average as possible.

Averages alter during a player's career. Some players start off with a poor average and as they improve technically, discover more about the game and gain experience they get better and their average becomes more respectable. On the flip-side, some players start off as bright stars only to fade away.

Twenty20 matches are over very quickly and often too little time exists for a batsman to make a really big score. Therefore, the benchmarks for deciding whether batsmen and bowlers are any good have to be qualified. A batting average of over 30 and a bowling average under 30 can be considered pretty handy in twenty20 games.

Wicket-keepers are measured by the number of catches and stumpings they make. They are also measured in the same way as batsmen, according to their batting average. For example, in the 1970s England had two world-class wicket-keepers in Alan Knott and Bob Taylor. In terms of wicket-keeping there was little to choose between them – they were both excellent at taking catches and executing stumpings. However, when it came to batting Knott was streets ahead. He averaged 32 runs per innings, while Taylor averaged a rather limp 18. As a result, Knott is widely recognised as the better player and went on to star in nearly 100 test matches.

Following the cricketing tweeters

Twitter and tweeting has taken the media world by storm with stories breaking, politicians resigning, revolutions being nutured and controversies coming to light all through the powerful social media. Twitter has been embraced too by the world of cricket. Here are some of the prominent cricketing tweeters who are informative, sometimes anarchic but never dull.

✔ **David 'Bumble' Lloyd:** The veteran Skly commentator is frankly as mad as a box of badgers his tweets are funny, knowledgeable and always worth checking out. 'Start the car', as Bumble would say!

✔ **Graeme Swann:** Swannie has a reputation as the dressing room wag and he has carried that onto the social media platform. His tweets – like the man – are irreverent and fun.

✔ **Damien Martyn:** The Ex Aussie ace batsman has taken to social media in the same way that he used to devour bowlers around the globe. His comments are bright, lively and always on the money: @dmartyn30

✔ **Kevin Pietersen:** KP, as he's known, is never shy of an opinion and is wont to let off steam on Twitter. He has been reprimanded more than once by the ECB as a result. It's always worth checking out whether KP has gone too far today.

✔ **Shane Warne:** Arguably the greatest cricketer of the last twenty years and a shrewd observer of the game, able to cut through the coach speak and get to the heart of cricketing issues. Follow him on @warne888.

Part IV
The Part of Tens

Go to www.dummies.com/extras/cricket for online bonus content.

In this part . . .

✔ Getting the low-down on ten of the game's greats.

✔ Running the rule over ten of the greatest ever matches.

✔ Being amazed by ten prodigious cricketing achievements.

✔ Go to www.dummies.com/extras/cricket for online bonus content, including an extra Part of Tens chapter: 'Ten Great Cricket Controversies'.

Chapter 14

Ten Greatest Ever Cricketers

In This Chapter

▶ Bowing to master batsmen

▶ Gazing in awe at the great all rounders

▶ Looking at brilliant bowlers

*W*herever you find a couple of cricket fans spending an evening together you can bet your bottom dollar that at some point – normally after the second bottle of wine has been opened – the conversation will turn to who were the greatest players ever.

The fans are bound not to agree but they will have a lot of fun discussing which players deserve to be called great.

In this chapter, I look at some of the cricketing superstars from past and present who have a good chance of being considered truly great.

Sir Donald Bradman, Australia

Most cricket lovers would rank Donald Bradman as the greatest cricketer of all time. This is because in one discipline of cricket – batting – he is undoubtedly head and shoulders above anyone who has ever played the game. In fact, you've to go a long way to find anyone who has dominated their sport as much as Bradman did in the 1930s and 1940s. Perhaps Jack Nicklaus in golf and Michael Johnson in 400 metre running are two other examples.

Time and again Bradman won matches and test series for Australia, literally off his own bat. His batting average is about 50 per cent better than any other batsman in the 130-year history of test cricket. Normally a player who scores one century every four tests is considered a legend. Bradman hit 29 centuries in 52 test matches. He would have played far more tests and set ever greater records if the Second World War hadn't meant that test match cricket wasn't played for six years.

Bradman was more than just a cricketer, he was a national icon. Some would argue that he was the most important Australian of the twentieth century because around his magical exploits a new nation found a focal point and a figure from whom they could derive immense pride.

For this reason and many others it's difficult to argue that Bradman was simply the greatest of all time.

Sir Jack Hobbs, England

Up until the emergence of Bradman, Hobbs was undoubtedly the finest batsman cricket had ever seen. He was simply known as 'The Master' and some die-hard England fans argue that he was actually better than Bradman.

Statistically he was a colossus. He scored more runs and centuries than any other player in the history of the game (see Chapter 16 for more on his mind-boggling achievements.) Like Bradman he lost potentially the best years of his career to a World War. In Hobbs' case the First World War ate into his career as test cricket stopped for the duration of hostilities. It was said that only one player was finer than Hobbs after the First World War, and that was Hobbs before the First World War.

Despite scoring such a huge number of runs, Hobbs was never deemed a selfish player. He was very much a team player, playing aggressively or defensively according to the needs of the team and the match situation. England has produced many great batsmen such as Wally Hammond, Denis Compton and Ken Barrington, but Hobbs stands out as number one.

Sachin Tendulkar, India

At age 16 – when most youngsters are fretting about their acne or what ring tone to have on their mobile – Sachin Tendulkar was making his debut in a test match for India. He was an instant hit; a master batsman while still only a boy.

In the decade and a half since his debut, Tendulkar's bright light of talent has remained undimmed. He has won test matches almost single-handed and is an Indian cricketing and cultural icon. Donald Bradman said that Tendulkar plays the game as he used too – praise comes no higher than that. To date he has scored more than 15,000 runs and made 51 test match centuries.

To cap it all Tendulkar is one of the best one-day limited overs batsmen in the world. In fact, he has scored more than 18,000 runs in one-day limited over matches, reaching 100 runs in an innings nearly 50 times.

Against Bangladesh in early 2012 he became the first player to have reached a 100 runs in an innings in international cricket 100 times: A mind-boggling feat. In fact, Tendulkar's batting statistics – the sheer volume of runs he has scored – undoubtedly beat ever other batsman in cricket history. At the age of 39, though, Old Father Time is beginning to catch up with the 'little master' as Tendulkar is called. His career may be drawing to a close, but his feats will stand the test of time.

Sir Gary Sobers, West Indies

Garfied St Auburn Sobers – or just Gary Sobers for short – is probably the only man to have a justifiable case to be considered a greater cricketer than Donald Bradman.

He was a bit of cricketing freak, because he could do just about anything. He could bowl fast. He could swing the ball and he could bowl both varieties of spin. In addition, he was, undoubtedly, the finest left-handed batsman to have ever played the game. In test matches he scored more than 8,000 runs and took 235 wickets. But the raw statistics do not do full justice to how great a player Sobers was. As a batsman he was capable of laying waste the bowling. One of his most famous exploits was to hit six sixes in one over delivered by Glamorgan bowler Malcolm Nash in 1968.

Sobers was also a very astute captain of the West Indies and a top class fielder. In short, he had it all and stands out as a genius.

Imran Khan, Pakistan

Imran Khan has a strong claim to be considered the finest all round cricketer to emerge since Gary Sobers retired in the 1970s. Over nearly two decades his performances in test match and one-day international cricket were top drawer.

He was a great fast bowler, taking 362 test wickets. In fact, he may have made this list for his bowling alone. But when you consider that he was also a fine test batsman who scored nearly 4,000 runs and posted six centuries, you can see why he is a shoe in. In addition, he is widely seen as Pakistan's best ever cricket captain.

As a captain, he led the country to its greatest ever triumph, victory in the 1992 cricket World Cup.

As if all that ability wasn't enough, I'm reliably informed by female friends that Khan is a bit of a heart-throb, with movie star looks – he has even run recently for president of his country some people really do have it all.

Sir Richard Hadlee, New Zealand

Richard John Hadlee is the greatest New Zealand bowler ever, without doubt. He also has strong claims to being considered one of the planet's all-time greats. Hadlee's main claim to fame was his fast bowling. He was a wonderfully accurate bowler, seemingly able to direct deliveries wherever he wanted. For batsmen he was a nightmare because he could bowl fast, but also make the ball deviate dramatically once it hit the surface of the wicket. No wonder he became the first bowler in the history of the game to take more than 400 test wickets. If you add Hadlee's batting ability – he scored more than 3,000 runs in 86 test matches – you can see why in his pomp he was rated by many as the world's best cricketer. Hadlee emerged at a time when the game was blessed with great all round cricketers such as Imran Khan (see above), Ian Botham and Kapil Dev. He wasn't as natural a talent as the others but he made up for it with hard work and immense determination. For example as he approached his mid-thirties he cut down his run-up, in order to save energy yet was still able to bowl fast with unnerving accuracy. In fact, he reached the high watermark of his career in his final five years as a player. Hadlee retired in 1990 and was, like Gary Sobers and Donald Bradman, knighted by the Queen.

Adam Gilchrist, Australia

This Australian wicket-keeper batsman was the scourge of bowlers around the globe since he made his test debut in 1999 until his retirement in 2008. He hits the ball as hard and far as anyone in the history of the game. But Gilchrist isn't just a force of nature as a batsman. He is also a top drawer wicket-keeper. The fact that he is exceptionally talented at two cricketing disciplines makes him an all rounder. Richie Benaud, the former Australian captain and doyen of TV commentators, rates Gilchrist as one of the all-time greats. Time and again Gilchristdug his team out of a hole. He bats quite low in the batting order, at number six or seven, and just when the opposition thinks it is doing well Gilchrist strides to the wicket and hits a century. He averaged nearly 50 runs each time he batted and took 379 catches and stumped 37 hapless batsmen during his distinguished career, making him undoubtedly the greatest wicket-keeper batsman of all time.

Sadly, for the world of cricket, Gilchrist made his test debut in 1999 at 27, quite a late age, so he may not be around for too much longer. However, bowlers around the globe will sleep a lot easier when he eventually retires.

Dennis Lillee, Australia

Anyone fortunate enough to see Dennis Lillee bowl will not forget the sight. He was the embodiment of the perfect fast bowler. His precise, smooth run-up to the wicket, perfect balance when delivering the cricket ball and control over where the ball landed on the wicket were all A1. Lillee was a thoroughbred amongst fast bowlers, and he was quick too – very quick. In fact when he first burst on the scene in the early 1970s batsmen didn't know how to play him. He delivered the ball at lightning pace and with unerring accuracy. However, Lillee had serious injury problems and was kept out of test cricket for the best part of two years with a stress fracture of the back. When he returned to trounce England in 1974, he was back to his best. Between 1974 and 1976 Lillee and fellow Australian fast bowler Jeff Thomson laid waste to batsmen around the globe. For a brief time Australia became the best team in the world, largely thanks to this fiery pair of fast bowlers.

Jeff Thomson never reached such Olympian heights again but Lillee continued to be the world's number one fast bowler for the rest of the 1970s. When his career came to an end in 1983 he had taken a then world record 355 test wickets in just 70 test matches.

Malcolm Marshall, West Indies

If Dennis Lillee was the most feared bowler of the 1970s then Malcolm Marshall took over that mantle in the 1980s. He was the greatest of a set of great West Indian fast bowlers including Michael Holding, Joel Garner and Andy Roberts. He was short for a fast bowler, but used this to his advantage by bowling the ball at a low trajectory at the batsman's stumps. Often he would beat the batsman with sheer pace, hitting the stumps. Other times he would use guile, the combination of raw pace, swing and his trajectory of attack allowing him to capture 376 wickets in 81 test matches.

Malcolm Marshall's greatness as a bowler is indicated by his test bowling average. In test matches a bowling average below 30 is considered excellent: Below 25 and you're talking all-time great; Marshall's average was below 21.

Marshall's story has a tragic postscript. In 1999, he died of cancer aged just 41. He may have been feared by opponents but Marshall was also very popular. Anyone who was fortunate enough to attend the memorial cricket match in honour of the great Malcolm Marshall, at the Honourable Artillery Company Ground in London in 2000, will attest to the high regard in which he was held.

Shane Warne, Australia

Shane Keith Warne, the bleached blond Australian leg-spin bowler, showed himself to be a very special talent with the first ball that he bowled in an Ashes test match. Bowling to England's best player of spin Mike Gatting at Old Trafford in 1993, Warne produced what became known as the *ball of the century*. It pitched outside Gatting's leg stump, spun viciously on bouncing, and hit the top of Gatting's off stump. Gatting was bamboozled and Warne an instant star.

But this was only the start. During his fifteen-year test career Warne re-wrote the record books, taking more than 700 test wickets. Warne has an incredibly astute cricket brain. Mike Atherton, a former England captain, has gone on record to say that Warne's ability to out-think batsmen makes him the finest bowler he has played against.

In 2000 *Wisden Cricketers' Almanack* named Warne as one of the five most important cricketers of the twentieth century and some would suggest that he should be ranked number one. He re-invented the art of leg-spin bowling – see Chapter 6 for more on this type of bowling – and was key to Australia's success during the 1990s and 2000s.

Chapter 15

Ten Most Memorable Cricket Matches

Cricket as an organised sport has been going for well over a century. During that time tens of thousands of test, first class and one-day limited-overs matches have been played. Some of these matches have been poor contests with one team running out easy winners. Some have been really good games, keeping the spectators on the edges of their seats until eventually one team has grabbed the win. A few games, though, have been classic affairs featuring nail-biting finishes, improbable run-scoring feats or astounding fight backs by teams that had seemed out for the count.

In this chapter I offer a selection of ten classic matches. They may not be the greatest games that have ever been played in terms of quality of cricket, performance, or the skill standard of players competing but they are all matches that anyone who was in the crowd or watched on television is likely never to forget.

England v Australia: Third Test Match, Headingley, 1981

Bookmakers rarely get things badly wrong. And few thought they had when the electronic scoreboard at Headingley flashed up the odds during the third test match between England and Australia in 1981.

England were in dire straits. Australia, 1-nil up in the six match series, had managed to score 401 in their first innings. In response England floundered to 174 all out. The only player to perform was all rounder Ian Botham, who had resigned the captaincy after the previous test match.

In the second innings, England, at first, fared even worse. They were slipping to defeat, having had seven batsmen dismissed for 135 runs. They still needed a further 100 runs just to make Australia bat again.

No wonder the bookmakers were offering odds of 500-1 on an England win. Even the England team had given up hope. The team had checked out of their hotel the night before, expecting to be beaten the day after.

But then what became known as the miracle of Headingley occurred. Ian Botham, supported by Graham Dilley, Chris Old, and Bob Willis, went berserk, hitting boundaries and sixes galore. Botham finished 149 not out and England were finally dismissed for 356, leaving Australia 130 runs to win on the final day of the match. The Australians initially went well and scored 56 runs for just one wicket. Then England fast bowler Bob Willis roared in to produce the best bowling of his life. He bowled at lightning pace and decimated the Australian batting, taking eight wickets for 43 in the innings. They were dismissed for 111 and England had claimed probably their most famous victory ever. The match was dubbed the miracle of Headingley.

Australia v England: Centenary Test, Melbourne, 1977

This one-off test was played to mark 100 years of test matches between England and Australia.

At first the game looked like it would be a damp squib, with Australia dismissed for just 138 runs in their first innings. England's response was even more lamentable: They were bowled out for 95.

From here on in though the match caught fire. Some exciting batting by the Australians – in particular Doug Walters, David Hookes and Rodney Marsh – saw the home team notch up an impressive 419 in their second innings.

England were left needing 453 runs to win. No-one gave England a hope but a remarkable innings by Derek Randall, who hit 174 runs off 353 deliveries faced, saw England come within a whisker of pulling off a famous and unlikely win. In fact at the tea interval on the fifth and final day England looked favourites to carry away the glory. But some fine fast bowling by Dennis Lillie – see Chapter 14 for more on this bowling legend – saw Australia home by a margin of 45 runs. By a remarkable coincidence the victory margin was identical to that of the first match between the two countries played 100 years earlier.

Australia v West Indies: First Test, Brisbane, 1960

In nearly 2,000 test matches only two ties have occurred. A tie occurs when both sides have completed their two innings and the aggregate scores are level. The first tied match at Brisbane in 1960 was a classic encounter between two great sides. Both the West Indies and Australia had star players galore. All-time greats such as Gary Sobers, Frank Worrell and Wes Hall lined up for the West Indies, while the Australians could boast crackerjack performers such as Richie Benaud, Alan Davidson and Neil Harvey. The game went right down to the wire, with the final Australian batsman dismissed with minutes to go of the fifth and final day's play. Australia, though, should have won the match. At one stage they needed just seven runs to win with four wickets in hand but some great fielding by the West Indies and the fast, accurate bowling of Wes Hall ensured the game was tied. The match saw nearly 1,500 runs scored, and two great bowling performances from Australia's Alan Davidson and West Indian Wes Hall.

England v Australia: Test Match, The Oval, 1882

This match was only the ninth test match ever played but marked the start of cricket's oldest competition: The Ashes.

The game itself was a very low-scoring affair. Australia were dismissed for just 63 runs in their first innings and England faired little better in response, notching up a paltry 101. The Australian second innings total of 122 was poor again, but in the context of the match proved crucial. England were left just 85 runs to win but somehow managed to be bowled out for 77, with the legendary W. G. Grace top scoring with 32. Australia, therefore, won an incredibly close contest by just 7 runs. The hero for Australia was demon fast bowler F.S. Spofforth who took 14 wickets for just 88 runs during the match. The English sporting public were taken aback by England's first loss at home to Australia.

After the match a mock obituary was carried in the *Sporting Times*, stating that the body of English cricket would be cremated and the Ashes taken to Australia. The following winter an England cricket team toured Australia for the first ever Ashes test series (so called because while on tour the England captain was presented with an urn containing the ashes of a bail); refer to Chapter 10 for more on this ancient rivalry.

India v Australia: Test Match, Kolkata, 2002

This match ranks with England's triumph at Headingley in 1981 as one of the greatest comebacks in the history of the game. Australia were going for their seventeenth straight test match win. They had won the first match in the three match series comfortably. Halfway through the second test at Kolkata they were dominating again. In fact, they had enforced the follow-on and it seemed only a matter of time before the Australians would sweep to victory. Then the great Indian batsman Rahul Dravid joined V.V.S. Laxman at the wicket and a funny thing happened: The Australians just couldn't get either of them out. They batted, and batted, and batted some more. They put the Australian bowling to the sword, sharing a partnership of 376 in over a day's play. When, finally, Laxman was out for 281, the match and the series had turned around. On the final day of the match the Indian captain Surav Ganguly declared the innings and Australia were batting to save the match. This they couldn't do: They were bowled out for 212 and India had won by a mighty 171 runs. And to rub salt into Aussie wounds the Indians went on to win the final match of the series by two wickets and claim a 2-1 series triumph.

England v Australia: Test Match, Edgbaston, 2005

When Australian tail-end batsman Michael Kasprowicz was dismissed by Steve Harmison on the fourth morning of this crucial Ashes test match, the cricketing world was turned upside down. England had beaten their old foes by just two runs, the narrowest victory margin in over a century of Ashes contests. The series was levelled at one match all, and ultimately England went on to win the Ashes for the first time since 1987.

However, the result could have turned out so differently. An hour before play began on the first day, Australia's best fast bowler Glenn McGrath injured himself during fielding practice and had to withdraw from the match. Then Aussie captain Ricky Ponting confounded the experts by electing to field on what looked like a good wicket for batting (see Chapter 2 for more on the condition of the wicket). During the first day England rattled up 407 runs and took charge. In fact England bossed the game until the fourth morning when remarkable batting by Shane Warne, Brett Lee and Michael Kasprowicz brought Australia to the brink of an unlikely triumph. That is until Harmison's last ditch effort saw Kasprowicz caught behind off his glove, sending England cricket fans into rapture.

South Africa v Australia: World Cup Semifinal, Edgbaston, 1999

The drama in this match all came in the final over. South Africa were chasing 214 to beat Australia and book a place in the World Cup final. At the start of the final over, South Africa needed just nine runs to win but had lost nine wickets, and so couldn't afford to lose another one or else their innings would be over.

South African all rounder Lance Klusener smashed each of the first two deliveries of the over for four runs. This meant that the scores were level. South Africa had four deliveries left to score just one run and claim a famous win. Off the third delivery no runs were scored and the tension, it turned out, became unbearable for the South Africans. Klusener made contact with the fourth ball of the over and set off to run a single but his batting partner Allan Donald had no intention of going for the run. There was a horrendous mix up and Donald was run-out. The match scores were level but because the Australians had scored their runs at a faster pace earlier in the tournament, according to the rules of the competition they, and not the South Africans, went through to the final. The final was a rather sorry affair with Australia overpowering a woeful Pakistan team to claim the World Cup trophy. However, the 1999 World Cup will always be remembered for the final over of the semifinal when the South Africans threw away the chance of glory.

England v India: NatWest Trophy Final, Lords, 2002

Few of the 25,919 spectators who were at Lords on 13 July 2002 will forget what they saw during the final of the NatWest trophy. In the end India won the match by two wickets but the result doesn't really matter. The real winner on the day was the game of cricket. England started the day by batting superbly. Marcus Trescothick and Captain Nasser Hussain both scored centuries as the home team compiled a mammoth 325 runs from just 50 overs. In reply India seemed at first to subside as five batsmen, including the brilliant Sachin Tendulkar, were dismissed for just 146.

But then Indian raw recruits Yurav Singh and Mohammed Kaif turned the tables on England and went on the attack. In a matter of just a handful of overs the match was back in the balance as the two young guns hit the ball to all parts of the ground to get the scoreboard ticking along. However, just as it seemed victory was in the bag, back came England to dismiss Singh. But with three balls remaining a poorly directed throw by an England fielder allowed Zaheer Khan to scramble the winning runs. Victory was India's.

South Africa v Australia: One-Day International Match, Johannesburg, 2006

This match rewrote nearly all the one-day international match records. The highest team score record was broken twice in the match. First Australia notched up an incredible 434 for the loss of 4 batsmen in just 50 overs. This score broke the previous highest achieved in an international one-day match by 36 runs. Aussie captain Ricky Ponting led the way with a blistering 164 and it seemed at the halfway stage of the match, with South Africa yet to bat, that Australia were certain winners. But what was to follow was even more incredible as South Africa chased down the Aussie score. Helped by superb innings by Graeme Smith, and particularly Herschelle Gibbs (who hit 175), South Africa surpassed Australia's total to win the game with one delivery remaining. In total, the two teams between them had scored 872 runs in the match off just 99 overs and 5 deliveries in a little over six hours. This was a humungous 179 runs more than had ever been scored in a one-day match before. The cricket world was stunned, as were the thousands of spectators lucky enough to be there.

One player who probably wishes he could forget this unforgettable match was Australian fast bowler Mick Lewis. He bowled 10 overs in the match and conceded – you guessed it – a world record 113 runs. And you think you have bad days at the office?

Surrey v Glamorgan: One-Day Match, The Oval, 2002

Before the South Africa v Australia one-day run bonanza – see the previous section – this match had a good claim to be considered the most memorable, just plain freaky, one-day cricket match ever played.

The Surrey innings was dominated by a staggering 268 runs scored by opener Alistair Brown. To say he went crazy, hitting the bowling to all parts of the Oval pitch, is something of an understatement. He only faced 160 deliveries in making his mammoth score. Suffice it to say that Brown's individual run tally on the day was the highest ever scored by any professional cricketer in a one-day cricket match. Likewise, Surrey's score of 438 set a new world record.

But just like the titanic South Africa v Australia match the team batting second didn't take a beating lying down, not a bit of it. Glamorgan captain Robert Croft scored 119 and opener David Hemp 102 as the Welsh county side went about chasing Surrey's total. At one stage it looked as if the impossible was about to happen and Glamorgan may win, but some clever bowling by Surrey captain Adam Hollioake ensured that there was going to be no fairytale ending. Glamorgan finished their 50 overs having made 429 runs, an agonising 10 runs short of a miraculous victory.

Chapter 16

Ten Mind-boggling Cricket Feats

C ricket fans live and breathe statistics. They also love to treasure the great performances which embellish the history of the sport. In this chapter, I look at some of the 'They did *what*?' statistics and big-match per- formances that have lit up the history of cricket.

Brian Lara's Record High Scores

The English cricket team hate the sight of Brian Lara, the great West Indian batsman. Lara has broken the record for the highest-ever number of runs in an individual innings in a test not just once, but twice. Both times, when breaking the record, he was playing against England. Back in 1994, in Antigua, he broke Sir Gary Sober's 36 year-old record for the highest individual test innings score, when he scored 375 runs. A decade later, at the same ground, against another set of sorry England bowlers, he became the first man to score 400 runs in a test match innings.

As if these magnificent feats weren't enough, Lara also holds the record for the highest score in a first class cricket match (see Chapter 3 for more on this match format). Just a few weeks after his first destruction of England's bowlers in Antigua, Lara bludgeoned 501 not out for Warwickshire against Durham at Edgbaston, Birmingham. Sadly few spectators were in the ground to see this stupendous cricketing achievement.

Jim Laker's Destruction of Australia

During a few cloudy days at the Old Trafford cricket ground in Manchester in 1956, England off-spin bowler Jim Laker achieved cricketing immortality. Virtually single-handedly he won a test match for England against a great Australian team. He took 19 of the 20 Australian wickets to fall during the match at a cost of just 90 runs; by a long chalk the most successful individual bowling performance in any single match in the history of cricket. And if you consider that the Australian team was chock-full of star players, Laker's achievement gains even greater magnitude. Some of the Australian players complained that the pitch was treacherous for batting, and helped the spin-bowling of Laker, but this doesn't detract from what was a truly mind-boggling cricketing feat.

Incidentally, the one wicket Laker didn't take fell to his Surrey colleague, left-arm spinner Tony Lock.

Australia's 16-Test Winning Streak

Between October 1999 and March 2002, Australia won 16 test matches in a row. They beat all-comers to register the longest winning streak in test history. The Australian team, captained by Steve Waugh and containing star players Shane Warne, Glenn McGrath, and Adam Gilchrist didn't just beat their opponents, but hammered them. Not even poor weather could stop the Australians from carrying away the spoils and confirming their status as one of the greatest cricket teams of all time.

But this unprecedented winning streak came to an end in dramatic fashion. After beating India comfortably in the first match of a three-match series the Australian's looked set to register yet another win in the second test at Kolkata. However, a stunning fight back by India led by batsmen V.V.S. Laxmann and Rahul Dravid led to a win against the odds for India. Refer to Chapter 15 for more on one of the greatest cricket matches ever played.

Sir Jack Hobbs: The Ultimate Golden Oldie

The career of England's greatest ever batsman, Sir Jack Hobbs, is proof that life can get even better after 40.

Hobbs, an opening batsman, was arguably the greatest cricket player up to the emergence of Australian legend Donald Bradman in the 1930s. In a 29-year first class career, starting in 1905, Jack Hobbs scored a staggering 61,237 runs. In compiling this mammoth total, he registered a record 197 centuries. But what is perhaps most impressive is the fact that 97 of these centuries were made after the age of 40, when many cricketer's abilities are on the slide or they have already retired.

Hobbs scored many of his runs on uncovered wickets. This means that from the start of the game to the end the wicket was open to the elements. If, for example, it rained during the match the wicket could become very difficult to bat on. Nowadays wickets are covered during the match, protecting them from the elements. All-in-all, scoring runs on covered wickets is considered easier than on uncovered ones.

No wonder, therefore, that Hobbs makes it into this book's Ten Greatest Ever Cricketers list; refer to Chapter 14 for more.

Ian Botham's Miracle Ashes Triumph

The 1981 test series between England and Australia will always be known as Botham's Ashes. However, after the second match of the six-match test series, Australia were 1-nil up and Ian Botham, the great England all rounder, had resigned as team captain. It didn't look like a miracle was about to happen.

Then in the Third Test at Headingley (refer to Chapter 15 for more on this match) Botham inspired England to probably the most incredible comeback win of all time, scoring 149 in England's second innings and taking six wickets in the match.

In the next test match at Edgbaston, with Australia seemingly coasting to victory, Botham produced an amazing match-winning bowling performance, dismissing five Australian batsmen for just one run.

The legend of Botham's Ashes was confirmed in the fifth test match at Old Trafford. Again England were in danger of losing, only for that man Botham to pull another rabbit from the hat. He hit an innings of 118, widely recognised as one of the greatest of all time for its display of sheer power and aggression. The match was eventually won by England and so were the Ashes 3-1. Botham never quite reached the same heights again but any England cricket fan fortunate enough to witness his performances in the summer of 1981 is guaranteed to get misty-eyed over his exploits.

Australia's Backs to the Wall Triumph at Adelaide

The second test of the 2006–07 Ashes series is one that England supporters would sooner forget. England had come back well from a thumping in the previous test, and thanks to a double hundred from batsman Paul Collingwood had managed to post a mammoth 551 for 6 declared in their first innings. Australia then slipped to 70 for 3, at which point captain Ricky Ponting was dropped by England spinner Ashley Giles on the boundary. It was a very easy catch and from that moment the game turned on its head. Ponting made 142 and Australia posted 513, but when England came out to bat late on the fourth day it seemed the match was now headed for a draw. Ace Australian leg spinner Shane Warne had different ideas, and took 4 wickets for 49 as England collapsed to 129 all out (see Chapter 14 for more on this great bowler). Australia then had a couple of hours playing time to make the 168 required to pull off a famous victory, which they did with minutes to spare.

The manner of the defeat crushed England's spirit and the great Australian team went on to record a famous 5–0 whitewash in the series, gaining sweet revenge for their narrow loss in the pulsating 2005 Ashes series.

Sir Donald Bradman's Colossal Batting Average

The performances of Australian batsman Sir Donald Bradman are mentioned many times in this book, mainly because some would argue that they are of a different magnitude to those of any other player who has ever lived. During his test match career, interrupted by the Second World War, 'the Don', as he was known, played in 52 test matches, scoring nearly 7,000 runs at an average of 99.94. Just to put this into context the next highest batting average achieved by any batsman in test cricket is around the 60 runs an innings mark. This means that from a purely statistical basis the Don was nearly 50 per cent better than any other batsman in the long history of the game. And Bradman's average would have been even more impressive if it hadn't been for the fact that in his last innings at the Oval in 1948 he was dismissed for 0 by England leg-spin bowler Eric Hollies. If the Don had scored just four runs in his final innings his test batting average would have reached the magical 100.

Bradman's batting average is probably the most impressive single achievement in cricket or even perhaps any sport, and underlines the impression of a sporting genius whose achievements were almost superhuman. No wonder, therefore, he makes it easily into the *For Dummies* list of Ten Greatest Ever Cricketers; see Chapter 14 for more.

Denis Compton of Arsenal and England Fame

England's Denis Compton was a lucky, lucky man. Not only was he one of the greatest batsmen of all time but he was a soccer star too. He played cricket for England and soccer for Arsenal in the top flight of the English game. He even managed to represent England at both cricket and soccer. He would finish playing cricket in September and then start playing for Arsenal. In his day, Compton was England's sporting megastar. He even became the pin-up boy of the hair lotion Brylcream; the David Beckham of his day.

Nowadays cricketers doubling up as soccer players is impossible. The soccer season seems to start earlier and earlier each year. In fact, you find only a few weeks in the high summer when the soccer season has stopped and the cricket season is in full swing.

Kapil Dev Flays Zimbabwe for 175

Kapil Dev, the great Indian all rounder, proved that he was a man for a crisis in the 1983 World Cup match against Zimbabwe. The Zimbabweans had already pulled off a shock by beating Australia in an earlier match and seemed to be set fair to do the same to India. They had dismissed five Indian batsmen for just 17 runs. Defeat for India would have meant an ignominious exit from the tournament. Enter Kapil Dev. He hit 175 runs – then a record for a one-day international – bludgeoning the Zimbabwean bowling to all corners of the Tunbridge Wells cricket ground.

India managed to squeak home, beating Zimbabwe by just 31 runs and qualified, against the bookmakers' odds, for the semifinals of the tournament. Better was to come for the Kapil Dev inspired Indians when they beat England in the semifinal and a great West Indies side in the final.

Kapil Dev's amazing innings against Zimbabwe was seen as the catalyst for India's greatest ever cricketing triumph.

Wilfred Rhodes: Never Ending Career

These days most test cricketers look to hang up their boots in their mid to late thirties. The physical demands of top-class cricket are increasingly making it a young man's sport – which wasn't always so.

England all rounder Wilfred Rhodes enjoyed the longest test career ever. Rhodes began his career at the age of 21 in 1899 and ended it in 1930 aged 52 years 165 days. Rhodes is by a good distance the oldest player to ever play test cricket.

During the course of his test career – which included 58 test match appearances – Rhodes became the first England player to perform the double of scoring a 1,000 test career runs and taking 100 wickets.

By the end of his long, long career Rhodes registered more than 2,000 test runs and took 127 wickets.

In all first class cricket, Rhodes's career stats are nothing short of mind-blowing. He holds the record for the highest number of wickets in a first class career. In total, he took 4,187 wickets. He took 100 wickets and scored a 1,000 runs in a season no less than 16 times. Over his career he scored nearly 40,000 runs.

During his final few appearances for England, Rhodes was a long way from being at his best. He was batting at number ten in the batting order and only managed to dismiss a few batsmen.

However, simply to have been playing top-level sport in his 53rd year was a staggering achievement in itself.

Index

• *F* •

• H •

• I •

About the Author

Julian Knight was born in 1972 in Chester. He was educated at the Chester Catholic High School and later Hull University, where he obtained a degree in History. Since 2002 Julian has been the BBC News personal finance and consumer affairs reporter and has won many awards for his journalism. Before this, he worked for *Moneywise* magazine and wrote for the *Guardian* amongst many other publications. He has also authored *Wills, Probate & Inheritance Tax For Dummies* and *Retiring Wealthy For Dummies*.

Julian has played league cricket for 20 years. He is a former captain at Blackheath cricket club and has played for several clubs in London and the north west of England.

Dedication

This book is dedicated to my father for bowling endlessly at me in my back garden as a child, and helping me develop a love for the game. Also to the players and members of Blackheath, Westminister Park, Hainault & Clayhall, and Chester Water cricket clubs.

Julian Knight

Author's Acknowledgments

I would like to thank the Wiley publishing team, in particular Jason Dunne, Alison Yates, Wejdan Ismail and Simon Bell. Thanks also go to Gary Palmer for his technical review.

Publisher's Acknowledgments

We're proud of this book; please send us your comments at `http://dummies.custhelp.com`. For other comments, please contact our Customer Care Department within the U.S. at 877-762-2974, outside the U.S. at (001) 317-572-3993, or fax 317-572-4002.

Some of the people who helped bring this book to market include the following:

Acquisitions, Editorial, and Vertical Websites

Project Editor: Simon Bell
  (Previous Edition: Simon Bell)

Commissioning Editor: Mike Baker
  (Previous Edition: Alison Yates)

Assistant Editor: Ben Kemble

Development Editor: Simon Bell

Copy Editor: Martin Key

Technical Editor: Gary Palmer

Proofreader: Kate O'Leary

Production Manager: Daniel Mersey

Publisher: Miles Kendall

Cover Photos: © Syed Farhan Hussain / Getty Images

Composition Services

Sr. Project Coordinator: Kristie Rees

Layout and Graphics: Amy Hassos, Joyce Haughey

Proofreaders: Carrie A. Cesavice, Melissa Cossell, Jessica Kramer, Lauren Mandelbaum

Indexer: Riverside Indexes, Inc.

FOR DUMMIES®

Making Everything Easier! ™

UK editions

BUSINESS

978-1-118-34689-1

978-1-118-44349-1

978-1-119-97527-4

MUSIC

978-1-119-94276-4

978-0-470-97799-6

978-0-470-66372-1

HOBBIES

978-1-118-41156-8

978-1-119-99417-6

978-1-119-97250-1

Asperger's Syndrome For Dummies
978-0-470-66087-4

Basic Maths For Dummies
978-1-119-97452-9

Body Language For Dummies, 2nd Edition
978-1-119-95351-7

Boosting Self-Esteem For Dummies
978-0-470-74193-1

Business Continuity For Dummies
978-1-118-32683-1

Cricket For Dummies
978-0-470-03454-5

Diabetes For Dummies, 3rd Edition
978-0-470-97711-8

eBay For Dummies, 3rd Edition
978-1-119-94122-4

English Grammar For Dummies
978-0-470-05752-0

Flirting For Dummies
978-0-470-74259-4

IBS For Dummies
978-0-470-51737-6

ITIL For Dummies
978-1-119-95013-4

Management For Dummies, 2nd Edition
978-0-470-97769-9

Managing Anxiety with CBT For Dummies
978-1-118-36606-6

Neuro-linguistic Programming For Dummies, 2nd Edition
978-0-470-66543-5

Nutrition For Dummies, 2nd Edition
978-0-470-97276-2

Organic Gardening For Dummies
978-1-119-97706-3

FOR DUMMIES®

Making Everything Easier!™

UK editions

SELF-HELP

Cognitive Behavioural Therapy For Dummies

978-0-470-66541-1

Creative Visualization For Dummies

978-1-119-99264-6

Mindfulness For Dummies

978-0-470-66086-7

LANGUAGES

Spanish For Dummies

978-0-470-68815-1

Polish For Dummies

978-1-119-97959-3

British Sign Language For Dummies

978-0-470-69477-0

HISTORY

The Tudors For Dummies

978-0-470-68792-5

Medieval History For Dummies

978-0-470-74783-4

British History For Dummies

978-0-470-97819-1

Origami Kit For Dummies
978-0-470-75857-1

Overcoming Depression For Dummies
978-0-470-69430-5

Positive Psychology For Dummies
978-0-470-72136-0

PRINCE2 For Dummies, 2009 Edition
978-0-470-71025-8

Project Management For Dummies
978-0-470-71119-4

Psychology Statistics For Dummies
978-1-119-95287-9

Psychometric Tests For Dummies
978-0-470-75366-8

Renting Out Your Property For Dummies, 3rd Edition
978-1-119-97640-0

Rugby Union For Dummies, 3rd Edition
978-1-119-99092-5

Sage One For Dummies
978-1-119-95236-7

Self-Hypnosis For Dummies
978-0-470-66073-7

Storing and Preserving Garden Produce For Dummies
978-1-119-95156-8

Teaching English as a Foreign Language For Dummies
978-0-470-74576-2

Time Management For Dummies
978-0-470-77765-7

Training Your Brain For Dummies
978-0-470-97449-0

Voice and Speaking Skills For Dummies
978-1-119-94512-3

Work-Life Balance For Dummies
978-0-470-71380-8

FOR DUMMIES®

Making Everything Easier!™

COMPUTER BASICS

978-1-118-11533-6

978-0-470-61454-9

978-0-470-49743-2

DIGITAL PHOTOGRAPHY

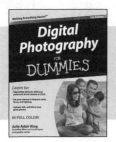

978-1-118-09203-3

978-0-470-76878-5

978-1-118-00472-2

SCIENCE AND MATHS

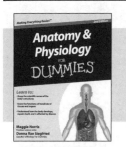

978-0-470-92326-9

978-0-470-55964-2

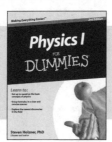

978-0-470-90324-7

Art For Dummies
978-0-7645-5104-8

Computers For Seniors For Dummies, 3rd Edition
978-1-118-11553-4

Criminology For Dummies
978-0-470-39696-4

Currency Trading For Dummies, 2nd Edition
978-0-470-01851-4

Drawing For Dummies, 2nd Edition
978-0-470-61842-4

Forensics For Dummies
978-0-7645-5580-0

French For Dummies, 2nd Edition
978-1-118-00464-7

Guitar For Dummies, 2nd Edition
978-0-7645-9904-0

Hinduism For Dummies
978-0-470-87858-3

Index Investing For Dummies
978-0-470-29406-2

Islamic Finance For Dummies
978-0-470-43069-9

Knitting For Dummies, 2nd Edition
978-0-470-28747-7

Music Theory For Dummies, 2nd Edition
978-1-118-09550-8

Office 2010 For Dummies
978-0-470-48998-7

Piano For Dummies, 2nd Edition
978-0-470-49644-2

Photoshop CS6 For Dummies
978-1-118-17457-9

Schizophrenia For Dummies
978-0-470-25927-6

WordPress For Dummies, 5th Edition
978-1-118-38318-6

12-47776–187x234mm